Y0-BOS-872

THE BAJA BOOK II

A Complete New Map-Guide to Today's Baja California

By TOM MILLER

and

ELMAR BAXTER

With Foreword By RAY CANNON

Mike Glover

Art Director

Charles Larson

Illustrations

Cover Photo Courtesy
Dr. C. W. Larson

Photographs for Baja Spacemaps®
From NASA Earth Resources Technology Satellite

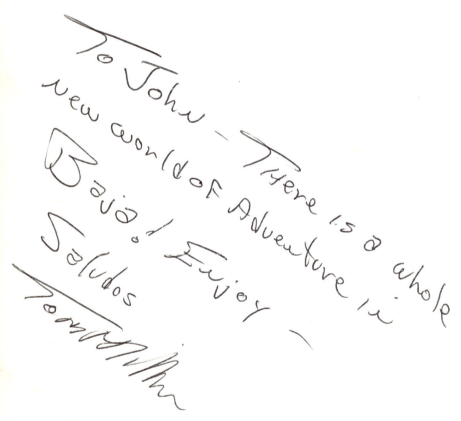

To John — There is a whole
new world of Adventure in
Baja! Enjoy —
Saludos
Tom Miller

BAJA TRAIL PUBLICATIONS, INC.
P.O. BOX 6088, HUNTINGTON BEACH, CALIFORNIA 92646

THE BAJA BOOK II...A Complete New Map-Guide to Today's Baja California. Published by Baja Trail Publications, Inc. ISBM 0-914622-03-5. All rights reserved. No part of this book may be reproduced in any manner whatsoever without written permission from the publisher, except by reviewers who may quote brief passages for publication or broadcast.

COPYRIGHT © BY TOM MILLER AND ELMAR BAXTER 1982.

DEDICATION

THE BAJA BOOK II is dedicated to all the individuals who have pioneered the development of the Baja California peninsula . . . to those who settled and struggled to survive during the centuries . . . to the travelers who have followed to enjoy this incredibly beautiful frontier land . . . and most importantly, to the friendly people of Baja, who are now our hosts below the border.

The authors would also like to recognize the 30,000 Baja aficionados whose faith in THE BAJA BOOK established it as the best-selling guidebook ever written on the peninsula — as well as to the many travel authorities who have been most generous with their counsel and in their reviews.

ABOUT
THE AUTHORS

Tom Miller is a lifelong **aficionado** of Baja California, a record-holding saltwater fisherman, participant in many International Spin Fishing Association tournaments, and active in numerous conservation programs.

For many years, Miller has maintained a trailer home at Corona Beach, south of Ensenada. During that time, he has driven thousands of miles throughout the entire peninsula—exploring, charting, photographing, taking notes against the day the long-awaited transpeninsula highway, Mexico 1, would be opened.

Scores of his articles on Baja California have been published in **Western Outdoors** magazine and **Western Outdoor News,** where his columns appear weekly. He is undoubtedly one of the leading authorities on Baja today.

Elmar Baxter, a long-time friend of Miller's, has been an outdoor and travel writer, editor and photographer since 1946, including 20 years with the Hearst newspapers. He has traveled well over one million miles to all parts of the world and lists Mexico as his favorite country, Baja as his favorite place.

An early-day advocate of light spinning tackle for billfishing, he helped popularize the tag-and-release policy now followed by many top tournaments. He has fished in Hawaii, Tahiti, Bora Bora, New Zealand, Panama, Canada, Alaska and Iceland, as well as Baja. Baxter also pioneered the use of short skis in the West, and is editor of California's SKIER newspaper.

When the two friends realized they were proceeding on parallel paths, they pooled their talents and knowledge. First came THE BAJA BOOK, and now the completely revised THE BAJA BOOK II.

FOREWORD
By RAY CANNON
Author of "THE SEA OF CORTEZ"

There is a wondrous feeling about driving down the full length of the new 1000-mile highway through the mountain that forms the Peninsula of Baja California.

The casual observer can read much of the history of the earth in the vast stretches of volcanic pinnacles and craters—primordial formations created as lands cooled, catastrophic earthquake escarpments, primitive fossilized life forms, and on down to the middens of aboriginal man, remnants from advent of the Spaniard—and finally to a period shortly after the 1849 Gold Rush, when Baja California and its past was all but forgotten for almost a century.

But even emptiness has left its thumb prints on the unrecorded history. Once-thriving mining towns are now seen as ghost towns. Roaring, bellowing cattle ranches are today heard as the lowing of stragglers on distant hills. Camino carretillas (cart-roads) have been eroded into gullies and gulches. Former haciendas and mine structures are crumbling rapidly.

Observers who examine closely can find excitement in all that's old and be enthralled by the ageless enchantment of nature's untouched beauty.

While seeing is rewarding beyond appraising, there is even more joy in the deep inner feelings of breathing clean-scented air and the delights of a warm, tropical climate, all in a freedom unique to most Norteamericanos.

Most of the good, the wondrous, the enchanting that Baja California has to offer would be missed without a knowledgable guide. This book provides that guidance.

"THE BAJA BOOK II" and its mapping was done by knowledgeable men who studied the roads, especially the new Transpeninsula Highway, for the express purpose of creating this fine, informative volume. No one should venture into Baja California without a copy in hand.

ACKNOWLEDGMENTS

We are most grateful for the encouragement provided by the Governors and their staffs of both the State of Baja California and the State of Baja California Sur. Their cooperation over the years has been most helpful.

Roberto de La Madrid, former Director of Tourism for the State of Baja California and now its Governor, provided much information vital to the book. The same is to be said for the Mexican National Tourist Council, headed by Lic. Miguel Aleman, and for the Mexican Government Ministry of Tourism under the direction of Arc. Guillermo Rossell de La Lama.

Juanita Roland of the EROS Data Center, U.S. Department of the Interior, was extremely helpful in providing the ERTS satellite space photographs of Baja California.

Walt Wheelock of La Siesta Press was very generous in sharing his considerable knowledge of the northern back country and in extending access to one of the finest of all Baja libraries.

Credit must go to the many engineers and architects throughout the peninsula who made available the maps and construction plans necessary to assure the utmost accuracy of these Baja Spacemaps and the Baja Roadlogs.

Others who made significant contributions include Tom Banks, Antero Diaz, Anita Espinoza, John Fitch, Bud Lewis, Manual Munoz, Tom Payne, Ed Pearlman, Charlie Rucker, Arnold Senterfitt, Harold Smith, Mac Shroyer, Ed Tabor, Bobby Van Wormer, Al and Dorothy Vela, Chuck Walters, Anita Williams and Clemente Wilson.

The authors would particularly like to express their deep appreciation to Shirley Casey Miller and Pat Brumm, who spent endless hours trying to make sense out of our extensive notes. Their role in the completion of this book can never be fully expressed.

The outstanding illustrations throughout THE BAJA BOOK II are the work of a very talented young artist, Charles Larson, who accompanied us on our final inspection tour of the newly completed Baja Highway.

Design and layout are by Mike Glover, an RV and fishing fan who has won more than a dozen national graphic design awards in the last few years.

Lastly, our thanks to Ray Cannon, author of THE SEA OF CORTEZ, who kindly offered to write the foreword to THE BAJA BOOK II. Ray—a long-time personal friend—has been an inspiration to many thousands of Baja travelers for two decades through his words, wisdom and contagious enthusiasm.

Muchas Gracias, to you all.

CONTENTS

HIGHWAY 1
NORTH OF
SANTA INES

MEXICO 1 . . . WHAT'S IN A NAME?

Romanticists call it "The 1000 Mile Dream." Patriots have named it for Benito Juarez. Geographically speaking, it is the Transpeninsula Highway. In Spanish it is the Carretera. The Padres knew it as Camino Real. Mapmakers officially label it Mexico 1. Campesinos speak of it as Numero Uno. Wags label it the Frijole Freeway. To those of us who have waited for its completion for more than 20 years, it is simply the Baja Highway.

For 1058 miles it threads serpentinely like a narrow black band from the United States Border at Tijuana along the 800-mile length of the Baja California peninsula. Sometimes it skirts the cool blue Pacific, other stretches carry it up arroyos, across barrancas, rising to an elevation of 2600 feet before it plunges again to alkaline deserts. Much of its mid-section touches the warm waters of the Gulf of California, now officially designated the Sea of Cortez. Finally, it crosses the Tropic of Cancer, south of La Paz, en route to Cabo San Lucas, land's end, where sea finally meets ocean.

Baja California is like Alta California in the U.S.—cut on the bias. Once part of the Mexican mainland, it angles sharply to the east as it juts southward. La Paz near the tip is actually east of Phoenix, Tucson and Salt Lake City.

A two-lane paved highway designed primarily to open "La Frontera" and to link both Bajas to the U.S. with truck transportation, the Baja Highway is, for nearly 400 miles, about 20 feet wide. Much of this stretch, between El Rosario and San Ignacio, has no shoulders. Turnoffs are few and far between. While all of Mexico 1 must be driven with extreme caution, this particular portion must be approached with extra care. Most of the Peninsula is open range and one must always watch for livestock.

Driving is extremely hazardous after dark, as witness the crosses and monuments frequently seen along the roadside. If an approaching vehicle flashes its lights at a bridge or narrow area, it means that they intend to proceed through. You had better slow down or even stop, pull as far over on the right as possible and allow the oncoming driver to pass. Rules of the road regarding who has priority on the up or down-grade mean little here. Caution is the only rule to follow.

The State of Baja California, occupying the northern half of the peninsula nearest the border, is on Pacific Time. The State of Baja California Sur is on Mountain Standard Time.

BAJA—A FRAGILE PARADOX

The 800-mile long peninsula known as Baja California has long had the reputation of being rugged and hostile, and with good reason. It took the Spaniards more than 150 years to establish their first permanent settlement in Baja. After another 150 years, their penetration was still limited to small clusters of Indians around the few active missions, plus several hundred tiny ranchos. Chroniclers of those times repeatedly commented on the inhospitality of the land, which has been known as "La Frontera" for more than four centuries.

Nothing is more awesomely rugged than raw desert land. While Baja boasts snowy two-mile-high peaks in its northern portion and a few green oases, it is largely desert—with rainfall figures ranging from under 10 inches in the southernmost regions to less than 2 inches in many areas further north.

The peninsula has often been characterized as being barren . . . yet Baja, and especially the ocean around it, is full of life.

As those who find their recreation in the great deserts of the Southwest have discovered, the environment of a desert is one of the most fragile of all. Often the destruction of only a few plants which were barely clinging to life will leave scars for generations.

If you are drawn to Baja for its uncluttered landscapes, remember to keep them that way — uncluttered. One of the great fears of many Mexicans and others who have come to love the stark beauty of Baja is that the great increase in the numbers of visitors will destroy this beauty.

Bring with you to Baja an open mind and an open eye. Mexico is different from California and the United States. Baja is even different from the rest of Mexico, and it is this difference that draws us south of the border in the first place. Cherish, protect and enjoy.

Baja California will, over the next few years, move from a primitive environment demanding great resourcefulness from its residents . . . to a modern effective society through the development of a transportation network, communications, industry, housing, education — and tourism.

But none of these changes has or probably will alter the basic friendly attitude of the Baja campesinos. "Mi casa es su casa" is a way of life to the Mexican. "My house is your house" is an offering of friendship and respect that is well to remember.

If you enter Mexico without preconceived prejudices, if you can throw away the key to the clock and forget the calendar in this land of little hurry or worry, if you can embrace the Baja Californian for what he is, a pioneer in a poncho not very different from our own Western past . . . then you will love Baja, perhaps even as much as we do.

CIRIO

BAJA IS BORN

There was a time, 20 million years ago, when no peninsula extended 800 miles southeastward from the western edge of the North American continent. What was later to become a peninsula was at that time a part of the land which supported great jungles and life forms typical of that era. Palms, ferns and other lush vegetation towered over the 50 foot duckbilled hydrosaur, a gigantic tyrannosaurus-like creature and many other reptiles in a setting of volcanoes, torrential rains and stiffling humidity.

But 20 million years ago, the earth was not at rest. Her uneasy writhings tore loose a great chunk of the continent, and caused convulsive liftings of rocky strata and ocean bottom. From time to time, entire ranges would collapse into the sea, to rise again and become covered with deep layers of volcanic outpourings.

The tip of Baja California is believed to have once been located on the west coast of Mexico between Acapulco and Puerto Vallarta. It has taken these 20 million years for Baja to move the 300 or more miles west and north to form the unique gulf known as the Sea of Cortez. Even today it moves northwestward along with California toward the Bering Sea at almost one inch per year.

THE HISTORY AND PEOPLE OF BAJA

Baja has answered the many challenges to its existence by creating an environment completely unique in the western hemisphere. It affords a ruggedness, magnificence and variety of scenery to delight anyone with a love of the outdoors. From unexpected alpine meadows near the 10,126-foot high Picacho del Diablo to the barren excarpments plunging downward toward the Sea of Cortez, there are countless places of scenic and scientific interest throughout Baja, both north and south.

The millions of years have left stories for all to read: the towering cinder cones, strange plants and jagged granitic and basaltic outcroppings are obvious to the untrained eye, while the skilled observer has studied the history of Baja through the fossil beds and Indian middens near such towns as Ensenada, San Quintin, San Felipe and the mountains south of La Paz.

Conservative estimates place the arrival of man on the Baja California peninsula about 10,000 years ago. The land forms were basically as they are now, but there was more water in this post ice-age period. Increased vegetation and animal life around lakes and their drainages provided the hunters and gatherers with a varied food supply.

By the time the Spaniards arrived over 400 years ago, the peninsula was considerably drier, and the lakes had for the most part disappeared.

In 1535, Hernan Cortez led a colonization attempt near La Paz, but his followers were driven out within two years by natives made hostile from severe treatment, lack of water and inadequate supplies.

Stories of great treasures of gold, pearls, and a race of beautiful Amazons ruled by Queen Calafia continued to excite explorers, and in 1540 Hernando de Alarcon visited the northern peninsula when he sailed into the mouth of the river now known as the Rio Colorado. He wrote of the native people there, was well treated and received food from them— as did Don Juan de Ornate, who visited the same area in the early 1600's and called the river people Cucapa. Ornate received gifts of corn, beans and squash from the Cucapa, which indicates that at this early period these northern Baja California people were practising agriculture.

In 1697, Jesuit padre Juan Maria Salvatierra established the first permanent non-indigenous colony on what was still thought by many to be the "Island" of California.

Padre Eusebio Kino attempted to missionize the native people of the southern peninsula in 1683 and 1685. He also visited the Colorado River delta in 1702 observing small rancherias near the river growing corn, beans and pumpkins. Padre Kino charted the region as a peninsula in 1705, but his map was rejected in Europe. It was not until Padre Fernando Consag sailed completely around the Gulf of California in 1746 and Jesuit Weneslaus Linck traveled from California across the Colorado River into Sonora that the dispute was finally settled.

It is generally believed that most of the earliest inhabitants of Baja California arrived via gradual or spasmodic immigrations from the north.

caused by cultural pressures or climatic changes. Some scholars, however, pursue the possibility of ancient trans-pacific contacts with Baja California, especially in the southern portion.

The native people of the peninsula were accustomed to using stone for their tools: in ancient times, crudely formed scrapers and choppers, later, fine projectile points and equipment for grinding foods, portable metates and bedrock mortars. They used wood to make dart throwers, spears, and later bows and arrows—as well as hunting sticks similar to the Australian boomerang.

Along the coasts on both sides of the Baja California peninsula there are numerous middens of clam shells many feet deep. These are particularly in evidence in the vicinity of Ensenada south to San Quintin and in the region north of Bahia Magdalena. The piles of shells graphically tell the story of a tribe's arrival in the area and their subsequent harvesting of the larger clams. As the supply diminished, smaller and smaller ones were taken until it became unprofitable to remain. They then moved to another spot, to return again after the clams had replenished themselves.

Little clothing was used. Women wore simple skirts of agave cactus fiber cordage or willow bark, and people protected themselves from winter's cold with deerskins or rather intricately contrived capes made of the skins of small animals, mostly rabbits. Historians and anthropologists also mention unique capes of human hair which were used by shamans for ceremonial purposes.

Native housing consisted of simple brush or rock shelters, some of them open to the sky, and caves. Household equipment included carrying nets of agave fiber in the northern and central peninsula and nets and mats of palm fiber in the southern portion.

In the north, over 2,000 years ago, the people learned to make thin-walled, hard-fired ceramic pots and bowls for cooking and storage. The northern and central people were also familiar with the art of basketry.

Mexico has recently expanded its program of archaeological investigation in the peninsula, and it is important that visitors be aware that all archaeological pieces (such as stone tools and arrowpoints) are considered part of the national heritage and may not be removed. A campaign is underway seeking the return of archaeological material already out of the country.

Ethnobotanists are learning from the surviving Indian people of northern Baja California that they possessed a vast knowledge of plant usages for food and for medicinal purposes—from wild grass seeds, to pine nuts, acorn and cactus fruit, as well as various roots. Protein sources in the past varied from insects to large animals such as deer and bighorn sheep.

These insects and animals—as well as fish, human figures and geometric forms—appear in paintings and carvings on rocks in many places along the peninsula. The most unusual and impressive paintings are those found in the central section, where larger-than-life figures of men and animals are painted in red and black. The figures dominate whole landscapes from the walls and ceilings of their rock shelters.

Radiocarbon dates on material from these caves have been reported by Dr. Clement Meighan to indicate the presence of people there 500 years before the coming of the Spaniards. Several excellent books have been written about the rock art of Baja California by Dr. Clement Meighan, Campbell Grant, and Harry Crosby.

As resident Indians in the missions of the southern two-thirds of the peninsula died off, their places were taken by people from the mainland, who have lived and worked in Baja ever since at fishing, cattle herding and mining.

Over the years, immigrants from Spain, England and France joined a number of Americans, Russians, Germans and Chinese to form the present-day population of Baja California.

The thousand or more surviving descendants of the original population of Baja California are now concentrated in the northern third of the peninsula—for the most part living in the mountains of the San Pedro Martir and the Sierra de Juarez and along the Hardy River (Rio Hardy). They identify themselves as Kiliwa, Pai Pai, Cochimi, Cucapa and Kumyai, many of them still speaking their ancient Yuman-Hokan dialects. Some of them even retain their several thousand year-old heritage, which enables them to survive in the natural environment independent of an otherwise hostile environment.

BEFORE THE BORDER
YOUR TOURIST CARD

To drive the new Transpeninsula Highway, Mexico 1, beyond Ensenada, you will need to obtain a Mexican Tourist Card. These are also required if you plan on driving anywhere beyond the 60-mile border zone, or if your stay in Mexico will be more than three days (72 hours).

Mexico considers the tourist to be "any foreigner who visits for recreation, health or scientific or sports activities, provided they are neither remunerative or lucrative." So, if your trip to Baja is for business, be sure to apply for a Business Visa, obtainable from Mexican Consulates for $5. You'll need a valid passport and letter from your company stating you are authorized to buy or sell in Mexico.

Mexico issues two types of Tourist Cards. Both are free. One is valid for single visits of up to 180 days; you can fill it out beforehand and have it validated upon proof of U.S. citizenship. The Multiple Entry Tourist Card allows for as many visits as you want in the same 180 days, but requires three 2 x 2 inch passport photos.

In either case, you may obtain the simple form from the Mexican National Tourist Council or Travel Department offices in major cities and Mexican Consulates. Single entry permits may also be obtained through airlines, auto clubs or travel agents when booking reservations.

Proof of citizenship can be a passport, birth certificate, voter registration, naturalization papers, baptismal certificate, affidavit of birth, discharge papers, or armed forces ID card. Such proof must be presented for every member of your family and should be carried throughout the trip.

Children under 15 may be included on their parent's card, but separate cards are advisable just in case they should return home with someone else.

Minors under 18 traveling alone or with persons other than their parents must not only obtain a Tourist Card but also present a notarized letter of consent from both parents or guardians. If the minor is with only one parent, a notarized letter of consent from the other parent is required.

To avoid a possible delay at the Border, you can mail the forms with proof of citizenship in advance to one of the Mexican offices named above. Enclose a self-addressed stamped envelope and allow about one week. This makes sense, particularly if you plan on driving to Baja during a weekend or holiday when traffic may be heavy.

Canadians and citizens of other lands must present passports or birth certificates for their tourist cards.

PERMITS APLENTY

Normally entry permits are required for each vehicle, including trailers and boats, entering Mainland Mexico. However, under current regulations, if you plan to stay within the confines of the Baja California peninsula you need only concern yourself with a boat permit.

If you decide to use one of the modern ferries linking Baja to the Mainland you will be required to take out a permit for all of your equipment. There's no charge for these permits but you must present your U.S. driver's license and proofs of ownership on automobile, motorhome, trailer, boat, etc. If you don't own them carry a Notarized Affidavit from the legal owner(s).

HUNTING AND FISHING LICENSES

The quality of wing shooting for dove, quail, duck , geese and black brant in Baja California and nearby Sonora/ Sinaloa is such that it attracts hunters from all parts of the U.S. and Canada.

The procedure for obtaining hunting licenses, gun permits, etc. is taxing, to say the least, and few people take it upon themselves to do all of the running necessary to get the papers. We strongly recommend that the leg-work be left to people in that business, such as: Mexican Hunting Association, 3302 Josie Ave., Long Beach, CA 90808, Phone 213/421-1619 or Romero's Mexico Service, 1600 W. Coast Highway, Newport Beach, CA 92663, Phone 714/548-8931. They can arrange the whole thing quickly and for a reasonable fee. Should you want to do it yourself, here are the steps involved:

You will need 12 passport-size full-face photos, proof of citizenship, and a character reference (in duplicate) from your local police department. Also have the serial numbers, calibers and makes of the firearms you wish registered. Next, go to any Mexican Consulate—where you will be issued a multiple-visit tourist card at no charge—and request a Consular Gun Permit application.

Once filled out, the gun permit is taken to the Mexican Department of Agriculture in either Tijuana or Mexicali. There you will receive a Military Gun Permit which is then taken to the Military Commandant's office to be signed by the General. (Here you may have to leave the papers and return another day.) Then you go back to the Department of Agriculture where a Wildlife Tax Stamp is affixed and validated. All fees must be paid for in pesos and vary from year to year. A truly exhausting experience! Total cost for the 1982-83 season was approximately $105, including one extra state. (e.g.—Baja California and Sonora)

Latest information on seasons, bag limits and United States boarder regulations regarding the importation of game is available through the two above-named organizations, or at the Mexican Consulates and U.S. Customs offices.

Permits necessary to fish from a commercial passenger-carrying sportboat in Mexican waters are included in the price of the trip. However, if you are going to fish on your own boat, or from the shore, you will need to buy a standard Mexican fishing license. At the time of this printing, there are one-day and one-month licenses available for 100 and 500 pesos respectively. They are available through a number of tackle stores near the border (including some in the Los Angeles area), and at the Mexican Department of Fisheries, 1010 2nd Ave., #1605, San Diego, CA 92101, though here administrative delays can sometimes be lengthy and parking can be a problem. Some Mexican insurance offices, such as Instant Mexico Auto Insurance in San Ysidro also have them for their customers. They are also available from some fisheries offices in Mexico. The dollar price of these and the boat permits vary with the peso exchange rate and, thus, may be different from month to month.

Each person over 14 years of age on a private boat must have a license, whether he fishes or not.

Additionally, possession of totuava, cabrilla, lobster, oysters, Pismo clams or shrimp is forbidden. Anglers may catch a total of 10 fish per day—no more than five of one species—but only two roosterfish or dolphinfish (dorado), one sailfish, marlin, swordfish or black sea bass. Releasing of fish is encouraged and is widely practiced. Fishing and boating is restricted at times in the areas where the California gray whale comes in to calve, such as Scammon's Lagoon and Black Warrior Lagoon. Check with local authorities for current regulations.

ABOUT INSURANCE

Automobile insurance in Mexico is confusing to many tourists, yet it is of vital importance. Simply stated, Mexican law does not recognize ANY insurance except that written by licensed Mexican insurance companies and their representatives, no matter what your American policy says.

To be fully protected while in Mexico, you must carry Mexican insurance on your car, trailer, boat (if trailered) or any other item you might be hauling. If the car but not the trailer is insured and you are in an accident, your car insurance is no longer valid—same as in the United States.

Should you become involved in an accident while in Mexico, you are considered liable under Mexican law—both parties are held equally guilty, regardless of the circumstances, until legally resolved. Lacking proper coverage, your vehicle can also be impounded and fines levied. Your Mexican policy guarantees, **in Spanish**, that you are able to pay damages up to the limit on the policy in case you are found to be at fault.

In the event of an accident and you are without Mexican insurance you may be brought to the police station for a hearing. If no one was injured or killed, you will be allowed to leave if you can pay for the damage and possible fines. If you are unable to pay, you probably will remain in custody and your car will be impounded.

If the accident involves injury or death to any party, you may be placed in protective custody until responsibilities are established by the authorities. Legally you can be held for up to three days before your case is heard. Bear in mind that an accident of any kind in Mexico is considered a felony, not a misdemeanor.

All of the above is based on the legal code known as the Napoleanic Code wherein one is held to be guilty until proven innocent as opposed to our English Code where the reverse is true. The Napoleanic Code is prevalent through much of Europe and most of Latin America.

Mexican insurance rates are based on the value of the vehicle and length of stay. For example, a 10 day trip in a $5,000 car costs about $60, though members of the Mexico West Travel Club can qualify for substantial savings through special group rates. (See supplement at end of book.)

If you return sooner, you may request a refund for the portion not used or receive credit by staying in a recognized trailer park and have manager sign a statement that your trailer/motorhome was not moved over a certain period. Ask your insurance carrier for details.

There are also available a number of types of policies allowing for multiple entries over a 12 month period, etc. Again, check with your carrier for the alternatives.

REGARDING ACCIDENTS IN MEXICO

1. Report any accident you may have to the nearest authorities.

2. City police have jurisdiction only in cities, not on highways.

3. Do not panic and do not pay anyone.

4. Show your Mexican insurance policy to competent authorities, but do not surrender your Mexican policy without a receipt for same.

5. If anyone is injured or killed, the parties involved must go to jail until guilt is established. This is a matter of legal procedure and cannot be changed.

IT'S THE CUSTOM

Mexican Customs regulations are similar to those of other countries. The whole of Baja California, however, is a Free Zone and your vehicle or goods will be searched only under special circumstances. Later should you board a ferry to the Mexican mainland, you will be subject to luggage inspection.

Time was when the "mordida," which translates as "death bite" and means a small bribe or tip, was common practice around larger towns, particularly along the border. The Mexican Government has been cracking down on this tradition in recent years and at the same time increasing incomes of officials to discourage "mordida." It is still possible, however, that the outstretched palm could appear at times, so be prepared to occasionally part with ten or twenty pesos to speed you on your way. Reporting such incidents to the tourism authorities will further discourage this practice.

By law you may take only one quart of liquor into Baja with 2 cartons of cigarettes, 50 cigars and 3 pounds of pipe tobacco. However in actual practice you are permitted to bring in a "reasonable amount" of these products for personal consumption. Don't bother to take your own beer or wine; both are reasonable in cost in Baja and the beer especially is world famous. Inexpensive too are rum, brandy, gin, vodka and, of course, tequila. Scotch, bourbon and Canadian whiskeys are more expensive.

You are only supposed to have one still camera and one movie camera per person, plus 12 rolls of film for each. Usually you may carry more, but professional photographers are supposed to have permits.

Americans may not take large quantities of new goods south across the border without paying duty if it appears they might be for resale. However, a supply of simple gifts like paper and pencils, erasers, gum, candy, cookies or balloons will not be questioned and they will make a hit with the children you meet. Used but clean clothing in smaller sizes are always appreciated and may find you a friend for life.

Tips are appreciated by adults for services rendered, but don't be surprised if they are refused with a smile in this *simpatico* land.

When returning to the U.S. you may bring back up to one liter of any liquor per person. This is a federal law and applies to all persons over 21 crossing the border, whether in a car, bus, plane or walking. Currently each individual may bring back into the United States $300 worth of Mexican goods duty-free. Special regulations apply to most handcrafted items, thus you may bring even more should this type of product be included. Check with U.S. Customs for up-to-the-minute regulations.

FUEL FOR THOUGHT

All gasoline in Mexico is sold through the government production and marketing monopoly, Pemex (Petroleos Mexicanos). When planning your trip into Baja California, you should consider the following:

FIRST—Once out of the border towns, you should have pesos to buy gasoline as dollars are rarely accepted.

SECOND—Gasoline is usually plentiful along Mexico 1 and Pemex stations are rarely more than 50 miles apart but we recommend that you work off the top half of the tank in case a station should be temporarily out.

THIRD—The premium, or "EXTRA" gas in the silver pump costs the equivalent of about 68 cents per U.S. gallon, while the regular, or "NOVA" in the blue pumps sells for around 48 cents. The EXTRA contains no lead and is designed for engines requiring unleaded fuel. Though rated at 92 octane on the pump, its actual motor octane number is closer to 81, according to tests made on samples.

FOURTH—Pemex NOVA (regular) does contain tetraethyl lead and the 82 octane marked on the blue pump is close to its tested 79 octane. In spite of its low rating, it appears to work satisfactorily in almost any car if the spark is retarded. This will reduce the "ping" with only a small power loss. We also suggest that you use one of the commercially available gasoline additives such as Moroso (found in many speed shops, it is the best we have tested) or J. B. Gas Treatment, as per recommendations on the container. You can also try mixing EXTRA and NOVA in various combinations to improve performance.

A special note to owners of air-cooled engines—excessive pinging, or pre-ignition, can burn up the pistons in a hurry. Be careful not to allow those pesky noises to persist. Follow the recommendations above and keep geared down during conditions of engine load.

FIFTH—Diesel fuel in Mexico is truly a bargain. At present it is about 24 cents per gallon and is available at most major stations.

SIXTH—Butane supplies are best found in the larger towns near the border or in La Paz. There are only limited supplies in between and shortages sometimes occur everywhere during the winter months. We do not recommend attempting to drive any butane powered vehcle into Mexico—the supplies are not reliable enough for this form of use. White gas is also difficult to obtain but kerosene (petroleo para lampara) is usually found in the smaller native grocery stores.

ONE ANSWER TO THE ENERGY CRISIS

A few miles south of Mexicali there is a region of geothermal activity being tapped by the Mexican Government to produce a significant portion of the electrical energy for the residents of the Mexicali Valley.

The intense heat that underlies the region is manifested on the surface by varicolored bubbling fumeroles, some of which emit high-pitched whistles and high plumes of steam. In the future, it could become more important by supplying even greater amounts of pollution-free energy.

THE GREEN ANGELS OF BAJA

Motorists in need of a helping hand on Baja's paved roads will find that and more in the fleet of "Green Angels" which patrol at frequent intervals, searching out motorists in trouble.

Each of these vehicles carries a crew of two, at least one of whom speaks English. They carry a limited supply of spare parts, gas, oil and water. Minor repairs can often be made right on the spot, at no charge, except for parts, which are at cost.

A push or a tow is also available, again without charge. This motorists' service is provided by the Mexican Government as part of its program to make the visitor welcome and help make his stay as carefree and enjoyable as possible.

However, we must emphasize that this complimentary service should not lull the motorist into driving in Mexico with a vehicle in need of repair or service. If you plan any off-road sidetrips, make sure that your tires are in top shape, have a five-gallon can of water, another of gas, and an adequate tool kit.

The Green Angels patrol the highways in Baja several times daily, so you may have to be patient. Fortunately, many of the truck drivers of Baja are generous with their time and talent, and often beat the "angels" at their own game.

The Green Angels or "Angeles Verdes" of Mexico are another way of saying "welcome" to Baja.

HEALTH HINTS

The United States Public Health Service does not presently require a smallpox vaccination certificate from Americans returning from Mexico, provided they have been nowhere else in the last 14 days. Neither do the Mexican authorities require visitors from the States to have proof of vaccination for entry.

If you are venturing off-road in Baja, or are going fishing, hunting, diving or where you could be exposed to puncture wounds, a tetanus booster is advisable.

You would also be wise to take along a First Aid Kit (see section on First Aid). Extra eye glasses and sufficient medical prescriptions to last your stay are also suggested. You'll be able to obtain most drug prescriptions, or their Mexican counterpart, in Baja's larger towns, along with medical and dental aid. Yes, U.S. Medicare benefits follow you to Mexico.

Everyone leaving home for a strange land should be sure they are in reasonable health. Don't risk spoiling your trip. Schedule your medical and dental checkup before departure.

Contrary to widespread belief, the same type bacteria and viruses that can cause the tourist intestinal problems flourish on both sides of the border. The villain is called E. coli, and is found all over the world, but with varying severity of symptoms. In Mexico, it is simply called "turista."

That particular intestinal affliction endured so frequently by tourists has almost as many colorful names as victims. And it may well be avoided completely, if certain simple precautions are taken.

Mostly, it is a matter of not overdoing in strange surroundings. Don't go overboard on heavily spiced dishes, don't overindulge, overexert, undersleep. Avoid water unless bottled, go easy on fruit and vegetables. Enjoy the great fresh seafood of Baja.

Should E. coli (with a Mexican accent) get to you, the illness may last up to three days. Symptomatic treatment can be made with Tincture of Paregoric or one of the diarrhea medications. Small amounts of fluid at frequent intervals, consomme, beef tea, soda pop are helpful to get you over the worst. Avoid spicy foods, milk, dairy products, orange juice and eggs for a few days.

Amoebic Dysentery is far more serious, and a physician should be consulted immediately. But this malady is far rarer even than the infrequent "tourista" in Baja California.

There are a number of preventatives and remedies readily available almost anywhere in Mexico. Lomotil is considered among the best . If caused by infectious bacteria, Oxabid is considered preferable.

Remember, it is most likely the change in your entire environment that is the cause, not just the water. Most cases occur during the first few days; after that your system adapts.

Interestingly, Mexicans encounter E. coli when they travel north into the United States. Wonder what they call it?

A WEATHER REPORT

Much of Baja California has a climate similar to that of Southern California. Both are basically semi-tropical desert, with verdant valleys and high mountains which catch the winter snow.

The Pacific coast of Baja is much cooler than the same latitude on the Sea of Cortez, just across the mountains that form the spiny backbone of the peninsula. That's why the Pacific is far less developed for tourism.

Climate in the north coastal region of Baja, with Ensenada as the hub, offers warm days and cool nights in summer — cool days and chilly winter nights . There is considerable fog along the beaches, while a ten-inch annual rainfall is restricted to the December-April period.

Along the Cortez, Baja is pure desert from Mexicali south to Bahia de Los Angeles. Summers range from 90 to 110 degrees, with warm and sometimes humid nights. Temperatures cool off to a more comfortable level in spring and fall, with winters occasionally cold, and often windy.

From just south of Parallel 28—the border between the two States of Baja Norte and Baja Sur—the climate becomes more sub-tropical. Summers are hot and humid, winters a bit cool for shirtsleeve comfort but still enjoyable. Spring and fall are close to perfect. Rainfall is scant, being restricted to summer storms, which are brief but sometimes violent and deposit up to 30″ annually in the mountains.

Most Baja resorts are now air conditioned, while the rest are so situated that they make the most of prevailing breezes. Generally, the peninsula is less humid than its counterpart across the Cortez on the Mexican mainland.

WHAT WOMEN WEAR

What to wear is always a problem for the ladies, and Baja is no exception.

If you are a guest at one of the more expensive resorts clustered around the Cape, wrap-around sundresses and bikinis are very much in order. However, if you are staying at a downtown hotel, it is better to dress more conservatively, and to wear a robe when heading for the beach. Hot pants, bra tops and the like are not yet completely accepted in urban or rural Mexico, only in the resorts.

Guests tend to dress casually even at the fancier places and ties are rarely seen. Guayabera shirts of Yucatan are popular with men, while Mexican lace dresses, blouses, shirts and rebozos (shawls) keep the women in a Baja mood. Sports clothes from home fit in very well here.

Aside from clothing, you should take along your favorite cosmetic and sunscreen products, insect repellant, toiletries, vitamins and prescriptions, extra eyeglasses, plus any first aid items you might need.

Campers should be sure to carry along a good quality sun shade—a tarp or one of the newer nylon ones—which can be securely tied down should a wind come up. Remember that you are going to need some shelter from the sun.

BYOB — BRING YOUR OWN BOAT

Mexican law states that any trailered or cartop-carried boat may be brought into the Republic of Mexico upon the purchase of a boat permit. Yearly licenses are available through many insurance companies and currently range from 200 pesos for a cartopper to 1000 for a trailered one. They also may be purchased through the offices of the Mexican departments of fisheries. Again the dollar values vary with the peso exchange.

Any private ocean-going yacht or cruiser which carries passengers and crew must be cleared by the Mexican Consul or a yacht clearance broker. One such experienced broker is Romero's Mexico Service, 1600 W. Pacific Coast Highway, Newport Beach, CA 92663, 714/548-8931. Passengers are listed on the crew list as "seaman." The papers are then presented to authorities at the first Mexican port of entry.

Insurance for small boats may be purchased when you buy policies for your car and trailer. This covers the boat for damage in the event of an accident on land. At present there is no hull coverage on the water except a liability policy covering others.

A boat being towed and not insured violates the terms of your Mexican auto policy, rendering it null and void. This same regulation applies in the United States.

Any boat operated within the 200-mile limit is considered under Mexican jurisdiction.

FOR YOU PILOTS

If you pilot your own plane, another set of rules applies concerning entry to Baja. When flying to mainland Mexico, flight plans must be sent in writing to the nearest International Airport, even if you plan to overfly it for a more distant destination. Your final ETA should be included. This is a FAA requirement, to aid the U.S. Air Force radar in monitoring your "blip" as you cross into Mexico.

Flying to Baja California, you must file a flight plan with the FAA, then clear immigration, customs and health at Tijuana, Mexicali, or La Paz. No intermediate stops are permitted enroute to La Paz if you overfly the border.

BROWN BOOBY

If the plane's owner is not aboard, carry a notarized authorization from the registered owner. Tourist cards and proof of citizenship are also required, just as they are if you drive. Upon leaving Mexican territory, clearance must be obtained from FSS.

Check with your nearest Mexican Consulate regarding other regulations. **Airports of Mexico and Central America** by Arnold Senterfitt is a valuable reference for pilots heading for the peninsula.

Most airports indicated on our Baja Photomaps® are merely dirt landing strips, usually maintained by the nearest resort. Their condition varies with weather and other factors. Always make a fly-over before heading in for a landing. Senterfitt suggests you give these a High Look — Low Look — Close Look approach. You can't be too careful when approaching small Baja landing strips.

International Airports are presently located only at Tijuana, Mexicali and La Paz, though there are plans for several others in Baja in the immediate future, including Loreto, Ensenada and San Jose del Cabo.

As with your automobile, you should carry Mexican insurance on your aircraft. This is available through most Mexican insurance carriers, with MacAfee and Edwards in Los Angeles specializing in servicing pilots. Rates are relatively low for liability and most U.S. aircraft policies cover damage to the plane in Mexico.

OSPREY

DIVING IN BAJA

The reefs and coves of the Sea of Cortez number among the premier places in the world for the diver. Hundreds of species of sealife may be found in sometimes bewildering abundance. There are, however, a number of restrictions that must be heeded.

It is illegal to possess a speargun if you also have Scuba equipment. However, it is permissible to use one when free diving. You may **NOT** take any lobster, abalone, pearl oysters or cabrilla under any circumstances. It is also necessary to have a valid Mexican fishing license if you take any form of sealife. The rules are strictly enforced and the penalties can be severe, so confine most of your activities to looking; it is still great.

TALE OF A PEARLER

Most noted of the early Cortez pearlers was Francisco de Ortega, who in 1633 produced his chart of the Sea of Cortez in which he named the larger islands, bays, points, etc. His nameplaces are still in use to this day, despite later attempts by other navigators to rename the landmarks in the Cortez.

—From Ray Cannon

SURFING

There are a number of popular surfing spots south of the border where the crowds are light enough to allow rides without concern as to whether a board is bearing down on you. Such nearby areas as K39, La Mision, San Miguel, Three M's and Corona Beach are well known to any avid surfer.

Some of the more adventuresome surfers have been working such spots south of Ensenada as San Isidro and Cuatro Casas over the last few years. A few, with rugged vehicles, have made it as far as Punta Santa Rosalillita. Here a heavy west-southwest set is storied to have a right break that can be surfed up to 1-1/2 miles. Summer storm systems create good conditions on an isolated beach just west of San Jose del Cabo.

Improvement of more side roads to the Pacific side of the peninsula will afford the exploration of hundreds of miles of heretofore untested breaks.

IF YOU TAKE A CAMERA

Take plenty of film—you'll need it. Hot weather can play havoc with your color film and it is important to store it in as cool a place as possible—not in direct sunlight or in the glove compartment. The bright sunlight of Baja makes it advisable to have a skylight filter along. A medium yellow filter is a plus for black and white photography. Be extra careful to protect your camera from the fine dust found almost everywhere in Baja.

PET PROBLEM

To bring a pet into Mexico, you should have a veterinarian's certificate of good health and rabies shot within the last six months entered on a visa form by the Mexican Consulate ($4). This may or may not be enforced at the border when heading into Baja.

THE PESO STORY

In mid-1982, Mexico's economic policy caught up with her for the third time in the last 6 years and she was forced to devaluate the peso. For decades it was considered the most stable monetary instrument in Latin America, and may be again in the near future. As we go to the printers the peso is hovering about 70 to the dollar, or about 1.4 cents each. It is our feeling that it will gradually drop further, maybe even past the 100 to 1 mark during the next year or two. What this does for the Mexico traveler is increase his buying power, while hopefully funneling more foreign exchange into Mexican banks.

(On the insert in the back, a Peso Exchange Barometer will show you how to compute pesos to dollars at a variety of exchange rates.)

Though dollars are still accepted through most of Baja, but less so on the mainland, we recommend that you exchange dollars for pesos during your travels by obtaining a few days supply at a time at the banks. Open weekdays from 9 to 1:30, they exchange at the going official rate, while hotels, etc., tend to offer a bit less.

In early 1980 Mexico instituted a Value Added Tax (EVA) of 10% on the mainland and 6% in Baja. This is added to almost all goods and services purchased in Mexico (except gasoline). This is not a ripoff, just a way of raising money, like our state sales taxes.

TOURISTIC TRIANGLES

The Mexican Government in their opening of the Baja Californias to tourism is endeavoring to establish scenic, recreational and commercial routes that will fit into a variety of preferences. Several side roads into such areas have been completed and others are in the planning stage, giving the visiting traveler additional views of this fascinating peninsula. Some Mexican officials have dubbed the interconnecting roads Touristic Triangles.

Triangle Number One has about five hours of driving in its path along the Pacific Ocean from Tijuana to Ensenada, then north again through rich farmland past Guadalupe's former Russian colony and miles of vinyards into Tecate, fast becoming a touristic center in its own right. Then the driver has the option of returning to Tijuana on the Mexican side or following winding roads northwest to San Diego.

Triangle Number Two is best taken over several days. Starting again in Tijuana, one would follow the Pacific coastal shores to Ensenada, then inland via BC Highway 16 into the mountains past huge boulders, cattle ranches and farms and miles of mountain vistas southeastward toward the Mexicali-San Felipe highway (Mexico 5). As the road drops into the desert bordering the Sea of Cortez an almost-manicured desert comes into view with the magnificent two-mile high Picacho del Diablo as a backdrop. San Felipe is only 30 miles south of this intersection and has numerous accommodations for most types of travelers. 127 miles to the north is Mexicali and California's Imperial Valley. For a spectacular drive follow Mexico Highway 2 west from Mexicali up the precipitous eastern escarpment of the Sierra Juarez and then through pine studded highlands, finally arriving in Tecate.

It is likely that Triangle Number Three will be only for the hardiest of equipment for some years to come, those adventurers with four-wheel drives and rugged dunebuggys have been driving it for years. Before Mexico 1 portions of it were along the old trail which wandered south from the border toward La Paz. Though much of the road in this circuit is paved there is a stretch of nearly 170 miles which is a little-traveled trail through arroyos, across searing desert sands and along treacherous mountainsides.

The attractions of this inhospitable portion of the peninsula are many for the adventuresome—beaches and bays ideal for the camper/fisherman/beachcomber, old mining areas, arroyos lined with palms, elephant trees and cirios. Forests of giant cardons along with rocky scarpments that defy the survival of even the tiniest shrub add to the stark beauty of the region. Water is scarce and the climate harsh but its day will come.

Touristic Triangle Number Four too is only in the planning stage although the paved road from Mexico 1 into popular Bahia de Los Angeles has been completed for several years. The region has great promise and someday will likely be visited by large numbers of Americans. Today the rocky trails around the road's terminus are only for the most hardy.

Touristic Triangle Number Five is located below La Paz and opens the Pacific side of the tip to visitors. Currently, only the portion from Pescadero to Cabo San Lucas is unpaved. Completion is anticipated within two years. Today that unpaved portion is passable to most vehicles, however, it is easier to go north out of San Lucas because of several sandy grades.

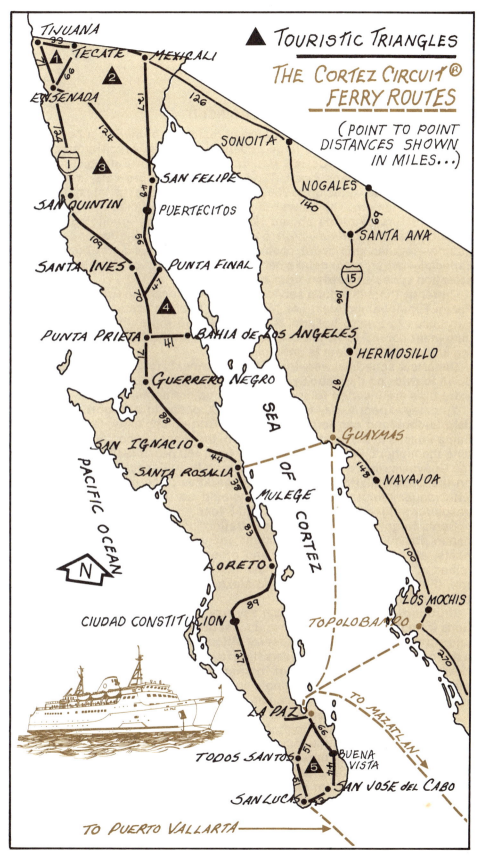

▲ TOURISTIC TRIANGLES

THE CORTEZ CIRCUIT®
FERRY ROUTES

(POINT TO POINT
DISTANCES SHOWN
IN MILES...)

TIJUANA
TECATE
MEXICALI
ENSENADA
SONOITA
NOGALES
SAN FELIPE
PUERTECITOS
SAN QUINTIN
SANTA ANA
PUNTA FINAL
SANTA INES
PUNTA PRIETA
BAHIA de LOS ANGELES
HERMOSILLO
GUERRERO NEGRO
SEA
SAN IGNACIO
GUAYMAS
SANTA ROSALIA
NAVAJOA
MULEGE
OF
CORTEZ
LORETO
PACIFIC OCEAN
LOS MOCHIS
N
CIUDAD CONSTITUCION
TOPOLOBAMPO
LA PAZ
TO MAZATLAN
TODOS SANTOS
BUENA VISTA
SAN LUCAS
SAN JOSE del CABO
TO PUERTO VALLARTA

33
66
127
126
134
124
81
140
99
95
109
70
47
41
7
88
44
39
83
89
137
87
149
106
100
270
66
51
34
147
52

1
2
3
4
5

15
1

25

THE CORTEZ CIRCUIT

An important part of the way of life of residents of the lower half of the Baja peninsula are the large oceangoing ferries which regularly crisscross the Sea of Cortez. Designed and built in Europe, these ships are by no means small. They hold fifty or more cars, trucks, trailers and boats—plus up to 250 passengers and have the latest navigational equipment. The crews are courteous and efficient.

The creature comforts aboard range widely: *Salon*—reclining, airplane-type seats; *Turista*—bunk beds in cubicles on the lower deck; *Cabina*—regular ship-board cabins with beds, toilets and showers; *Especial*—larger, more deluxe cabins on the upper deck. Number and selection varies somewhat from ship to ship.

Currently there is regular service from Santa Rosalia to Guaymas, La Paz to Topolobampo (near Los Mochis), La Paz to Mazatlan and Cabo San Lucas to Puerto Vallarta. Another planned route, Puerto Escondido (near Loreto) to Topolobampo, has been shelved for the time being and no starting date is anticipated.

Departure schedules vary from six times weekly for La Paz-Mazatlan down to twice on the Cabo San Lucas-Puerto Vallarta run. On occasion extra runs are inserted to accommodate requirements.

You may expect to pay from $500 to $900 pesos to transport a standard 20-foot-long car across the Sea of Cortez. Logically, Guaymas-Santa Rosalia is the least expensive, with the longer Cabo-Vallarta running the highest. Passenger rates vary from $60 pesos (*Salon* class on the Guaymas run) to $800 pesos per person in an *Especial* class cabin on the Cabo-Vallarta voyage. A representative price range for those with longer motorhomes or trailers would be from $1400 to $2500 pesos for a rig with a total length of 35 feet.

Don't forget to take along registration and proof of ownership papers for all of your RV equipment, including motorbikes, trailers, boats, etc. Automobile permits and other permits may then be obtained at the ferry docks if you have not received them earlier in the trip. (For example—if you entered Mexico through a mainland state such as Sonora.)

Unfortunately there is no longer any way that you can make reservations from the United States so you must go to the port of debarkation and purchase your ticket at the ferry office. This may cause a delay of a day or two if schedules or reservation loads are heavy, so try and stay flexible and enjoy the sights of the region. Most are located so that pleasant and scenic camping spots are within an easy drive. The thing to remember is to get that reservation and ticket right away.

Many passengers aboard the Cortez ferries find the atmosphere around the stern-located lounge and restaurant much like a mini-cruise ship and spend the sunset hours watching the sea glide by. A welcome break while someone else does the driving.

NOTE: Once you have parked the car on the ferry, you will not be allowed to return to it for any reason, so remove whatever you might need during the trip. A partial list of accommodations near Puerto Vallarta, Mazatlan, Los Mochis, Guaymas and Hermosillo are included in the "Resort" section on page 161.

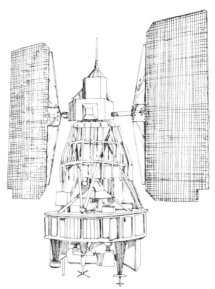

FIRST SPACE AGE PHOTOMAPS

When the authors began the preparation of this book they found that while a broad selection of maps of the peninsula existed, the physical contours, shorelines, landmark locations, etc. varied widely in most cases. It became obvious that all were incomplete by today's standards. Clearly, the time for guess-mapping had passed.

About that time, NASA launched the first U.S. program devoted exclusively to the study of earth resources from space. In 1972 the ERTS (Earth Resources Technology Satellite) Pathfinder satellite was sent into a 568-mile-high orbit around the globe, carrying special cameras and sensors to provide data relating to agriculture, forestry, land use, geology, hydrology, geography, oceanography and environmental science.

From its platform in the sky ERTS looked down on a Baja California as never seen before by man. Constantly recording the electronic EKG's of the earth with its bank of camera systems, Pathfinder radioed back thousands of images for study by scientists throughout the world.

For the first time in man's history, the long narrow peninsula that encompasses the State of Baja California and the lower Territory could be clearly seen at a single glance — a great ragged finger clawing the Pacific. Using special films, virtually every land detail was captured.

The authors discovered that they could visually detect surf breaking on the shallow beaches, even hundreds of miles of highways and towns could be seen. Surely, the key to mapping Baja was to be found in these remarkable photos.

From thousands of prints a complete set of photos of the peninsula, made on days of good visibility, was selected. Once secured, these photographs were pieced into a great nine foot high montage of Baja California.

Next came the painstaking process of transferring the many notes and sketches secured over thousands of miles of driving through virtually every corner of the vast peninsula into an easily-understood map. Using a second color, the data was overlaid onto the actual photographs, thus preserving every detail of the original pictures.

The end result was scaled into 45 full-page Baja Spacemaps®, each covering about 70 air miles of Baja at a scale of one inch to 8 miles.

BEFORE
YOU CROSS THE BORDER CHECKLIST

Make sure you have the following items, if applicable:

- Proof of citizenship . . .
- Tourist Card . . .
- All vehicle registrations and/or proof of ownership or notarized permission . . .
- Notarized permission for children other than your own if they are under 18 . . .
- Mexican Insurance . . .
- First aid kit . . .

- Emergency water . . .
- Propane tanks filled—it's hard to find in Baja . . .
- Hotel and ferry reservation proof . . .
- Fishing and Hunting licenses, guns and tackle . . .
- If you have any doubts, reread the BEFORE THE BORDER section!

NOTE . . . Don't forget to turn off the gas and lights; lock the house, put out the cat—and take THE BAJA BOOK II . . .

HOW TO USE THE BAJA SPACEMAPS®
AND BAJA ROADLOGS®

All Baja Spacemaps have been coordinated with matching Baja Roadlogs in a mile-by-mile manner on facing pages so that you can find and follow your exact location on the appropriate photomap at any time. Your position in relation to the nearby towns, peaks, arroyos and beaches is readily found, as is the nearest location of surfing, camping, fishing spots, etc. . .

Baja Roadlogs have been broken into convenient segments of about two hours drive between easily recognizable landmarks. All of the Baja Spacemaps are shown in the same relative relation to North—as indicated by the compass arrow—so that your view of the countryside will always be consistent.

The small maps of Baja in the margin of each roadlog page are marked to show your general location in the peninsula. Page numbers of connecting maps are given in the margins of every spacemap page.

We found it necessary to repeat three maps (pgs. 30&32, 62&64, 120&122) in order to accommodate the roadlogs. Notice that in several instances the roadlogs appear in reverse order because of the East to West path of the highway (Tecate to Ensenada, pgs. 34, 32; Loreto to Ciudad Constitucion, pgs. 108, 106, 104; and San Jose del Cabo to San Lucas, pgs. 124, 122).

Baja Spacemap keys are listed below:

Major Highway, paved	⚓ **Anchorages**	★ **Gas Stations**
	⊣ **Airports**	🏃 **Hunting**
Major road, unpaved	🦅 **Beachcombing**	**Missions**
	⊂ **Clamming**	🌴 **Resorts**
Minor Highway, paved	◪ **Diving**	⌐ **Surfing**
Minor road, not for standard cars	🐟 **Fishing**	🚐 **Trailerparks and Campgrounds**

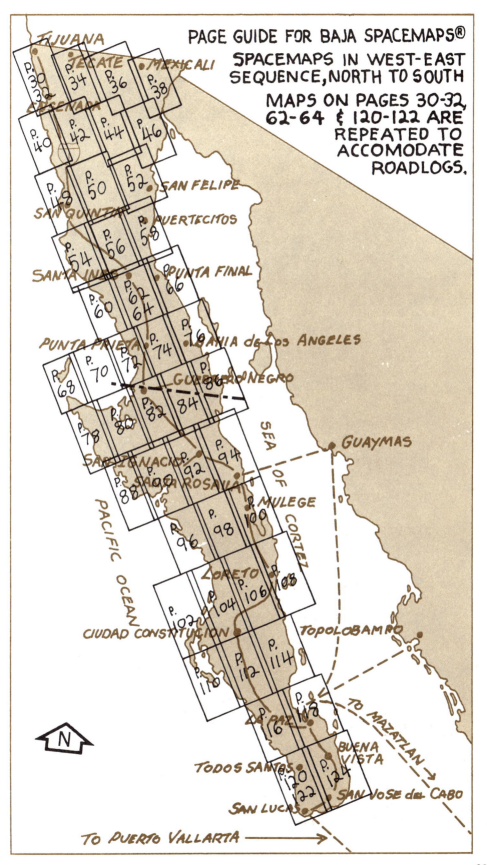

PAGE GUIDE FOR BAJA SPACEMAPS®
SPACEMAPS IN WEST-EAST
SEQUENCE, NORTH TO SOUTH

MAPS ON PAGES 30-32,
62-64 & 120-122 ARE
REPEATED TO
ACCOMODATE
ROADLOGS.

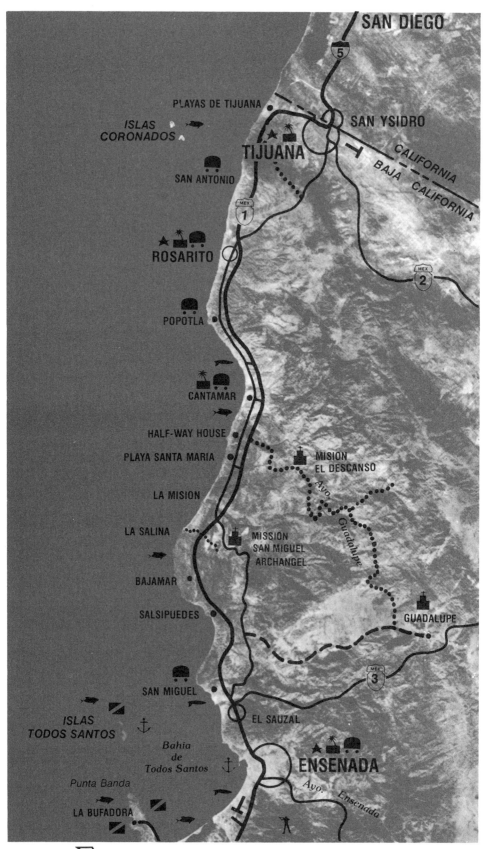

SEE PAGE 34

 SEE PAGES 40 & 42

TIJUANA — ENSENADA

Total Mileage	Running Mileage	
0	0	As you cross the border you will pass through American immigration, then Mexican customs. Last chance to get tourist permit at "Migracion" building to right as you cross border. Follow signs through new "semi-cloverleaf" indicating Ensenada toll road until you are going east along border fence. A sharp eye may be required to accomplish this as the area seems to be perennially under some sort of construction program. By the time it is all completed it is the author's opinion that this book will probably have already turned to dust!
5	5	After a steep up and down grade on divided road bear right toward the ocean.
6	1	1D highway curves south to toll gate. Road west goes to bullring and rapidly growing suburb of Playas de Tijuana.
6½	½	Toll gate is closed, probably permanently. No need to stop here at this time.
14½	8	San Antonio del Mar is to right, site of several hundred vacation homes, a KOA campground and modest motel.
16	1½	Curve gently left past truck gardens. Visible to right is a power plant, a desalting facility for Tijuana's drinking water and a Pemex tank farm complex.
19¼	3¼	Rosarito Norte sign; road to right passes through Rosarito Beach. This road rejoins toll road after passing Rosarito Beach Hotel and other services. (3 mi.)
22¼	3	Road right to Rosarito Sur and non-toll road that parallels divided 1D and goes for the next 20 miles past the many resorts. Additional turnoffs from toll road ahead at Cantiles, Cantamar and La Mision. **Stop at toll gate—about $.25 or 18 pesos per car.**
31	8½	Cantiles turnoff onto Highway 1 and several resort developments.
33½	2½	Cantamar turnoff.
42	8½	La Mision turnoff. Take full right back up free road to Plaza Santa Maria. "Libre" road continues south past American colony of La Mision and under "Cuota" 1D highway and heads inland across the arroyo, past the ruins of Mision San Miguel and winds up onto a mesa. "Libre" road rejoins 1D at 63½. The old road is scenic and winds through scattered farms. Distance 20 mi.
46¼	4¼	La Salina turnoff to several beaches with camping facilities and good fishing (perch and corbina).
49½	3¼	Jatay turnoff, to Bajamar resort development. Highway curves gradually through rocky terrain with scattered brush and agave cactus.
53½	4	El Mirador turnoff. Just past here is a curve to the left that should be taken with caution....30 to 40 mph. To the right is an almost vertical 600 ft. drop into the Pacific Ocean giving a spectacular view of the coastline. Road follows the ocean as it gradually drops to 100 ft over the next 10 miles.
63	9½	Last toll gate—around $.35 or 20 pesos per car. San Miguel Village is to right.

(continued on page 33)

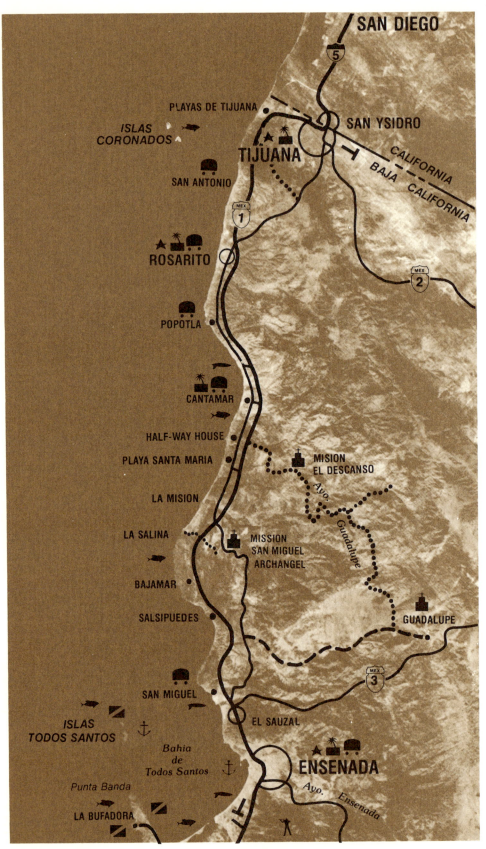

SAN DIEGO

5

SAN YSIDRO

PLAYAS DE TIJUANA

ISLAS CORONADOS

TIJUANA

CALIFORNIA

BAJA CALIFORNIA

SAN ANTONIO

MEX 1

MEX 2

ROSARITO

POPOTLA

CANTAMAR

HALF-WAY HOUSE

PLAYA SANTA MARIA

MISION EL DESCANSO

Avo. Guadalupe

LA MISION

LA SALINA

MISSION SAN MIGUEL ARCHANGEL

BAJAMAR

SALSIPUEDES

GUADALUPE

MEX 3

SAN MIGUEL

ISLAS TODOS SANTOS

EL SAUZAL

Bahia de Todos Santos

ENSENADA

Punta Banda

Avo. Ensenada

LA BUFADORA

SEE PAGE 34

N

SEE PAGES 40 & 42

Total Mileage	Running Mileage	

TIJUANA — ENSENADA (continued from page 31)

Total Mileage	Running Mileage	
63½	½	Ensenada "Libre" road rejoins highway. Proceed past cotton storage sheds. 3 M's surfing spot is to right. San Miguel Village and more surfing is several hundred yards back to the northwest.
64½	1	Side road to right is Tecate road. Proceed past a number of motels, campgrounds and the cannery community of El Sauzal.
69½	5	Curve right at fork to Muelle and Ensenada after passing Granada Cove Motel.
71	1½	Enter downtown Ensenada past more cotton sheds. (See Ensenada map page 130)

TECATE — ENSENADA (continued from page 35)

49	8½	Road right to Guadalupe, 1 mi. Continue past farms and ranches. Road winds at times but easy driving.
61	12	Pass small settlement and cross narrow bridge. Road goes sharply to left, 30 mph then follow canyon down toward Mexico 1, 7 miles north of Ensenada.
66	5	Junction with Mexico 1.

TIJUANA — MEXICALI

0	0	As you pass the Mexican Customs officials at the border, note the "Migracion" office on the right. Follow signs along new divided highway that say "Racetrack" and "Mexico 2".
4	4	Road right is to racetrack, hotels, etc. Continue east through La Mesa, a suburb of Tijuana.
11½	7½	Wind uphill and turn sharp to left, 25 mph.
12	½	Rodrigues Dam—flood control for Tijuana and some of water supply. Continue upgrade.
24	12	Road continues winding uphill past sign on right, "Canada Verde". Giant boulders next 5 miles on both sides of Mexico 2.

(continued on page 35)

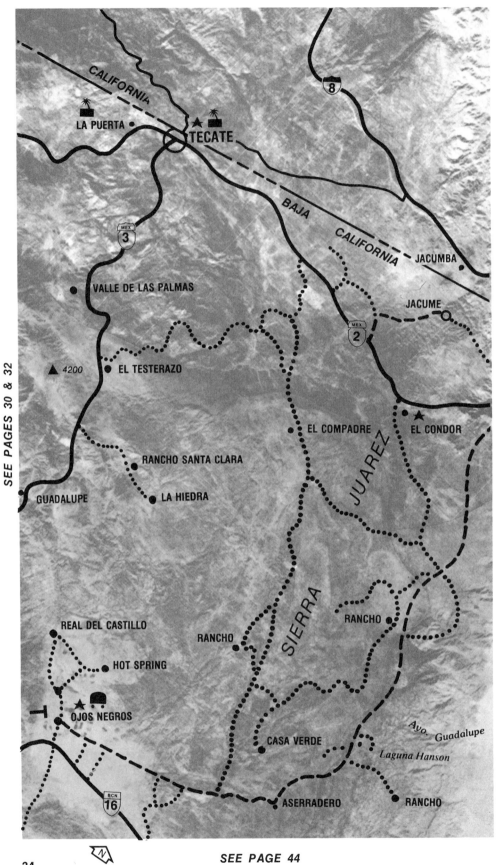

SEE PAGES 30 & 32

SEE PAGE 36

CALIFORNIA

8

LA PUERTA

★ TECATE

BAJA

CALIFORNIA

JACUMBA

MEX 3

VALLE DE LAS PALMAS

JACUME

MEX 2

▲ 4200   EL TESTERAZO

EL COMPADRE   ★ EL CONDOR

JUAREZ

RANCHO SANTA CLARA

GUADALUPE   LA HIEDRA

SIERRA

RANCHO

REAL DEL CASTILLO

HOT SPRING

RANCHO

★ OJOS NEGROS

Ayo. Guadalupe

CASA VERDE

Laguna Hanson

BCN 16

ASERRADERO   RANCHO

34   N   SEE PAGE 44

Total Mileage	Running Mileage	**TECATE—ENSENADA**
0	0	Leave Tecate heading south past park and several large buildings on left.
2	2	Begin climb out of valley. Winding, 30 mph.
5½	3½	Rancho San Lorenzo on right.
8½	3	Road winds up hill, 30 mph.
10	1½	Top of grade.
18	8	Small community of Valle de las Palmas on right.
19½	1½	Road right to Cerro Bolas 12 km. Road winds up hill and back toward NE, following canyon.
25½	6	Top of grade, road now heading generally south.
28	2½	Downgrade, winding, 35 mph.
31½	3½	Road left to El Testorazo.
32	½	Sign: Colonia Guadalupe 32 km. Continue through open range country and a winding stretch up hill.
40½	8½	Pass sign: Ej. Ignacio Zaragosa and begin downgrade, steep in places and sharp turns. 25-35 mph.

(continued on page 33)

TIJUANA—MEXICALI (continued from page 33)

28½	4½	Road on right is to orphanage. Vineyards along road.
30	1½	Famous health spa, Rancho La Puerta is on right.
32¾	2¾	Enter Tecate and straight ahead at fork. Right branch parallels other and leads to Ensenada road at signal past brewery. (see Tecate map page 123).
35	2¼	Leave Tecate and begin winding upgrade.
37½	2½	Sharp turn left, 25 mph.
40	2½	Large auto junkyard on hill to north.
44½	4½	Road right goes to Rosa de Castilla, 43 miles.
47	2½	Wind uphill through well-kept vineyards. Grapes go to Santo Tomas winery in Ensenada for processing.
51	4	Several ranches along road.
55½	4½	Colonia Luis Echiverria Alvarez on right.
60½	5	Road left to Ejido Jacumbe, 10 km (6 miles).
65	4½	El Condor—several small houses, gas station and cafe, road to the south by gas station goes to Laguna Hanson and beyond, but best road to Laguna Hanson is from La Rumerosa.

(continued on page 37)

THE ROADS TO THE SOUTH

The high tableland that extends south of El Condor and La Rumerosa is a maze of paths, trails and roads that date variously back to the Indian tribes of pre-Spanish days, the Padres and explorers of the 18th century and the gold seekers of the 1880's. Many of the isolated ranchos of the region had their beginnings as a village, mission waystation or mining camp.

Today the single lane dirt road south from La Rumerosa past Laguna Hanson (Laguna Juarez) is passable to standard cars, with more rugged vehicles recommended for the others. The great pine forests, broad grassy meadows and the sparkling lake are somewhat of a surprise to visitors. It is a region that offers much to the hiker and camper.

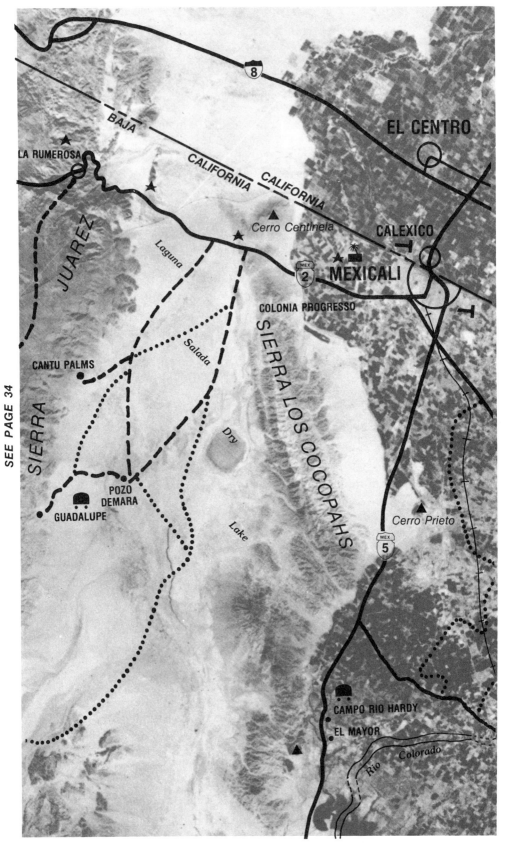

SEE PAGE 34

SEE PAGE 38

EL CENTRO

LA RUMEROSA

BAJA

CALIFORNIA CALIFORNIA

JUAREZ

Cerro Centinela

CALEXICO

Laguna

MEX 2

MEXICALI

COLONIA PROGRESSO

CANTU PALMS

SIERRA

Salada

SIERRA LOS COCOPAHS

Dry

POZO
DEMARA

GUADALUPE

Cerro Prieto

MEX 5

Lake

CAMPO RIO HARDY

EL MAYOR

Rio Colorado

36

N

TIJUANA—MEXICALI (continued from page 35)

Total Mileage	Running Mileage	
73	8	After passing through area of small mining operations of various sorts, arrive at La Rumerosa. Here, easily travelled dirt road goes south to Laguna Hanson (39 miles).
74	1	Begin twisting descent to desert floor down Cuesta La Rumerosa grade. Many sharp turns and spectacular views of Mexicali and Imperial Valleys. Make sure brakes are in good order.
89½	15½	A Pemex station is just ahead on N. side at bottom of grade.
101½	12	Marked road south across lakebed is to Canon Guadalupe. Cantu Palms is 19 mi., and Canon Guadalupe, 35. (See page 141)
103	1½	Reach top of low pass into Mexicali Valley. Watch for sharp curve near top.
115	12	You pass a number of small Ejidos as you approach Mexicali. In Colonia Zaragosa, there is a small charro ring on south side of highway.
117	2	Intersection of Avenida Guadalupe and Mexico Highway 2. Go North to border or straight for San Felipe and Sonora. (see Mexicali map page 128)

MEXICALI—SAN FELIPE

0	0	Begin from border crossing in Mexicali, turn left at first signal, left again at next corner and follow road east along border fence. (See Mexicali map page 128).
2½	2½	Turn right onto divided avenue "Justo Sierra".
4	1½	After passing stores and PepsiCola bottling plant, continue south past monument in center of street.
6	2	Highway, Mexico 2, goes left to San Luis and Guaymas.
7	1	Highway, Mexico 2, on right to Tecate and Tijuana.
17½	10½	Paved road left to Cerro Prieta geothermal steam plant, largest in North America, supplying much of the electrical requirements of Mexicali Valley. Continue through farmlands.
31	13½	Paved road left to Coahuilla, Riito and El Golfo.
41	10	On the left is Campo Rio Hardy, a trailer camp with rustic vacation homes for a number of Americans. The area boasts fine hunting plus fishing in canals and river. 1 mile south is El Mayor, home for a number of Cucapa Indians, original inhabitants of the lower Colorado delta region.
46	5	Enter alkalai flats of the Laguna Salada, extending about 50 miles to NNW.

(continued on page 47)

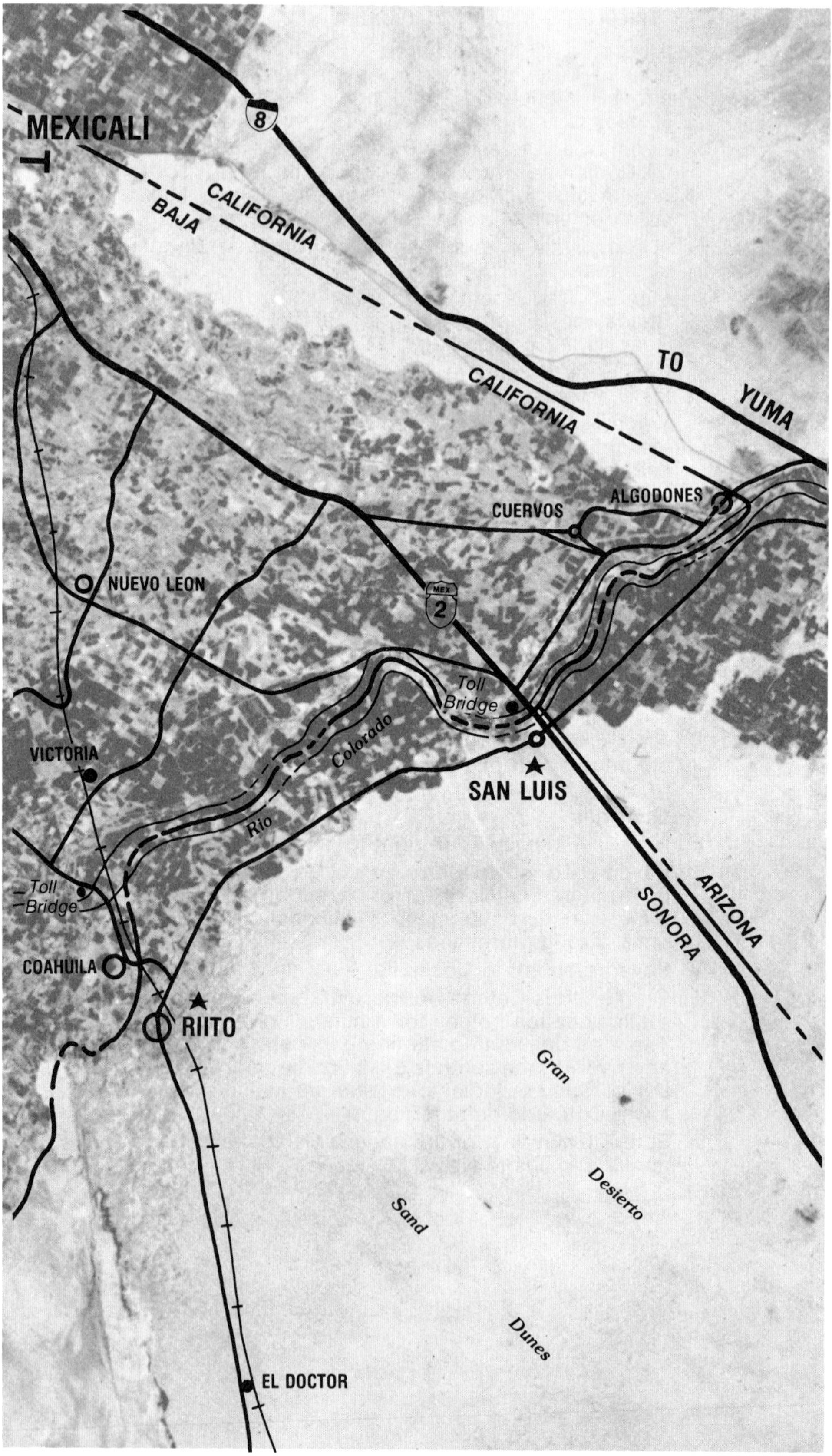

SEE PAGE 36

MEXICALI

BAJA CALIFORNIA

CALIFORNIA

TO YUMA

8

ALGODONES

CUERVOS

NUEVO LEON

MEX 2

Toll Bridge

VICTORIA

Colorado

Rio

SAN LUIS

Toll Bridge

ARIZONA

SONORA

COAHUILA

RIITO

Gran

Desierto

Sand

Dunes

EL DOCTOR

38

N

SEE PAGE 46

A DUNE BUGGY PARADISE

Although not actually in Baja California, a town 45 miles south of Riito—El Golfo de Santa Clara—should be mentioned, especially for the benefit of the off-road buff.

This small fishing town is barely touched by the Norteamericano traveller. Facilities are minimal and there is little to do unless you are equipped to travel along the beaches that extend 40 miles to the southeast.

This undisturbed stretch of sand is a treasure trove of shells and clams. Behind the bluffs to the north are quantities of petrified ironwood and colorful rocks. It is not advisable to travel this back country alone, however, as help is a long way off.

Limited camping facilities are to be found just above and below town, while the several native restaurants serve fish and shrimp.

El Golfo is particularly popular with the residents of Mexicali and San Luis during the Easter holidays when El Golfo takes on a carnival atmosphere.

100 MILE SHORTCUT

The region east and south of Mexicali is the scene of extensive farming (seen on the map from 568 miles in space as tiny squares). Mexico Highway 2 passes through the many farms, across a toll bridge over the Rio Colorado and into San Luis in the state of Sonora. The road south from San Luis is paved all the way to El Golfo de Santa Clara and follows along the bluffs that rise to the east of the Rio Colorado.

Highway 2 extends eastward from San Luis to meet Mexico 15, which is the main route for those driving to Guaymas, Mazatlan, and Puerto Vallarta. Southern California motorists headed for Mexico's West Coast can save 100 miles by using Highway 2.

THE WILL TO SURVIVE

The early Indians who lived along the Rio Colorado below Yuma regularly made long pilgrimages across many miles of hostile desert in search of food. The ripening of the pinon pines would bring them across the Laguna Salada onto the mile-high plateaus of the Sierra Juarez. They also walked 75 or more miles through the barren salt flats to the beaches near San Felipe to gather clams and spear fish. Both trips required monumental endurance and emphasized the desperate will to survive exhibited by these people.

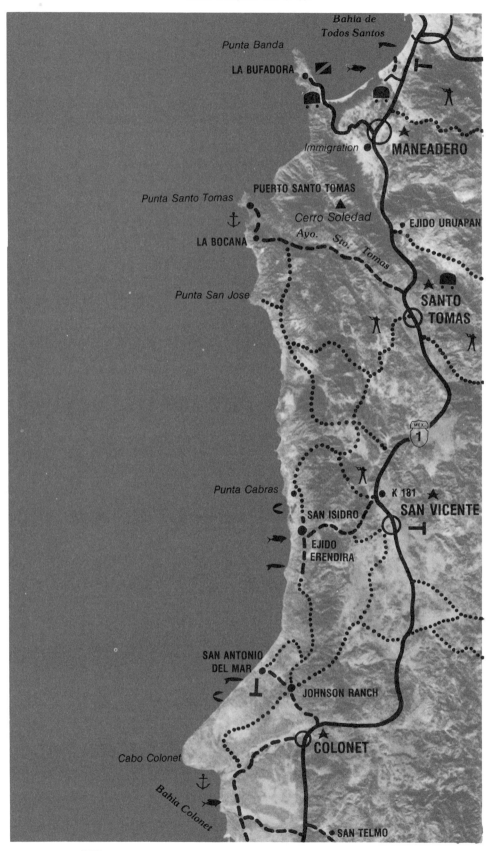

Bahia de
Todos Santos

Punta Banda

LA BUFADORA

Immigration

MANEADERO

Punta Santo Tomas

PUERTO SANTO TOMAS

Cerro Soledad

EJIDO URUAPAN

LA BOCANA

Ayo.   Sto.   Tomas

Punta San Jose

SANTO
TOMAS

MEX.
1

Punta Cabras

K 181

SAN VICENTE

SAN ISIDRO

EJIDO
ERENDIRA

SAN ANTONIO
DEL MAR

JOHNSON RANCH

Cabo Colonet

COLONET

Bahia Colonet

SAN TELMO

SEE PAGE 42

SEE PAGE 48

ENSENADA—PARADOR SAN QUINTIN

Total Mileage	Running Mileage	
0	0	Leave town from "Y" at south end of town, near Colonel Sander's Chicken stand. Proceed south past several hotels and trailer camps, El Cipres military camp and the airport.
5	5	Paved road right leads through Ejido Chapultepec to Estero Beach Resort (2 mi.) (left at winery) and Corona Beach Resort (2 mi.) (right at same intersection).
7	2	Dirt road left goes to San Carlos Hot Springs (12 mi.) through rows of tall trees.
9	2	Mexico 1 goes to left at fork at south end of Maneadero. Take right for paved road to Punta Banda and La Bufadora (12½ mi.).
10½	1½	**Site of recently closed "Migracion" check point. It is noted in case it reopens, in which case you will have to have tourist card validated. Continue SE up arroyo. Watch speed on curves next 8 miles.**
21	10½	Road left to Rancho Los Malcriados.
24½	3½	Ejido Uruapan to left.
26	1½	Sharp turns, begin descent into Santo Tomas Valley. Speed 30 mph.
28	2	Road right to Ejido Ajusco and Puerto Santo Tomas.
30	2	Pass El Palomar Resort and Campground, through Santo Tomas and follow valley floor 5 miles and begin ascent on south side of arroyo.
38	8	Reach top of grade and enter farming area.
47	9	Road right to Ejido Erendira, San Isidro and beach. After turning off highway, bear left at next 3 forks and follow arroyo and small streambed into main Arroyo de San Vicente, then to ocean (11 mi.). Surfing, fishing, shelling, camping, etc. Road right up hill at first fork is to Punta Cabra.
53½	6½	Enter San Vicente. Two Pemex stations and several stores with some supplies. 1 mile south of town is new motel El Camino.
58	4½	Rancho Santa Marta on right. Continue through rolling farmlands and small arroyo past Ejido Milton Castellanos (9½ mi.).
73	15	Green building on left is excellent bakery. Ovens are heated with firewood in centuries-old manner. It was originally purple but Baja Book readers brought so much business that the overworked baker decided to camoflage it.
75½	2½	Enter Colonet. Road right just before left curve goes to Johnson Ranch and San Antonio del Mar.
84	8½	Road left to San Telmo (2 mi.) Meling Ranch (31 mi.) and new National Observatory (approx. 53 mi.). Mexico 1 continues south through farmlands with a number of sideroads to ocean.

(continued on page 49)

Islas de Todos Santos ... help to provide calm anchorages in Bahia Todos Santos off of Ensenada. They are popular with locally-based sportfishing boats and yachtsmen from the U.S. There are several coves where a small boat can land for a look around. It is interesting, but watch out for the flies— they are persistent —and they bite.

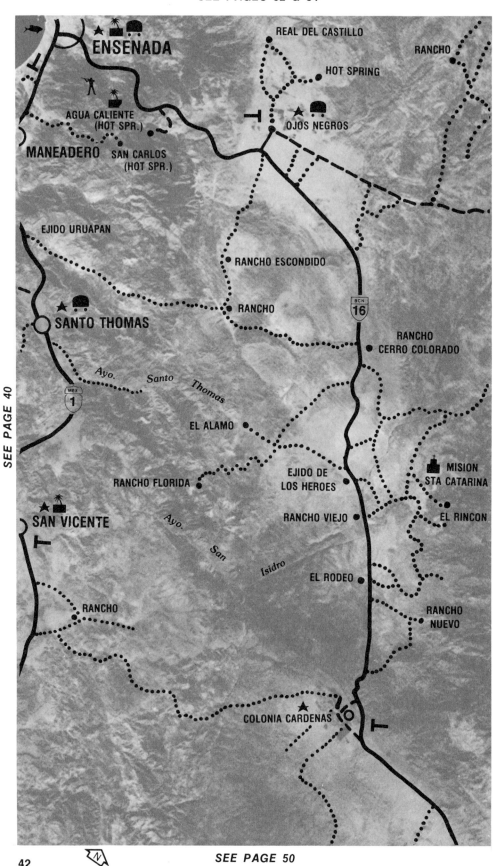

REAL DEL CASTILLO

RANCHO

ENSENADA

HOT SPRING

OJOS NEGROS

AGUA CALIENTE
(HOT SPR.)

MANEADERO   SAN CARLOS
(HOT SPR.)

SEE PAGE 40

EJIDO URUAPAN

RANCHO ESCONDIDO

RANCHO

BCN
16

SANTO THOMAS

RANCHO
CERRO COLORADO

Ayo. Santo Thomas

MEX
1

EL ALAMO

RANCHO FLORIDA

EJIDO DE
LOS HEROES

MISION
STA CATARINA

SAN VICENTE

Ayo.

San

RANCHO VIEJO

EL RINCON

Isidro

EL RODEO

SEE PAGE 44

RANCHO

RANCHO
NUEVO

COLONIA CARDENAS

42   N   SEE PAGE 50

Total Mileage	Running Mileage	
0	0	Leave Ensenada on Calzada Cortes near Benito Juarez Monument, heading east past a number of stores and homes.
1½	1½	Follow highway as it curves upward into hills. Roadbed is winding but easily travelled at 40 mph.
9½	8	Good view of Bahia Todos Santos and islands to west. Continue upward on winding road with several sharp curves.
17½	8	Dirt road to right is to Aguas Caliente Resort. Mexico 16 continues to wind, finally descending into Ojos Negros Valley. Watch for several well marked sharp curves.
26¼	8¾	Paved road left goes to Ojos Negros and to dirt road leading to Laguna Hanson and, eventually, La Rumerosa.
32	5¾	Poor road left leads past rancho and on to Laguna Hanson Road. Road continues southeast through several valleys and past a number of ranches and small farming colonies. Vegetation is typical of high plains—chaparral, mesquite and manzanita.
57	25	Ejido Heroes de la Independencia is to right. About 500 people live here. Gas and limited supplies available.
64½	7½	Road left, 1 mile, to agricultural community of El Rodeo.
73	8½	Road begins descent into Valle Trinidad, turning east and skirting north portion of this large agricultural settlement.
76½	3½	One of several roads into community of Lazaro Cardenas, but this one is paved. Pemex, stores and cafe here.
88	11½	Road right goes south into San Pedro Martirs and Mike's Sky Ranch (21 mi.). This is direct route to an interesting area, but not recommended for standard cars. Continue past small farm area.

(continued on page 45)

SCREECH OWL

SEE PAGE 34

SEE PAGE 42

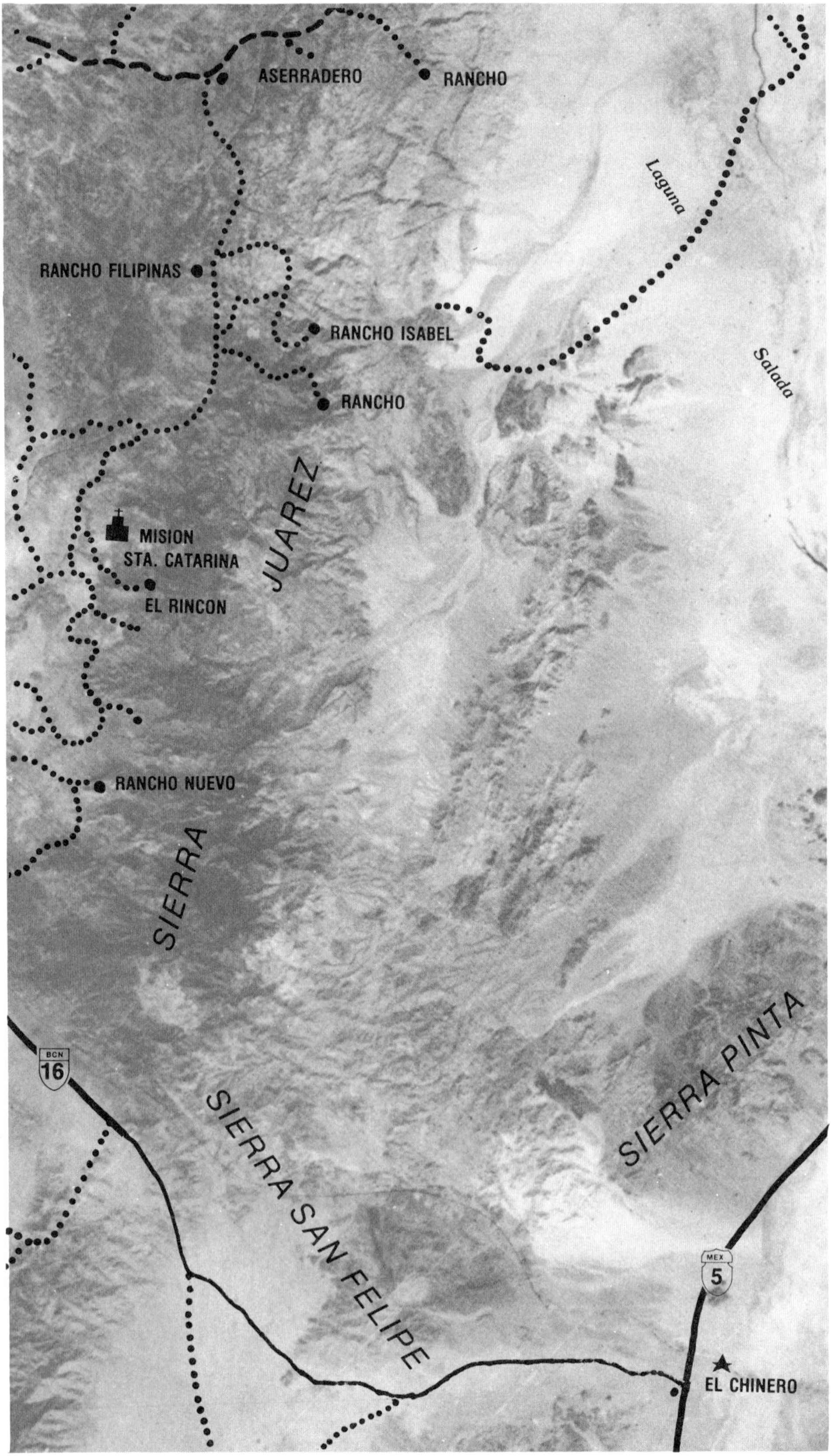

ASERRADERO
RANCHO
Laguna
Salada
RANCHO FILIPINAS
RANCHO ISABEL
RANCHO
JUAREZ
MISION
STA. CATARINA
EL RINCON
RANCHO NUEVO
SIERRA
BCN
16
SIERRA SAN FELIPE
SIERRA PINTA
MEX
5
EL CHINERO

SEE PAGE 46

SEE PAGE 52

92	4	Enter winding area along rocky side of arroyo. Several sharp curves ahead. At bottom of arroyo dirt road right goes through dry lake bed and dunes to San Felipe (46 mi.) but 4 WD advisable. Continue due east.
98	6	All around are varieties of desert plants and in distance to north is Picacho del Diablo (10,156 ft.) Continue in easterly direction.
111	13	First view of Sea of Cortez barely visible on horizon past salt flats. Follow paved road through series of shallow "vados."
121	10	Reach Mexico 5 at Crucero Trinidad. San Felipe is to south 31 miles.

YOUNG CARDON

LAND OF CONTRASTS

A flight over this portion of the Sierra Juarez shows an even more rugged landscape than that seen from the Ensenada-San Felipe road. Occasionally, among the rolling brush covered hills, a tiny ranchhouse will be spotted in the middle of a small clearing. Their only link with survival is often a laboriously dug well and a few head of cattle that live off of the grasses and shoots in the surrounding wilderness.

Spring and early summer brings numerous varieties of shrubs, cacti and wildflowers into bloom in patches of yellow, orange, red and blue. Deer, coyote and skunks are among the many species foraging through the head-high manzanita, scruboak, creosote bush and sage.

As you proceed south and east toward the pass leading onto the San Felipe plain, numerous varieties of cactus gradually replace the mountain flora as the climate becomes more arid.

A good supply of underground water has allowed the ranchers of Valle Trinidad to raise large crops of peaches, plums, almonds and potatoes. The challenge was not so much in raising the crop but in trucking it out of the valley over the long rough road without damaging it. Recent grading and the promise of a paved highway has encouraged new settlers to clear more land.

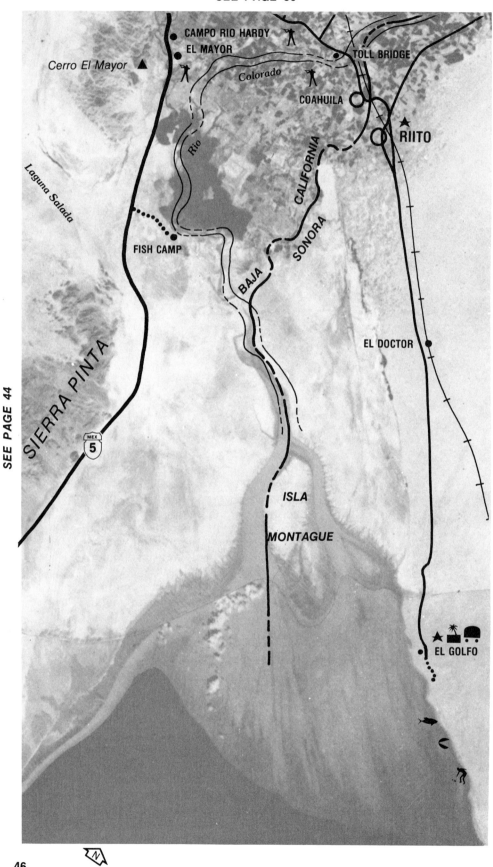

MEXICALI—SAN FELIPE (continued from page 37)

62	16	Enter area of dunes and brush that boasts beautiful wildflowers following winter rains. Road winds a bit here.
72	10	Pemex station and cantina "La Ventana". Road to south is straight and good as it passes through a number of shallow arroyos.
90	18	Ahead to left is black volcanic hill, El Chinero, named for a group of Chinese who died of thirst near here while trying to walk from San Felipe to Mexicali.

(continued on page 53)

WATCH THOSE HIGH TIDES

Solar and lunar forces that create tidal surges on the world's oceans cause something special to occur in the Sea of Cortez.

The three foot variation from high to low tide that occurs at Cabo San Lucas is transformed into a sometimes raging surge of nearly thirty feet at the mouth of the Rio Colorado, 600 miles to the north.

As the waters surge past the islands of the Cortez, many currents are developed that can either hinder the progress of a boat or speed it unexpectedly along its way.

The gently sloping beaches near San Felipe and El Golfo de Santa Clara may be exposed for more than a half-mile on a low tide, affording wonderful opportunities for the shell collector and clammer.

More than one boatsman has seen his craft floating merrily out to sea, unattended, because he went up to his camp for just a minute. He has also had his craft left high and dry hundreds of yards from the water after only a few hours.

Make sure that your activities in the North portion of the Cortez are done with an eye on the tide.

The University of Arizona in Tucson has available a tide table for the regions around San Felipe. Copies may be obtained by sending $2.50 to the attention of the Printing-Reproduction Department, University of Arizona, Tucson, AZ 85721 and requesting the tide table.

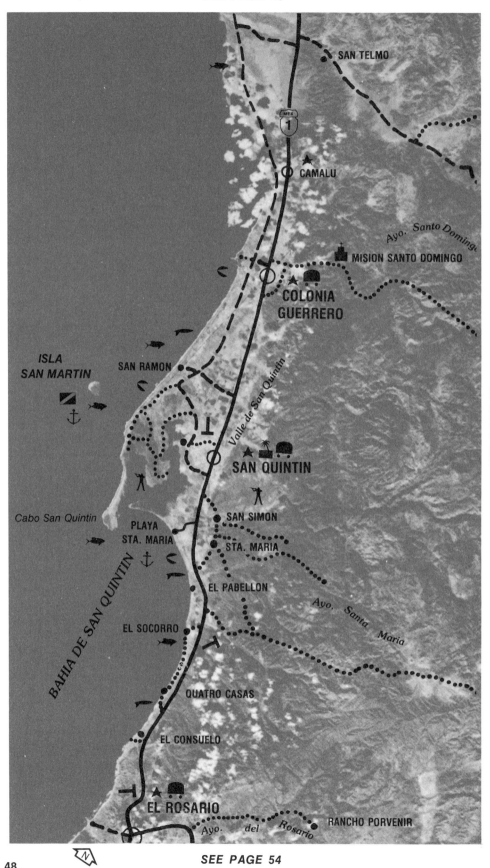

SAN TELMO

MEX 1

CAMALU

Ayo. Santo Domingo

MISION SANTO DOMINGO

COLONIA GUERRERO

ISLA SAN MARTIN

SAN RAMON

Valle de San Quintin

SAN QUINTIN

Cabo San Quintin

SAN SIMON

PLAYA STA. MARIA

STA. MARIA

EL PABELLON

Ayo. Santa Maria

BAHIA DE SAN QUINTIN

EL SOCORRO

QUATRO CASAS

EL CONSUELO

EL ROSARIO

RANCHO PORVENIR

Ayo. del Rosario

SEE PAGE 50

N

ENSENADA—PARADOR SAN QUINTIN

(continued from page 41)

Total Mileage	Running Mileage	
90½	6½	Rancho Ibarra on right. This was as far as road was paved in early 1972.
95½	5	Camalu; Pemex station on right. Road just north of tall green tanks goes to nice beach with clamming (rock clams) and good surf fishing. Camping sites available.
104½	9	Colonia Guerrero; Pemex station and store. South 1 mile is entrance to Posada Don Diego on right. Very good camping facilities and restaurant.
116	11½	Enter San Quintin. Several Pemex stations and stores with adequate supplies. 2 miles farther is new military camp on right. Road narrows shortly.
123	7	Road right is marked "Muelle Viejo", "old pier." It is also the best road into Old Mill Motel (Molino Viejo). Main road narrows—to 19½ ft.—with few shoulders. Watch opposing traffic. This is the narrowest stretch of the entire Baja highway. Condition continues for some miles.
127	4	Parador San Quintin, recently completed service center with gasoline, food, washrooms, tourist information, etc. Road right is into El Presidente San Quintin hotel and beach.

PARADOR SAN QUINTIN-PARADOR SANTA INES

0	0	Continue south on Mexico 1 from Parador San Quintin. In ¾ mile you pass road right leading to new 60 room Hotel San Quintin on wide sandy beach with good clamming and surf fishing. Beautiful, modern hotel with all facilities.
4½	4½	Right road to El Pabellon Beach (1½ mi.). Watch for sandy spots on this side road. Highway climbs sandy hills and follows south 2-3 miles from ocean.
8½	3½	Road right angles down to Rancho Soccoro. Good fishing and camping along here almost anywhere for next 11 miles. Bluffs above road are covered with fossil shells.
20	12	Turn uphill away from beach toward El Rosario. 30-35 mph on twisting portions of road. Climb to top of plateau through barren sandy hills.
27	7	Begin descent into Arroyo de El Rosario, steep and winding, 25 mph.
29	2	Arrive El Rosario. Gas, lodging and meals at Espinoza's place on left at corner. Right road at corner goes to ocean and across arroyo to old mission ruins. Main road goes out of town on north side of arroyo.

(continued on page 55)

Isla San Geronimo . . . a barren ¼ by ¾ mile pile of bird lime about ten miles south of Punta Baja and five miles offshore. Area for lobster, abalone and fishing, mostly by long-range boats.   (see page 54)

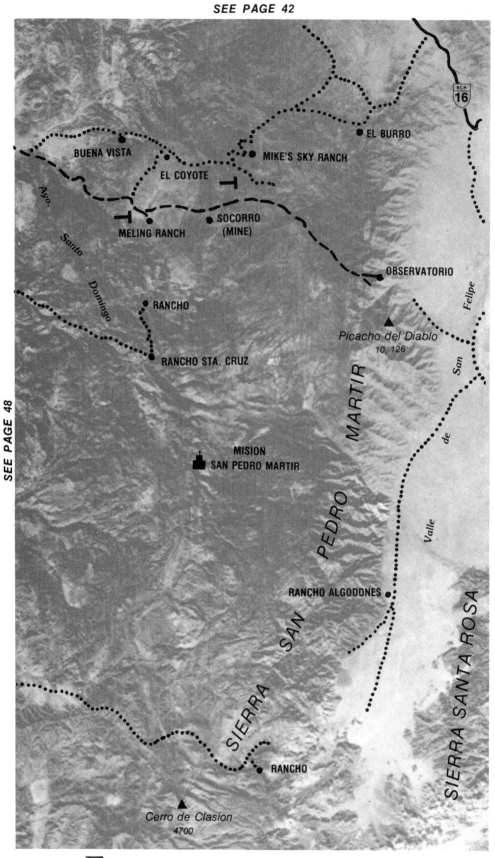

EL BURRO

BUENA VISTA

MIKE'S SKY RANCH

EL COYOTE

MELING RANCH

SOCORRO
(MINE)

Ayo.

Santo

Domingo

OBSERVATORIO

Felipe

RANCHO

Picacho del Diablo
10, 126

RANCHO STA. CRUZ

San

MARTIR

MISION
SAN PEDRO MARTIR

PEDRO

de

Valle

SAN

RANCHO ALGODONES

SIERRA

SIERRA SANTA ROSA

RANCHO

Cerro de Clasion
4700

N

SEE PAGE 48

SEE PAGE 52

TWO-MILE HIGH MOUNTAINS

The mountainous backbone of Baja California reaches its greatest heights in the Sierra de San Pedro Martir. A rocky forested tableland nearly seventy-five miles in length, it is in sharp contrast to the regions that surround it.

To the east, it drops precipitously for over one mile onto the San Felipe Plain and the Sea of Cortez. This side is scarred by a number of rocky, palm dotted canyons that once served as refuges for the nomadic Indians of the region. The small streams provided moisture for their survival and that of the desert bighorn sheep and deer that they hunted.

The six to nine thousand foot high plateau that makes up the central portion of the San Pedro Martir is well forested and contains abundant wildlife around the many springs and year-around streams that wind through the alpine meadows. It is here that a species of trout is found that occurs nowhere else. (see Meling Ranch in town section, page 132).

Dominating the entire range is the 10,126-foot high mountain variously called Picacho del Diablo, Cerro de la Encantada and La Providencia. Separated somewhat by the Canyon del Diablo, this picacho presents a challenge to the mountain climber that has been met only a few times during the last quarter-century. Its sometime-snowy escarpments may be seen from both the Cortez and the Pacific.

Just to the northwest on another high ridge, the Mexican government has built an observatory which boasts the clearest air of any in the world. To insure a minimum of interference with operation of the telescopes, the government has even limited the amount of outdoor lighting in the town of San Felipe, 40 miles to the east.

Each winter the high plateaus of both the Martir and Juarez ranges are visited by deep snows and travel during this time is not recommended. The balance of the year, however, offers great recreation to the hiker and back packer.

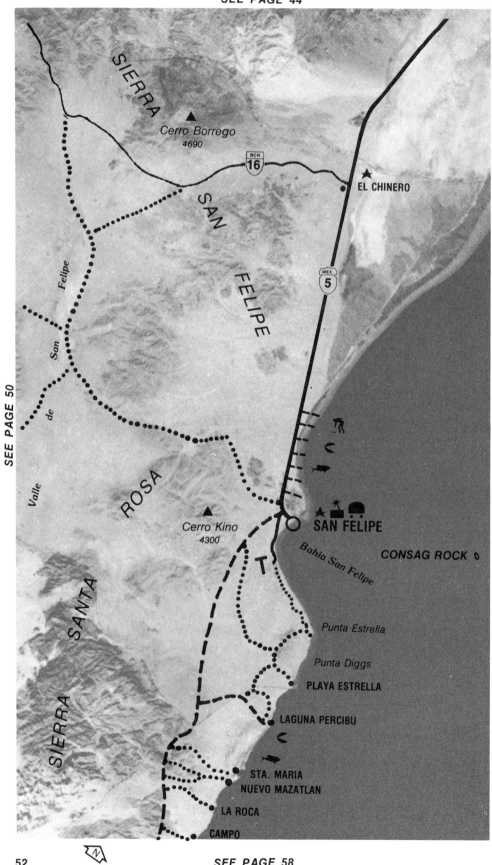

SIERRA

Cerro Borrego
4690

SAN

FELIPE

BCN
16

★ **EL CHINERO**

MEX
5

San Felipe

San

de

Valle

ROSA

Cerro Kino
4300

SANTA

SIERRA

○ **SAN FELIPE**

CONSAG ROCK ◌

Bahía San Felipe

T

Punta Estrella

Punta Diggs

PLAYA ESTRELLA

LAGUNA PERCIBU

STA. MARIA
NUEVO MAZATLAN

LA ROCA

CAMPO

N

MEXICALI—SAN FELIPE (continued from page 47)

Total Mileage	Running Mileage	
96	6	Road comes in from west from San Felipe. A good road to take in hot weather as much of it is through mountains.
116	20	Left to Playa Grande camp, one of a number of campos along gulf north of San Felipe. Road continues straight south.
120	4	Left to Playa del Sol camp.
125	5	Enter San Felipe past tall arch on divided road and paved road which leads to hotel, past beach and on to new airport.

SAN FELIPE—PUERTECITOS

0	0	The road leaves the highway south about 400 yards west of the main intersection in San Felipe, past a small plaza containing a few trees and a little patch of grass. It leaves town across a fairly stable sandy base.
3¼	3¼	Road left leads 11 mi. to Punta Estrella, then follows south behind dunes past Punta Diggs and Percebu, returning to Puertecitos road after about 20 mi. Don't try this in a standard car.
21	17¾	Southern end of road to Percebu described above. There are a number of sandy roads between San Felipe and here that go off to Gulf. A popular region with off-road vehicle set. There are a number of camps along the beaches.
22	1	Abandoned sulfur mine on right. There are a number of the strange, stubby elephant trees around here and on to the south. To left is road to small camping and fishing beach. (5 mi.)
22½	½	Road left to "Campo Nuevo Mazatlan", a well organized camp with water and toilets. (4½ mi.) This road is passable in standard car.

(continued on page 59)

LOVE IN THE AFTERNOON

Baja California and the Sea of Cortez is known to contain many things that are unique to this region alone . . . and one of these is a species of grunion that performs its beachside love dance in broad daylight!

Many residents of Southern California know the Pacific grunion as a small smelt-like fish that lays its eggs along the sandy beaches late at night.

North of Guaymas and Bahia de Los Angeles during the months of January to June, watch for these beachbound visitors in the late afternoons. They usually appear for several days following a new and full moon. Gulf grunion make an excellent bait, and they are also fine eating when scaled, rolled in flour or bread crumbs and deep fried.

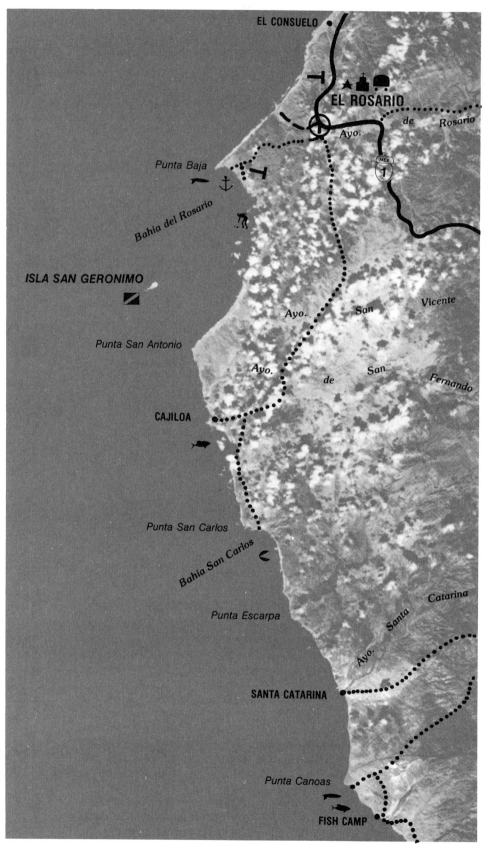

EL CONSUELO

EL ROSARIO

de   Rosario

Ayo.

MEX
1

Punta Baja

Bahia del Rosario

ISLA SAN GERONIMO

Ayo.   San   Vicente

Punta San Antonio

Ayo.   de   San   Fernando

CAJILOA

Punta San Carlos

Bahia San Carlos

Catarina

Punta Escarpa

Ayo.   Santa

SANTA CATARINA

Punta Canoas

FISH CAMP

PARADOR SAN QUINTIN—
PARADOR SANTA INES (continued from page 49)

Total Mileage	Running Mileage	
33½	4½	Road crosses streambed and climbs into a low range of hills. Road continuing up north side of valley leads to Rancho Provenir.
42	8½	Road goes through first stands of cirios and cardon cactus. You will see many more of these plants before you leave Baja. Watch for approaching traffic as road is still narrow and has no turnouts. Road often follows tops of ridges, winding up and down.

(continued on page 57)

CIRIO

THE WEIRD CIRIO

One of the most fascinating plants of Baja is the cirio tree, **Idria columnaris.** Occurring in a 150 mile wide east-west corridor from below El Rosario to just north of Guerrero Negro, it is a tree of great distinction. Not only does it survive in one of the harshest climates in the world but it provides, in its endless odd shapes, a natural subject for the photographer.

When young, the cirio is a roundish stubby plant that slowly elongates as it extends skyward, looking much like a carrot that has been turned upside-down. The larger specimens develop branches that look like wildly waving arms.

In mid-winter, tiny leaves appear that quickly die to leave a barren thorny stalk. Later, bunches of small yellow flowers appear on the tips of the branches.

Occasionally the cirio will be referred to as a "boojum" due to its resemblance, in the eyes of botanist Godfrey Sykes, to the description of a fanciful desert dwelling creature in Lewis Carroll's story "The Hunting of the Snark".

SEE PAGE 54

SEE PAGE 58

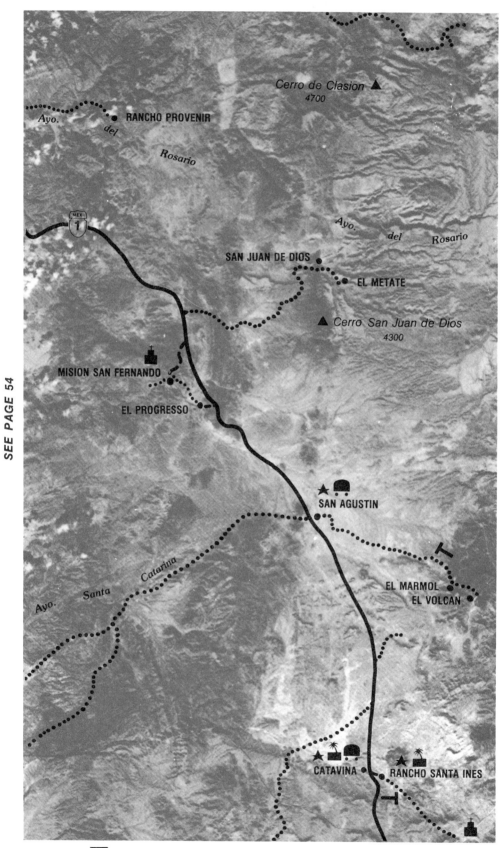

Cerro de Clasion ▲
4700

Ayo. del Rosario

RANCHO PROVENIR

MEX 1

Ayo. del Rosario

SAN JUAN DE DIOS

EL METATE

▲ Cerro San Juan de Dios
4300

MISION SAN FERNANDO

EL PROGRESSO

SAN AGUSTIN

Ayo. Santa Catarina

EL MARMOL
EL VOLCAN

CATAVINA

RANCHO SANTA INES

56

PARADOR SAN QUINTIN—
PARADOR SANTA INES (continued from page 55)

Total Mileage	Running Mileage	
55	13	About 1 mile to right there is a turquoise mine being worked. It is private property, but there are several other abandoned mines on hillsides to left. Continue winding through low hills.
65½	10½	Road right to Rancho Arenoso. This is open cattle range.
70½	5	New dirt road on right to ruins of Mision San Fernando. (see page 166)
75½	5	El Progresso to right. Take road past there to ruins of Mision San Fernando (2 mi.).
87½	12	San Agustin on left. The new buildings are part of Highway department maintenance system. Road leaves here and goes to El Marmol onyx works (10 mi.). New Pemex station and trailer court.
90	2½	Tres Enriques ranch is to left with a small store offering refreshments and limited supplies.
99	9	This region known as Las Virgenes . . . an area of spectacular rock formations and many varieties of cactus and other desert vegetation. Ahead is giant rock that was blasted in two in order to get the road through this particularly difficult spot. Altitude 2200 ft. The road continues with gentle curves and easy driving. Painting of Virgin in near road on right.
109	10	Arrive at Parador Santa Ines and Motel Santa Catavina.

THE HOME OF THE ONYX ELEPHANTS

From the new road maintenance camp at San Augusin a road leads to El Marmol, site of large deposits of onyx. The road has been badly eroded by recent rains and only an occasional visitor with off-road equipment ventures into the mine area.

For years the onyx was broken out in heavy slabs and hauled over 50 miles to Puerto Santa Catarina to be loaded on waiting ships. Later it was trucked directly to Tijuana.

There artisans fashioned many items from the beautiful onyx and sold them to the tourists. Not only were bookends, chessmen and elephants carved and polished but their endeavors included an occasional bathtub and birdbath.

Once the home of several hundred people, El Marmol is nearly deserted. Large slabs of the quarried rock are scattered about. A trail leads three miles northeast to El Volcan, where you can literally watch onyx being made. Due to the action of the soda springs on the side of the arroyo the material is being formed at the rate of a few inches each thousand years.

From El Marmol an even wrose road winds southward for about 10 miles before joining Highway 1 near La Virgen.

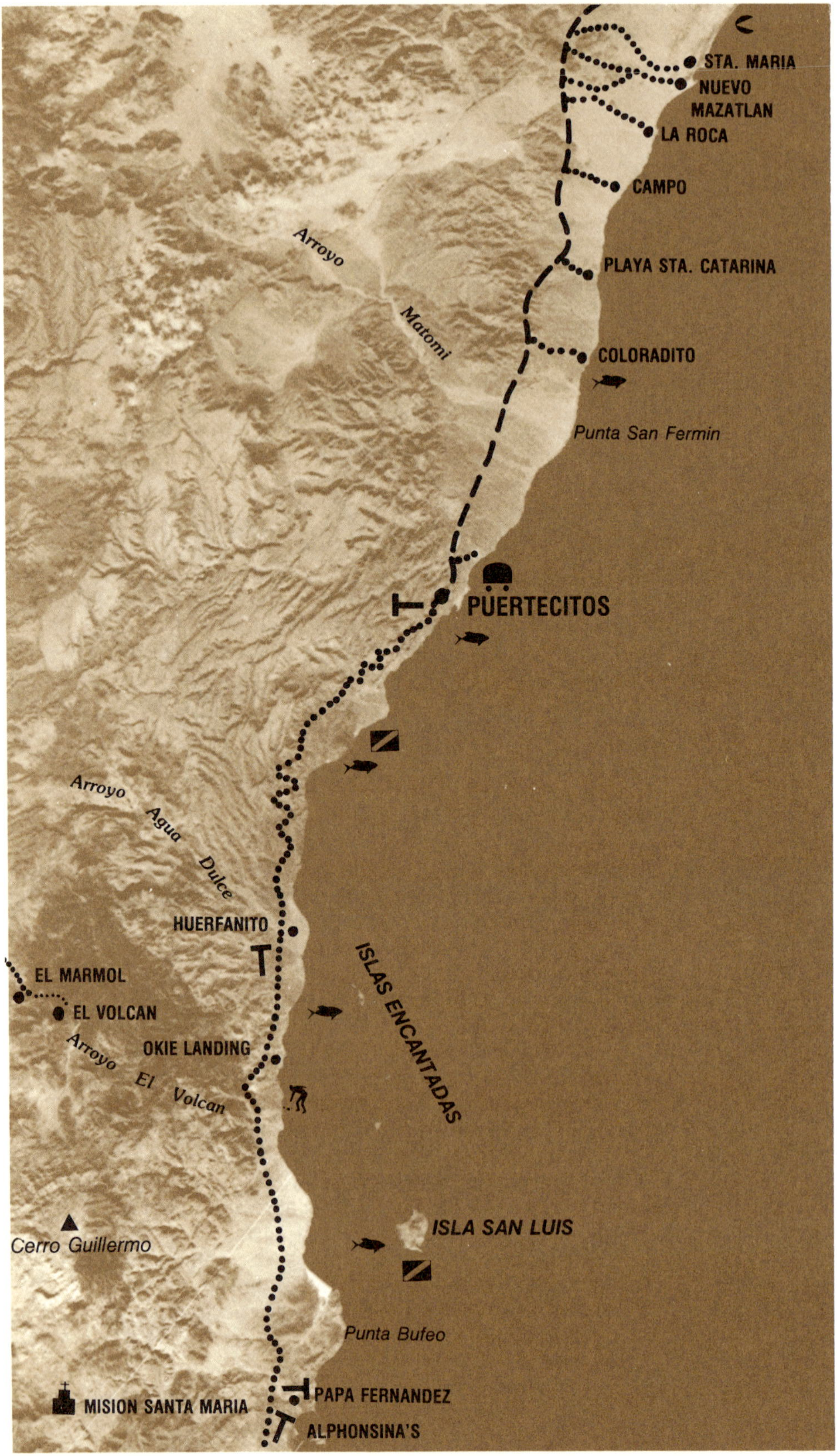

STA. MARIA
NUEVO
MAZATLAN
LA ROCA

CAMPO

PLAYA STA. CATARINA

COLORADITO

Punta San Fermin

PUERTECITOS

Arroyo

Matomi

SEE PAGE 56

Arroyo

Agua

Dulce

HUERFANITO

EL MARMOL

EL VOLCAN

Arroyo   *El   Volcan*

OKIE LANDING

ISLAS ENCANTADAS

Cerro Guillermo

ISLA SAN LUIS

Punta Bufeo

MISION SANTA MARIA

PAPA FERNANDEZ

ALPHONSINA'S

58

N

Total Mileage	Running Mileage	

SAN FELIPE—PUERTECITOS (contd. from pg. 53)

Total Mileage	Running Mileage	
34	11½	Side road left to Gulf and beach. Sandy.
41	7	Arrive in Arroyo Matomi. Several jeep trails lead past a well to east. Arroyo begins in southern portion of San Pedro Martir range and has palms and small stream at approx. 36 mi. Very rough going.
48	7	Side road to Corvina Beach Camp. Some camper sites and cantina. Road usually passable.
48	3	Downgrade into Puertecitos.

PUERTECITOS—PUNTA FINAL

The road below Puertecitos is NOT for a standard car; there are stretches where sharp volcanic take a heavy toll on tires. Plans are under way to pave the entire distance from San Felipe to Punta Final, but no timetable has been announced.

0	0	Leave Puertecitos and follow near coast for several miles before going slightly inland.
11	11	Top of grade with good view of Gulf and islands to the south. Next 8½ miles are very difficult, with a number of steep grades and sharp rocks.
17	6	Top of crest offers beautiful view of Sea and coastline in both directions. Begin descent onto coastal plain.
20½	3½	Road left to La Huerfanito. Limited facilities. Boats sometimes available to rent.
26½	6	Cross Arroyo Miramar. Several miles up arroyo are ruins of gold mining operation of early 1900's.
27	½	Stone ruins on left near beach are remainder of bldg. used during mining in nearby Arroyo Miramar.
29½	2½	Okie Landing. Site of ill-fated fishing camp for Americans. Good fishing around nearby islands. Caves behind camp were used to store fish in ice brought down from San Felipe.
32	2½	Small waterhole to right about ½ mi.—Agua Mezquitito.
35½	3½	Campo Salvatierra. Sign says that they offer "cafe, sodas, comidas, agua, cigarros". Here road goes across plain and makes gradual ascent to ridge overlooking bay.

(continued on page 63)

A ONE MAN GANG

The extreme grades beginning 11 miles below Puertecitos have gained notriety over the years, not only because of their steepness and sharp rocky surface but because that stretch of road had its own volunteer one-man maintenance crew. He was often seen filling in the holes and clearing the roadbed, using only simple handtools. The only pay he received was donations left by the grateful travellers.

Cerro Prieto and **Punta Prieta** are common names throughout Baja. There are numerous towns, ranches, hills and points of land bearing these names. **Prieto** or **Prieta** means "dark", while **Cerro** and **Punta** mean "hill" and "point" in that order. It was an easy way to describe a landmark and the names have carried on.

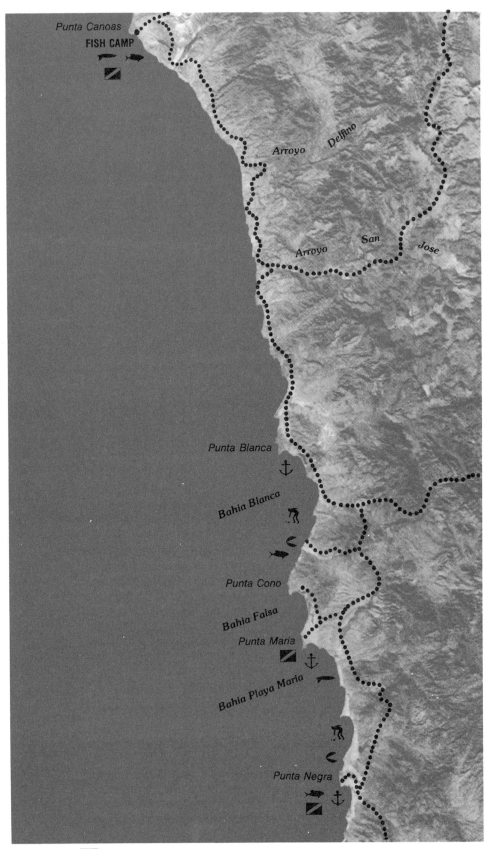

SEE PAGES 62 & 64

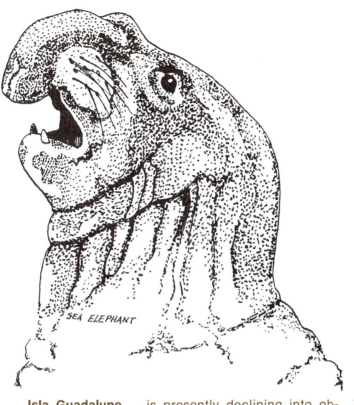

SEA ELEPHANT

Isla Guadalupe . . . is presently declining into oblivion as an island of flowers, birds and trees, thanks to earlier visitors to its shores. Due to its remote location—the nearest neighbor is Cedros Island 164 miles to the southeast—Guadalupe was a naturalist's dream with many species of flora and fauna found nowhere else in the world. Cypress, pine, palm and oak groves covered much of the northwest portion of the island, where they thrived in an often foggy atmosphere. This oak, incidentally, has an acorn fully two inches in diameter. The abundant bird life was reported to be so tame that most could be picked up with ease.

This all changed when early whaling expeditions loosed goats, cats and mice onto the land. They have multiplied and together have all but cleaned out the island. Efforts are planned to control these populations to encourage the return of a portion of the island's original beauty.

Guadalupe was once the scene of great slaughters of fur seals and sea elephants and presently serves as one of the few sea elephant rookeries left. Today the island is the site of a few abalone and lobster fishermen—plus a small military encampment—and is visited by numbers of sportfishermen in private and long-range boats from San Diego, as well as by cruiseships which take passengers near the beach in motor launches to ogle and photograph the giant sea elephants, who are seemingly oblivious to the tourist invasion.

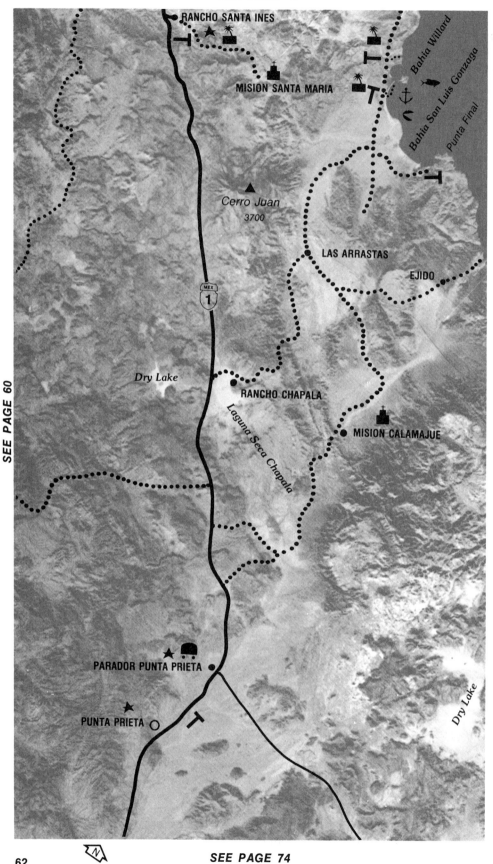

RANCHO SANTA INES

MISION SANTA MARIA

Bahia Willard

Bahia San Luis Gonzaga

Punta Final

Cerro Juan
3700

LAS ARRASTRAS

EJIDO

MEX 1

Dry Lake

RANCHO CHAPALA

Laguna Seca Chapala

MISION CALAMAJUE

Dry Lake

PARADOR PUNTA PRIETA

PUNTA PRIETA

N

62

Total Mileage	Running Mileage	
		PUERTECITOS—PUNTA FINAL (contd. from pg. 59)
46½	11	Begin twisting descent to Bahia Gonzaga.
47½	1	Road left to resort of Papa Fernandez, 0.8 mi. Camping, meals, gasoline, boats for rent and a nice beach for shelling and swimming. Prices reasonable. Road goes on out to Punta Willard, less than a mile east.
50½	3	Road left to Alfonsinas, 2 miles around estero. Popular with boaters and dunebuggy crowd. Camping, meals, meager supplies including gas. To south are the sandy beaches of Ensenada de San Francisquito.
56	5½	Road sharp to right goes to Las Arrastas and joins up with Mexico Highway 1, 48 mi. To left is Punta Final region, with nice beaches and good fishing along rocky shore. Road straight ahead deadends in cardon forest.

PUNTA FINAL—HIGHWAY 1

0	0	Head south up Arroyo de San Francisquito. Road gets progressively more sandy and as it narrows, steepens.
12	12	Road right goes to vicinity of an old turquoise mine. About 7 miles of rough driving and hiking.
15½	3½	Las Arrastas de Arriola. Small rancho near site of abandoned mill, which processed ore from nearby mines. Water well is located in wash behind bldg. A few hundred yards past here is road to Laguna Chapala. This 15 miles is considered extremely difficult, even for 4X vehicles.
18	2½	Road left to Molino de Lacy (4 mi.).
22	4	Road left to Puerto Calamajue. Little traveled, it goes past La Josefina mine (ruins), 1 mi., before descending into Arroyo de Calamajue and beach at 15 mi.
31	9	The site of Mision Calamajue (1766) and later of gold stamping mill for various mines in vicinity. The road then descends into the arroyo and follows up the canyon, crossing a little stream many times. Heavily mineralized at the bottom, the water becomes potable where the stream is crossed for the last time.
39	8	Reach top of grade and begin gradual descent through beautiful cirio and cardon forest.
47	8	Intersect Highway 1 at El Crucero, 18 miles north of the Parador Punta Prieta.

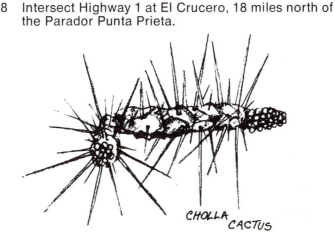

CHOLLA CACTUS

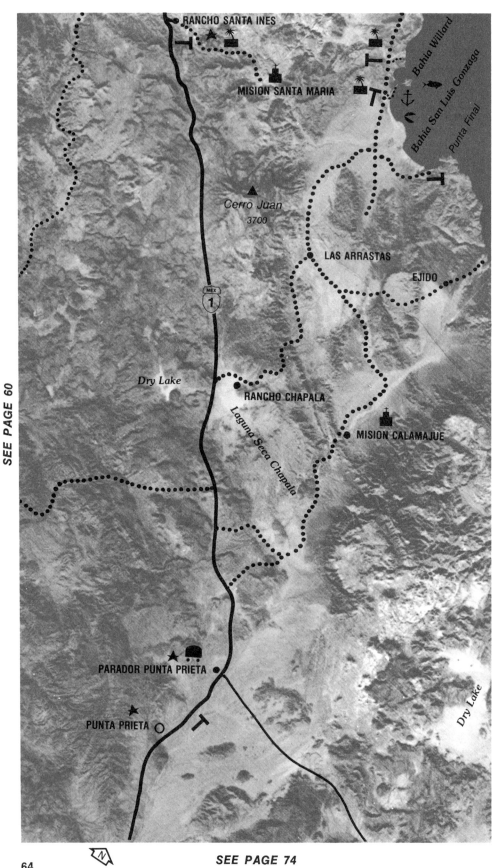

RANCHO SANTA INES

MISION SANTA MARIA

Bahia Willard

Bahia San Luis Gonzaga

Punta Final

Cerro Juan
3700

LAS ARRASTAS

EJIDO

MEX 1

Dry Lake

RANCHO CHAPALA

Laguna Seca Chapala

MISION CALAMAJUE

PARADOR PUNTA PRIETA

Dry Lake

PUNTA PRIETA

Total Mileage	Running Mileage	**PARADOR SANTA INES—PARALELO 28**
0	0	Start from Parador and Hotel Catavina southeast across arroyo. On other side of arroyo paved road on left leads to Rancho Santa Ines (1 mile).
3½	3½	Road heads ESE, 2200' alt, gently winding up and down through foothills.
8	4½	Road narrows slightly and becomes more winding (30-35 mph on curves) through forests of cirios and cardon.
9	1	Rancho Jaraguay. Refrescos. Begin steep ascent toward pass and onto plateau. Road on top is easy driving, good visibility.
24	15	Ahead to left is view of Laguna Chapala, a dry lake bed except following rare heavy rains.
32	8	Road left to Rancho Chapala. Road continues through sparse growths of cirio, cardon, yucca and cholla.
44	12	Road gradually descends through the Arroyo de Leon. Now there are a few agave and ocotillo to be seen. Road has few shoulders or turnouts.
52	8	High mesas visible on both sides of road. Still flat plain, altitude 1500'. Dirt road from left is Gulf road from San Felipe and Bahia Gonzaga.
65	13	Parador Punta Prieta. Pemex, and all services of other paradors. Paved road east leads to Bahia de Los Angeles, 41 miles.
70½	7½	Enter small ranch community of Punta Prieta. There is a large airstrip NE of town. Someone has built a small motel on right.

(continued on page 73)

NOPAL CACTUS

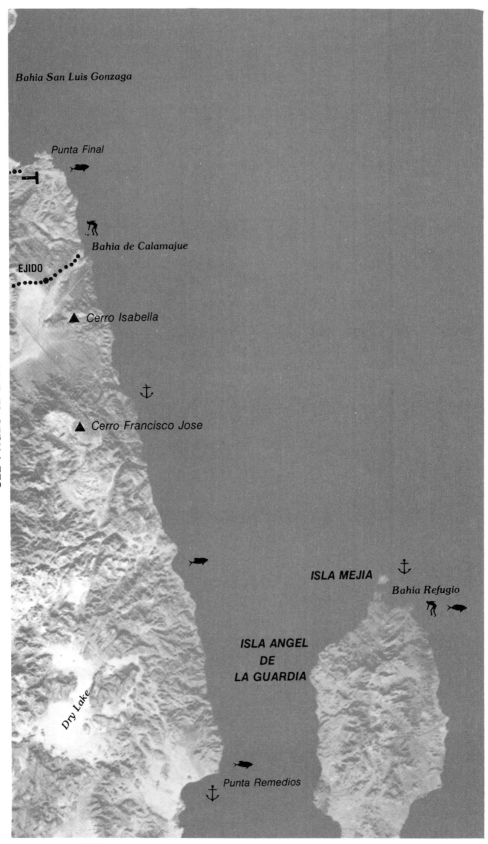

Bahia San Luis Gonzaga

Punta Final

Bahia de Calamajue

EJIDO

▲ Cerro Isabella

⚓

▲ Cerro Francisco Jose

SEE PAGES 62 & 64

Dry Lake

ISLA MEJIA

Bahia Refugio

ISLA ANGEL
DE
LA GUARDIA

Punta Remedios
⚓

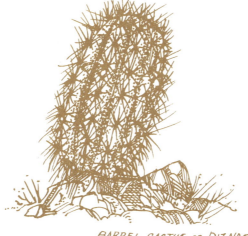

BARREL CACTUS OR BIZNAGA

NAMING THE SEA OF CORTEZ

That body of water which separates the Baja California peninsula from the Mexican mainland has been named many times since it was first visited by the Spaniards.

Starting in 1537, Francisco de Ulloa led three ships the entire length of the gulf. They found the mouth of the Rio Colorado and charted many of the landmarks from Acapulco around Cabo San Lucas to the giant bay now known as Bahia Magdalena.

Ulloa named it **Golfo de Cortez** or **Mar de Cortez** after his captain Hernan Cortez. On most charts the name was short lived, being replaced by **Mar Vermiglion, Mar Rojo** and **Mar Vermijo.**

Those three names all refer to the reddish color of the waters, quite probably due to the immense numbers of pelagic red crabs that periodically cover the surface in the southern half of the Sea.

Following the trek around its perimeter by Padre Eusebio Kino in 1700, it was known as **Mar Laurentano**, after the Virgin of Loreto, patroness of the California missions, as well as **Seno California** and **Mar California.**

Jesuit maps of 1730 and 1772 documented it as **Golfo de California** and this name has been in prominence since.

Recently there has been a move on the part of officials in Mexico City to return to the original name **Mar de Cortez** (Sea of Cortez). This is in large part due to Ray Cannon and the success of his classic book "The Sea of Cortez."

Whatever its name, this body of water is one of the most interesting in the world to the marine biologist, naturalist and angler, as it contains over eight hundred species of fish and thousands of other forms of sealife, many of which are found nowhere else on earth.

The islands offer almost totally isolated environments for the study of flora and fauna, and scientists from all over the world have visited Mexico for this purpose.

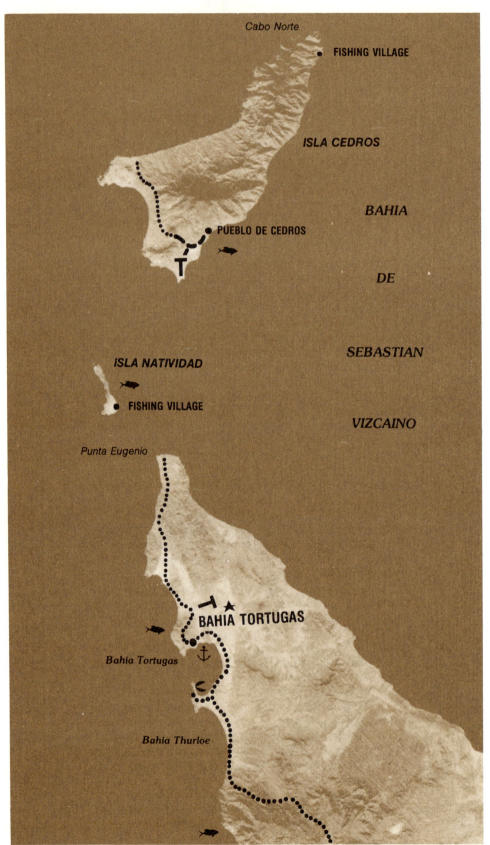

Cabo Norte

FISHING VILLAGE

ISLA CEDROS

BAHIA

DE

PUEBLO DE CEDROS

SEBASTIAN

ISLA NATIVIDAD

VIZCAINO

FISHING VILLAGE

Punta Eugenio

BAHIA TORTUGAS

Bahia Tortugas

Bahia Thurloe

SEE PAGE 70

SEE PAGE 78

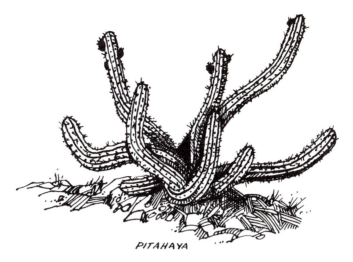

PITAHAYA

Bahia Tortugas (Ba-EE-a Tor-TO-gass) . . . is one of the most remote settlements on the entire peninsula. It is over 100 miles from the nearest paved road and its only access is by boat, plane or many miles of treacherous sandy trails. Yet it is a busy town—thanks to a major fishing and abalone industry. Its well protected anchorage is a popular spot for visiting yachts, and the sandy beaches yield many clams and surf fish. Over 4000 people live here in a climate that is cool and windy much of the time, with foggy weather to be expected from April to July.

Isla Cedros . . . is located about 12 miles northwest of Punta San Eugenio and was a popular port with the coastal explorers of the 16th century. Later, pirates hid here and at the nearby San Benito Islands, awaiting the rich Manila galleons (Silver Plate Fleet). The springs and the wild descendants of domestic goats released on the islands earlier provided 19th century whalers with fresh water and meat after long months at sea. Here too, the goats destroyed much of the unique vegetation and are still a staple in the diet of the several hundred residents. Their labors are divided between fishing, lobstering, diving for abalone, operating a cannery and loading great mountains of salt onto vessels from all over the world. The salt is brought on barges from the shallows of Guerrero Negro to be transferred in the deeper waters of Cedros. On the north end of the island, there is a small abandoned copper mine. The region is popular with the San Diego long-range sportfishing fleet.

Once the island was inhabited by Indians who would float in rafts over to the Baja mainland to gather clams and berries. It was a tough way to get a clam, though, and many Indians must have been lost due to the heavy currents in the area.

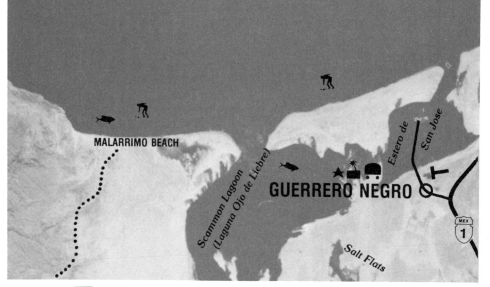

BAHIA DE SEBASTIAN
VIZCAINO

SEE PAGE 68

SEE PAGE 72

MALARRIMO BEACH

Scammon Lagoon
(Laguna Ojo de Liebre)

GUERRERO NEGRO

Estero de
San Jose

Salt Flats

MEX
1

N

SEE PAGE 80

TREE YUCCA

THE BEARDED DESERT

The coastal regions around the Bahia de Sebastian Vizcaino are dominated by a surprisingly cool and strong shoreward air movement. Much of the year, the nights and mornings are foggy, often for many miles inland.

Although the region is rarely visited by any major rainstorms—less than 3 inches per year—many of the desert plants are festooned with spanish moss, a plant most associated with regions of high humidity. Many of the cirios and ocotillos in this area have taken on a bizarre appearance because of the long "beard" supplied by the grey-green spanish moss.

Another plant common to this portion of Baja is the tree yucca. Although related to the joshua tree of the high desert north of Los Angeles, they are generally more slender and less branching. The Baja California tree yucca blooms during the summer, displaying masses of white blossoms in contrast to the springtime appearance of creamy flowers on the joshua tree.

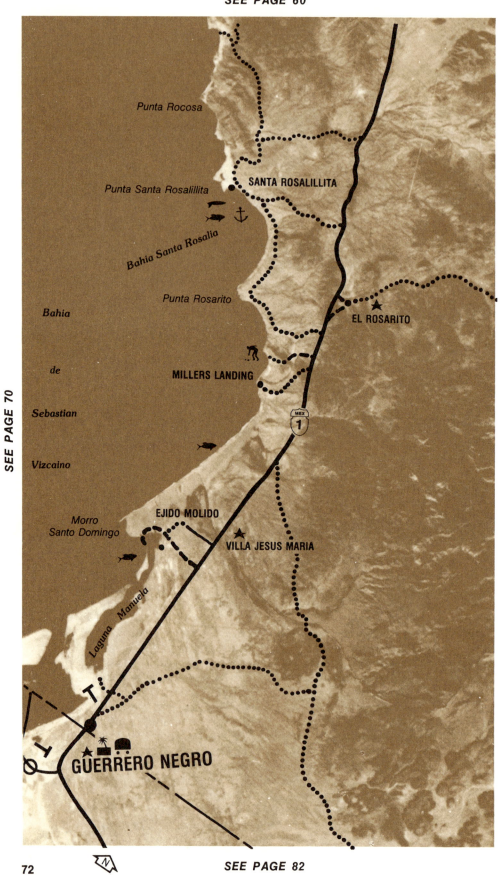

SEE PAGE 70

SEE PAGE 74

Punta Rocosa

SANTA ROSALILLITA

Punta Santa Rosalillita

Bahia Santa Rosalia

Punta Rosarito

EL ROSARITO

Bahia

de

MILLERS LANDING

Sebastian

MEX 1

Vizcaino

Morro
Santo Domingo

EJIDO MOLIDO

VILLA JESUS MARIA

Laguna Manuela

GUERRERO NEGRO

PARADOR SANTA INES—PARALELO 28

(continued from page 65)

Total Mileage	Running Mileage	
81½	8½	Adobe ranch house to left. Scattered stands of elephant trees. Cirios have bearded appearance from growths of a type of Spanish moss. Alt. 600'. Ahead you begin a steep winding ascent to ridge. Follow along the top for 2 miles, then into valley with sharp curves on downgrade (30 mph).
87½	6	Road straightens and passes through dips.
91	3½	Road right is to Punta Santa Rosalillita (approx. 8 miles) down Arroyo Santo Dominguito. Surfers say that the rides here can carry as much as a mile and a half with a good southwest swell. Road not good for standard cars. Large black butte is to left of highway.
98	7	Small town to east is El Rosarito. Gas and new trailer park.
99	1	Loncheria Terecita, just north of data palms and abandoned ranch house.
102	3	Road right is to Punta Rosarito (about 4 miles).
104	2	Begin steep downgrade, sharp curves, 25-30 mph.
105½	1½	Road west goes to Miller's Landing. A good camping spot with an interesting beach.
106	2½	Graded road to right leads to El Tomatal beach and fish camp, 3 miles.
118	10	Road right (paved) by Pemex station into Ejido Morelos. To go to Puerto Santo Domingo (5 miles) take graded road left one mile in from highway.
125½	2½	Continue straight south with dunes of Laguna Manuela in distance. There are several marginal roads leading to west in this area.
136	18	Paved road right into large airstrip. It was originally intended to be a refueling stop for transpacific passenger flights.
137½	1½	"Monumento Aguila", a huge stylized eagle built on the boundary between the states of Baja California and Baja California Sur. (See page 135)

PARALELO 28—PARADOR SAN IGNACIO

0	0	Leave hotel at Paralelo 28 and head south.
2½	2½	Main road curves left at intersection with paved road into Guerrero Negro, 2½ miles (See pages 81 & 135). Mexico 1 turns east-southeast through low dunes with a sparse covering of brush.

(continued on page 83)

CHOLLA

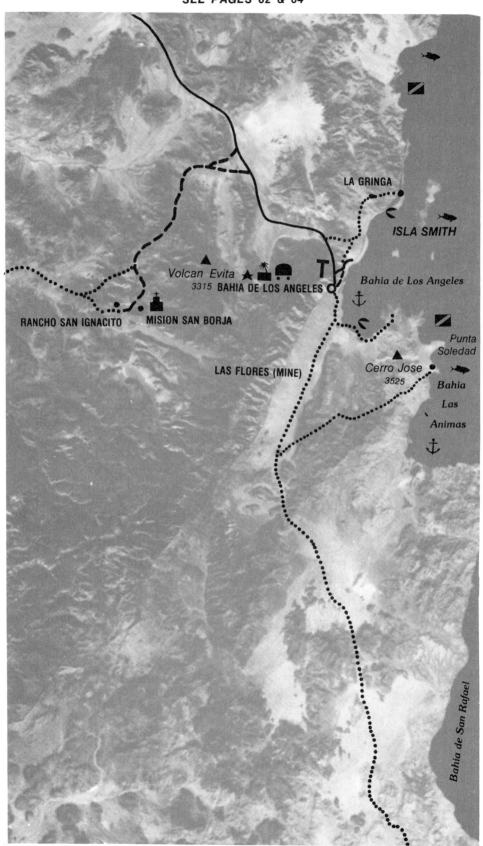

LA GRINGA

ISLA SMITH

Volcan Evita
3315 **BAHIA DE LOS ANGELES**

T

Bahia de Los Angeles

RANCHO SAN IGNACITO **MISION SAN BORJA**

Punta
Soledad

LAS FLORES (MINE) *Cerro Jose*
3525

*Bahia
Las
Animas*

Bahia de San Rafael

SEE PAGE 72

SEE PAGE 76

N

BLACK MUREX

Bahia de Los Angeles (Ba-E-a day Los-AN-hay-lace) is a beautiful harbor with shelter and anchorage for almost any size vessel. It is a popular anchorage for shrimp boats and visiting small boaters who trailer their craft to San Felipe or Kino Bay to head for the midriff islands, Mulege, Loreto and La Paz.

The bahia is protected by Isla Angel de la Guardia and a dozen smaller islands. The channel separating Angel de la Guardia and the peninsúla is filled with fish . . . Yellowtail, cabrilla and grouper are caught year-around, and are joined during the summer and early fall months by billfish and dorado. Large schools of porpoise and whales often move through the channel within sight of land. A few years ago, the Bahia was a productive turtle fishing region, but over-harvesting has badly depleted the supply.

The road from Parador Punta Prieta into Bahia de Los Angeles is now paved, opening one of the most interesting and accessible recreation areas in Baja. Rewards for visitors to the gulf here are many. Besides excellent fishing, there are beds of clams and oysters along shore. Shelling is very good. There are several old mining sites to be explored, and the scenery is beautiful. Trips to the adjoining islands and beaches will result in lots of "treasures".

The motel, Casa Diaz, offers comfortable accommodations, with large rooms and showers. Meals are good and reasonably priced, often consisting of seafood. Reservations should be made in advance, especially from November to May. There is a small store and gasoline is generally available. (See Resort Roundup on page 158)

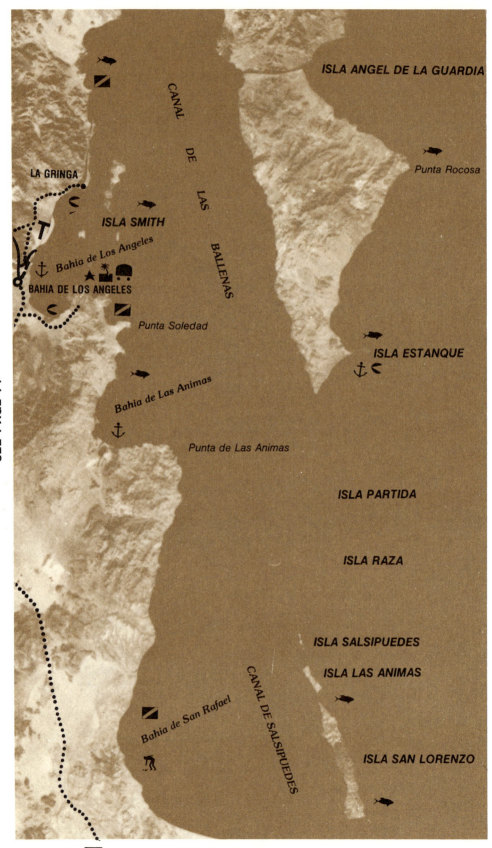

ISLA ANGEL DE LA GUARDIA

CANAL DE LAS BALLENAS

Punta Rocosa

LA GRINGA

ISLA SMITH

Bahia de Los Angeles

BAHIA DE LOS ANGELES

Punta Soledad

ISLA ESTANQUE

Bahia de Las Animas

Punta de Las Animas

ISLA PARTIDA

ISLA RAZA

ISLA SALSIPUEDES

ISLA LAS ANIMAS

Bahia de San Rafael

CANAL DE SALSIPUEDES

ISLA SAN LORENZO

Isla La Raza . . . is barely a third of a square mile, but this low island is of prime interest to naturalists as the breeding place of many species of sea birds. In 1964, President Lopez Mateos dedicated La Raza as a wildlife preserve. In years past, residents for miles around went to La Raza during the spring to take the eggs, which they sold in the surrounding settlements. Their efforts netted countless thousands of eggs and seriously threatened the survival of some of the species. Presently, the island is closed to visitors, except with permission from the Government. Arrangements may be made at Bahia de Los Angeles.

Isla Angel de la Guardia . . . is the second largest island in the Sea of Cortez—Tiburon on the eastern side of the Midriff is the largest. It's high peaks (to over 4,000 feet) and 42 miles length helps to provide generally calm waters for the peninsula coastline in the vicinity of Bahia de Los Angeles. The largely barren surface supports a few coyotes and rodents, plus abundant numbers of lizards and rattlesnakes. There are several seal rockeries along the northeastern coast. Many schools of fish patrol the rocky reefs and coves of La Guardia Angel.

The highlight of a visit to Isla Angel de la Guardia to me is fishing and exploring the scenic—almost surrealistic—Bahia Refugio at the northern end of the island. Here are pinacles of white and black rocks jutting from the water's surface, high cliffs of reds, browns, greys and whites. There are many coves and lees that afford protection in any weather.

Once, while fishing from the boat "Poseidon" out of San Felipe, we spent several days in Refugio waiting out gale force winds that were whipping the whole gulf to a froth. We experienced only a little wind in the sheltered coves and, at the same time, some of the best yellowtail fishing I have ever seen. Bernard and Ron Zwilling and I caught and released over fifty big yellows in one three-hour stretch—this kind of action continued for two days. We almost collapsed from exhaustion.

There are numerous other smaller islands in the Gulf of California, or the Sea of Cortez, but the ones mentioned will provide a most interesting visit—should you have an opportunity to navigate your own craft into the regions of the islands. Boats may also be chartered from nearby ports to take you to the islands of the Cortez. (Also see page 66)

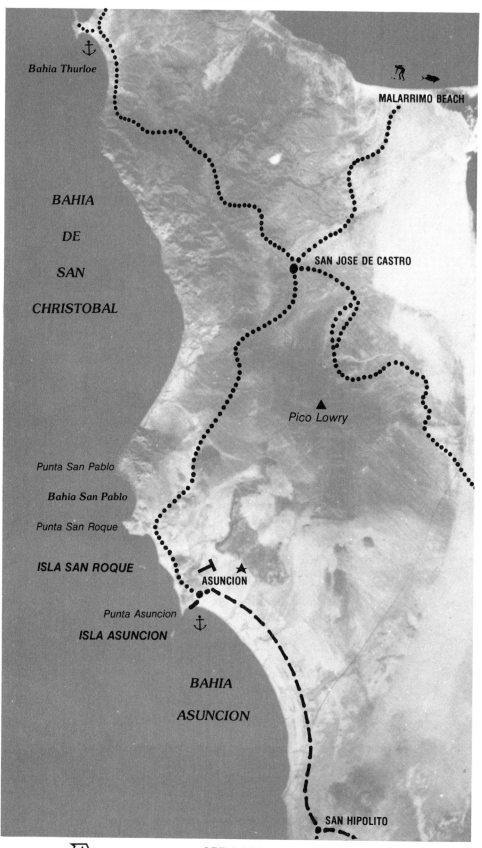

Bahia Thurloe

MALARRIMO BEACH

BAHIA

DE

SAN

CHRISTOBAL

SAN JOSE DE CASTRO

Pico Lowry

Punta San Pablo

Bahia San Pablo

Punta San Roque

ISLA SAN ROQUE

ASUNCION

Punta Asuncion

ISLA ASUNCION

BAHIA

ASUNCION

SAN HIPOLITO

N

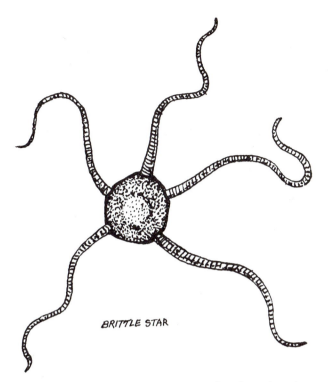

BRITTLE STAR

Isla Natividad . . . is almost four miles long by about one mile wide and lies four miles west of Punta San Eugenio. It is rather barren, with a small fishing village on the southern end.

Islas San Benito . . . is also a regular stop for anglers and has a small fish camp on the westernmost island. It is a good place to pick up lobster and abalone. Once while on a long range trip, we stopped for these goodies and were told that it would require "much work" to get what we wanted, but if we would be patient they would do their best. For two hours we fished the nearby kelp beds and visited with the residents. Finally they returned with a good supply of lobster and abalone, looking as though they had just run a four-minute mile. We learned as we left that the abalones had been in a shed nearby all the time, while the lobsters were in a receiver only a few yards away in the next cove. They just wanted company.

Asuncion (Ah-soon-si-OWN) . . . is similar to Tortugas, but with only 2000 residents who work in the taking and processing of abalone, lobster and fish. The beaches south of town afford excellent fishing and clamming, while the offshore reefs have abundant fish. There are only limited supplies available, but gasoline may usually be obtained. Water is scarce, as it is either distilled from seawater or brought in from Cedros Island by tanker.

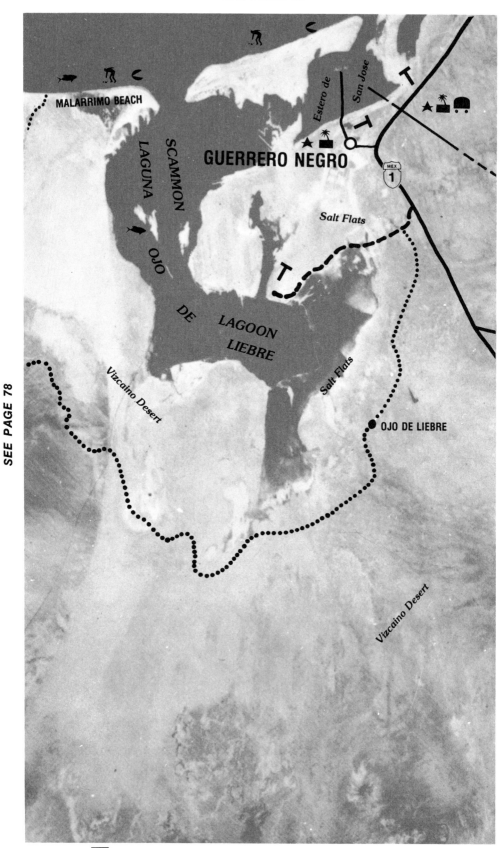

MALARRIMO BEACH

GUERRERO NEGRO

Estero de San Jose

SCAMMON LAGUNA

OJO DE LAGOON LIEBRE

MEX 1

Salt Flats

Salt Flats

Vizcaino Desert

OJO DE LIEBRE

Vizcaino Desert

SEE PAGE 78

SEE PAGE 82

CHARLES SCAMMON

THE WHALES OF SCAMMON LAGOON

From January through mid-March each year, over 6000 California gray whales turn Scammon Lagoon, San Ignacio Lagoon and the many miles of protected waterway in and north of Magdalena Bay into the world's biggest nursery.

The plankton-rich Arctic and Bering Seas are the homes of these fifty foot giants before they begin the longest migration of any mammal to their calving and mating grounds.

Fifteen feet long and 1000 pounds when born, these "babies" consume up to 50 gallons of milk daily and put on nearly 100 pounds of weight per day for two months before heading north to their summer feeding grounds.

There are a number of locations around Scammon Lagoon where the whales may be seen as they tend their young, court and frolic in the shallow protected waters.

Captain Charles Scammon discovered the entrance to the lagoon in the 1850's and proceeded to slaughter the giant beasts by the hundreds for their valuable oil. Others uncovered his secret and within a few decades the gray whale was considered to be nearly extinct.

From an estimated 100 whales remaining in 1937, the California gray whale has made a remarkable comeback.

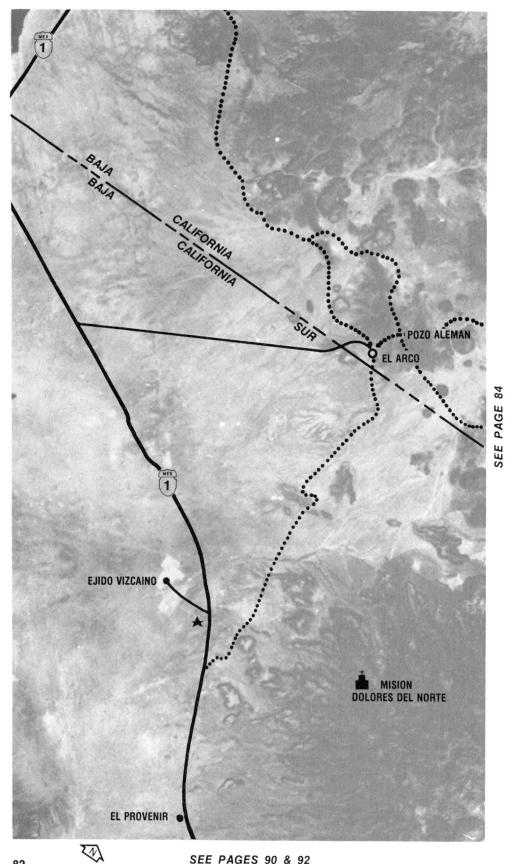

SEE PAGE 80

SEE PAGE 84

POZO ALEMAN

EL ARCO

BAJA
BAJA
CALIFORNIA
CALIFORNIA
SUR

EJIDO VIZCAINO

MISION
DOLORES DEL NORTE

EL PROVENIR

PARALELO 28—PARADOR SAN IGNACIO

(continued from page 73)

Total Mileage	Running Mileage	
17	14½	Road left to Ejido Benito Juarez (3½ miles).
19	2	Road left going straight NNE to El Arco (26 miles). It is paved all of the way into this tiny ranching and mining community. Continue through desolate flat country with gradually more cardon, ocotillo and yucca.
45	26	Dirt road right is to Ejido Vizcaino. There is a better road 2½ miles ahead. Road left is the old road to El Arco (31 miles).
47¼	2¼	To the right is the main road from Ejido Vizcaino (5 miles), location of a government agricultural experiment station. Continue straight through heavier stands of many kinds of cactus and into low foothills.
64	16¾	There are a number of dips through here that could be muddy after a storm.

(continued on page 91)

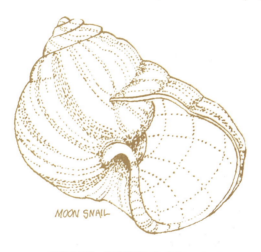

MOON SNAIL

FOSSIL WATERS OF BAJA

As you drive through the desolate flatlands southeast of Guerrero Negro, you will see large tracts of desert being cleared. Ejido Vizcaino—several miles west of the highway 45 miles below Paralelo 28—is the site of an agricultural experiment station where numerous crops are being tested for cultivation in this region.

One thing of particular interest about this project is that the water to be used for farming is many thousands of years old! It is not from the rains of recent times, but rather water which percolated into the substrata during an age when water was plentiful.

This phenomenon also accounts for much of the available water on the Magdalena Plain where vast regions are planted in grain and cotton.

Like oil and coal deposits, once it is gone it cannot be replaced and thus the size of the underground pool dictates the success of the project. Preliminary tests indicate sufficient reserves for many years of productive farming.

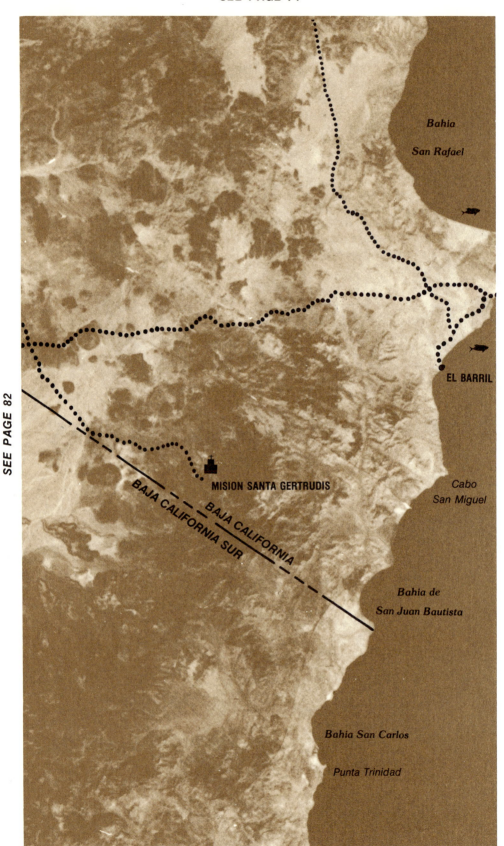

SEE PAGE 82

SEE PAGE 86

Bahia

San Rafael

EL BARRIL

MISION SANTA GERTRUDIS

BAJA CALIFORNIA

BAJA CALIFORNIA SUR

Cabo
San Miguel

Bahia de
San Juan Bautista

Bahia San Carlos

Punta Trinidad

N

BROWN
PELICAN

THE PELICAN WATCHERS

Anyone who has followed the plight of the pelican along the Southern California coast will be happy to see the many long flights of these awkward looking birds throughout the Sea of Cortez.

The Cortez flocks have yet to experience the effects of the deadly DDT that has nearly obliterated the nesting areas along the Pacific. The rookeries on the islands in the Cortez are still producing well.

The pelican is still the best harbinger of where to toss a lure when they begin their wheeling, hell-bent dive for the baitfish pushed to the surface by larger gamefish. The sight of circling birds and myriads of splashes and boils will make any angler's heart skip a few beats and cause his fingers to flub even the simplest cast.

Each year the U.S. Fish and Wildlife Service marks several thousand young pelicans to study their movements. It has been determined that a number of the birds traverse the mountainous Baja peninsula to patrol the Pacific shores as far north as San Francisco.

Variously colored streamers have been attached to the birds and any sightings should be reported to Dr. D. W. Anderson, PO Box C, Davis, CA 95616, giving the color of the streamer and the location and date of the sighting.

SEE PAGE 76

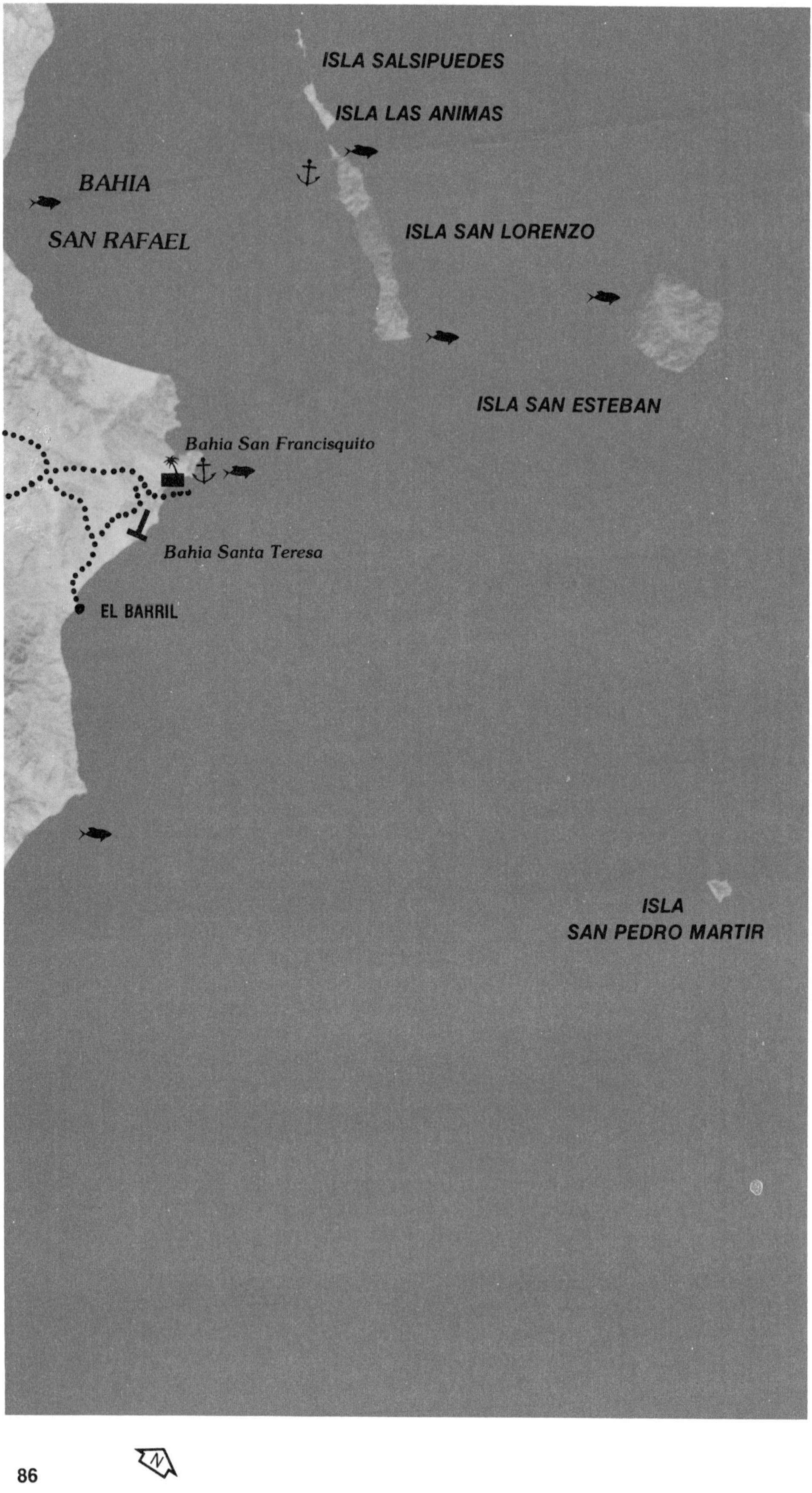
ISLA SALSIPUEDES
ISLA LAS ANIMAS
BAHIA
SAN RAFAEL
ISLA SAN LORENZO
ISLA SAN ESTEBAN
Bahia San Francisquito
Bahia Santa Teresa
EL BARRIL
ISLA
SAN PEDRO MARTIR
N

SEE PAGE 84

SAND DOLLAR

Isla San Lorenzo . . . is a closely situated narrow chain of three islands that comprise the southern-most of what is popularly known as the Midriff Islands. They extend for about 15 miles in a southeast-northwest direction and afford some pro-tection for the Salsipuedes Channel. Incidentally, Salsipuedes in Spanish means "get out if you can," and whenever this name is attached to a location it indicates that there is some reason to take extra care. In this instance, it is the currents which at times of great tidal change can literally make a boat progress **backwards!** The three islands have been dubbed, going from south to north, San Lorenzo—the largest at 10 miles by two miles, Las Animas—two by one, and Salsipuedes—a mile square. Fish-ing on both sides of the islands is generally good. However, the islands offer scant refuge in case of heavy weather and little of interest ashore except a few rattlers and lizards.

BAHIA SAN FRANCISQUITO

It's a tough fifty miles from El Arco to Bahia San Francisquito and El Barril, but well worth the effort for anyone with a good offroad vehicle. Those who make it to this region during the months of May through October will find that the yellowtail congre-gate just offshore in incredible numbers. Not only do most boats that venture into the channel be-tween here and Isla San Lorenzo load up on these gamesters but even those anglers who stay ashore have a chance to tangle with yellows to 25 pounds as they chase baitfish almost onto the sand.

March, April and May are good months for white seabass over the rocky reefs south of the point, and sierra make an appearance during July, August and September.

The white sand beaches have a wealth of shells, including the beautiful pink murex and the orange colored spiny rock oyster.

Several hundred feet back from shore there are a number of large mounds of pearl oyster shells, some dating back to the days of the Spaniards. Today, the pearl oyster is rarely found offshore but an abundance of other clams, scallops and conchs await the diver.

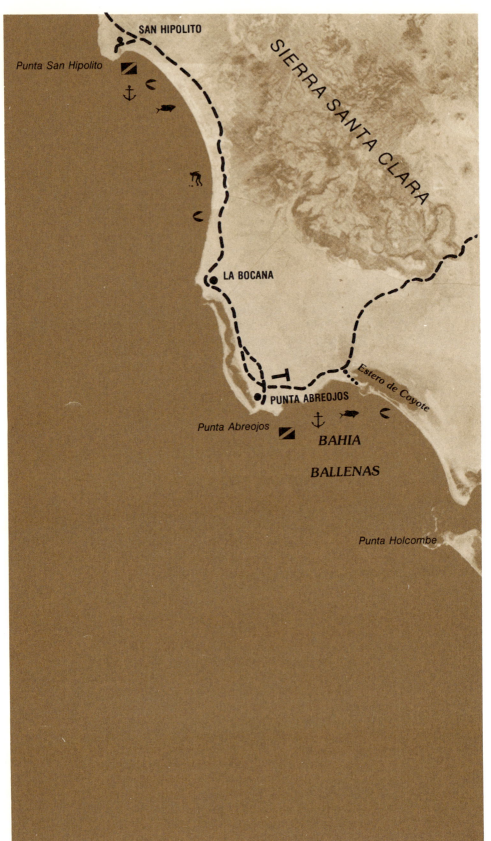

SAN HIPOLITO

Punta San Hipolito

SIERRA SANTA CLARA

LA BOCANA

PUNTA ABREOJOS

Estero de Coyote

Punta Abreojos

BAHIA

BALLENAS

Punta Holcombe

Abreojos (A-bray-O-hos . . . has great potential for development as the hub of a region that includes much sealife. Nearby Laguna San Ignacio is an important calving spot for the gray whale. Shore birds, migrating geese and ducks are plentiful. Unfortunately, even the water needed by the 1000 residents must be trucked in, but when this problem is solved it will become a popular spot for the vacationing Norteamericano to view nature at its best. As yet, there are no adequate roads into the town— unless a rugged recreational vehicle is used. There is a good airstrip here, but accommodations are minimal.

AN "UNOFFICIAL" ADVENTURE

An "unofficial" touristic triangle that may someday in the future become paved is the nearly 400 mile circuit from just north of San Ignacio to the Pacific at Abreojos, northward to Asuncion and Bahia Tortugas, then east toward Malarrimo Beach and finally, Guerrero Negro. It is currently for offroad vehicles only—and then you should not go alone.

The first leg, from the turnoff of Mexico 1 some 10 miles west of San Ignacio is through very desolate desert terrain that includes sand dunes, salt flats and more sand. The distance to Abreojos is about 62 miles.

South of the last portion of the road is Laguna San Ignacio. The lagoon and adjacent marshy areas are a haven for many varieties of waterbirds, clams and fish. Expeditions into the area by scientists have yielded astounding quantities of croakers, perch and other shallow water varieties.

The beaches along the Pacific harbor tremendous numbers of pismo and other clams, along with large quantities of surf fish, rays and small sharks. The offshore rocks are regularly worked for commercial quantities of abalone and lobster. Some of the warm water species such as the triggerfish, corvina and grouper are taken near Abreojos.

All of the water in this region must be trucked in from San Ignacio, so it is scarce. Fuel and groceries are available.

The rough and often sandy road closely follows the coastline northward another 68 miles past San Hipolito to Asuncion. There are many inviting beaches a short distance from the road through here, but rarely visited. Again they presumably offer good clamming and surf fishing.

One should expect to find the weather to be generally foggy and windy much of the year, so warm clothing should be taken "just in case".

Once past Asuncion, the road turns inland for about 36 miles to a small ranch, San Jose de Castro, built around a well of good water. It is a most welcome sight after crossing the barren Sierra Pintada.

(continued on page 91)

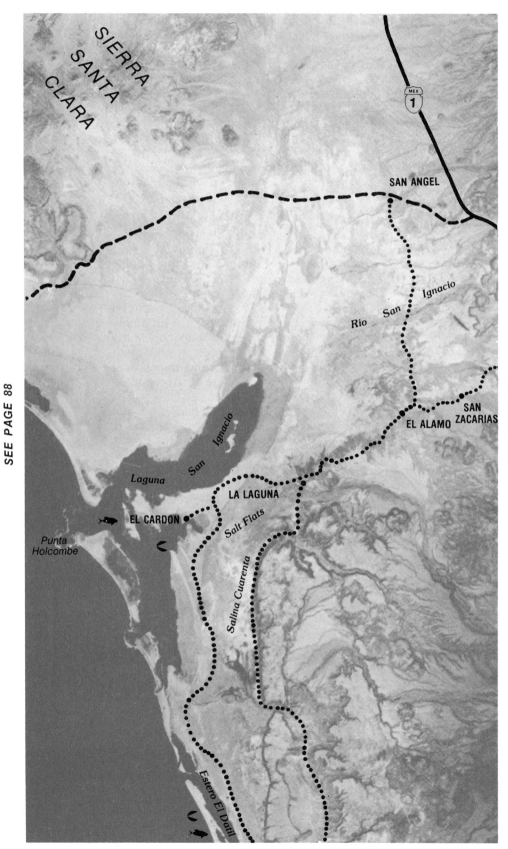

SIERRA
SANTA
CLARA

MEX
1

SAN ANGEL

Rio   San   Ignacio

SEE PAGE 88

SEE PAGE 92

SAN
ZACARIAS
EL ALAMO

San Ignacio

Laguna   San

LA LAGUNA

EL CARDON

Salt Flats

Punta
Holcombe

Salina Cuarenta

Estero El Datil

90

N

PARALELO 28—PARADOR SAN IGNACIO

(continued from page 83)

79   15   The poorly marked turnoff to the right is to Abreojos (63 miles), Bahia Asuncion (160 miles) and Bahia Tortugas (260 miles). The road is BAD. It is presently only for experienced 4-wheel drivers travelling in tandem. There is some talk of improving, and possibly paving, the route in 2 or 3 years. Once you get to the ocean, it is an exciting area. (See page 89)

(continued on page 93)

THE BAJA 1000 ROAD

A road out of San Ignacio to the south goes through a desolate, waterless plain—past the southern shore of Laguna San Ignacio to eventually connect with the road across the Sierra Gigantas from Canipole to La Purisima. It is this road that has been used by the Baja 1000 racers and is generally suited for just that—a Baja 1000 type vehicle.

Shortly after joining the La Purisima road, you reach a well-graded straight road that goes through the northern farmlands of the Magdalena Plain. Total distance from San Ignacio to this point is about 145 miles.

AN "UNOFFICIAL" ADVENTURE

(continued from page 89)

Just past San Jose de Castro, the road to Bahia Tortugas takes off to the left. The road straight ahead goes north to Malarrimo Beach and the one heading east goes past Scammon Lagoon and into Guerrero Negro.

The settlement of Bahia Tortugas is entered 45 miles after leaving the intersection and following an arroyo to the beach (30 miles) and then proceeding north along the coast and around the bay. Portions of the road are quite rough but passable. This stretch is fairly well traveled by trucks bringing in supplies to the people of the town.

The road north to Malarrimo Beach is 26 miles of soft sand, according to some who have tried it. If you can make it to the beach, however, there is an almost unlimited treasuretrove for the inveterate beachcomber. (see Beachcombing, page 142)

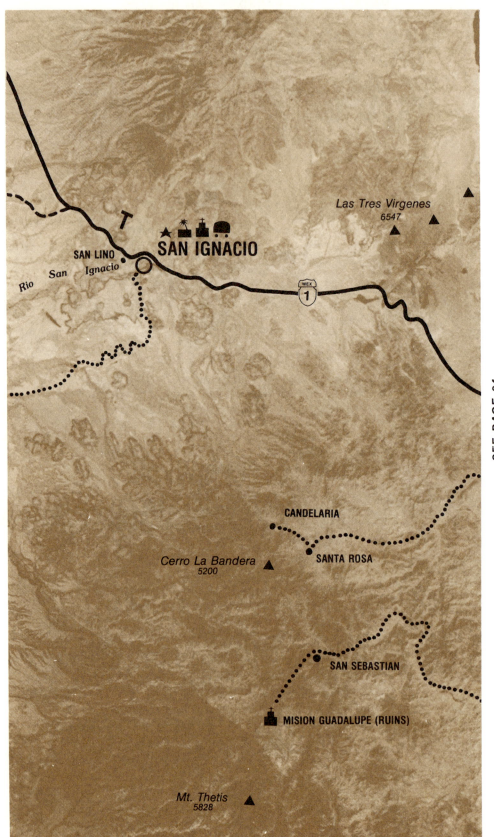

SEE PAGE 90

SEE PAGE 94

Las Tres Virgenes
6547

T

SAN LINO
San
Rio   Ignacio

SAN IGNACIO

MEX 1

CANDELARIA

Cerro La Bandera
5200

SANTA ROSA

SAN SEBASTIAN

MISION GUADALUPE (RUINS)

Mt. Thetis
5828

N

92

PARALELO 28—PARADOR SAN IGNACIO

(continued from page 91)

Total Mileage	Running Mileage	
81½	2½	Small house is on left. Just past the house there is a dip, then road goes up a short hill. Alt. 700'.
87	3	Road left is to paved landing strip.
90	3	Small ramada on left sells gas. There is a Pemex station at San Ignacio Parador.
88½	2	San Lino. This small community might be termed a suburb of San Ignacio. Take road to the right into San Ignacio over a small dam. Motel and parador is located just before you enter town.

PARADOR SAN IGNACIO—SANTA ROSALIA

0	0	Leave San Ignacio, return to Mexico 1 and proceed east toward Santa Rosalia.
1	1	To right is the upper end of oasis of San Ignacio. Road winds eastward up and down through hills. Many curves—30-40 mph.
4	3	At top of grade (alt. 900 ft.) road straightens out. There is much evidence of volcanic action throughout area. Extensive stands of elephant trees are among the dark red lava rocks.
21	17	You approach a small ramada with refrescos as road becomes winding again (alt. 1500 ft.). Start downgrade ahead with sharp turns and narrow shoulders, 30-35 mph. Ahead to the left are three tall volcanic mountains, Tres Virgenes.

(continued on page 95)

IGLESIA SANTA ROSALIA

Shortly after Santa Rosalia was settled in the 1880's with the discovery of rich copper deposits, the French owners shipped from France a prefabricated church building consisting of large sheets of galvanized iron. Its designer was one of the most famous in the world—he also designed and built the Eiffel Tower.

SEE PAGE 84

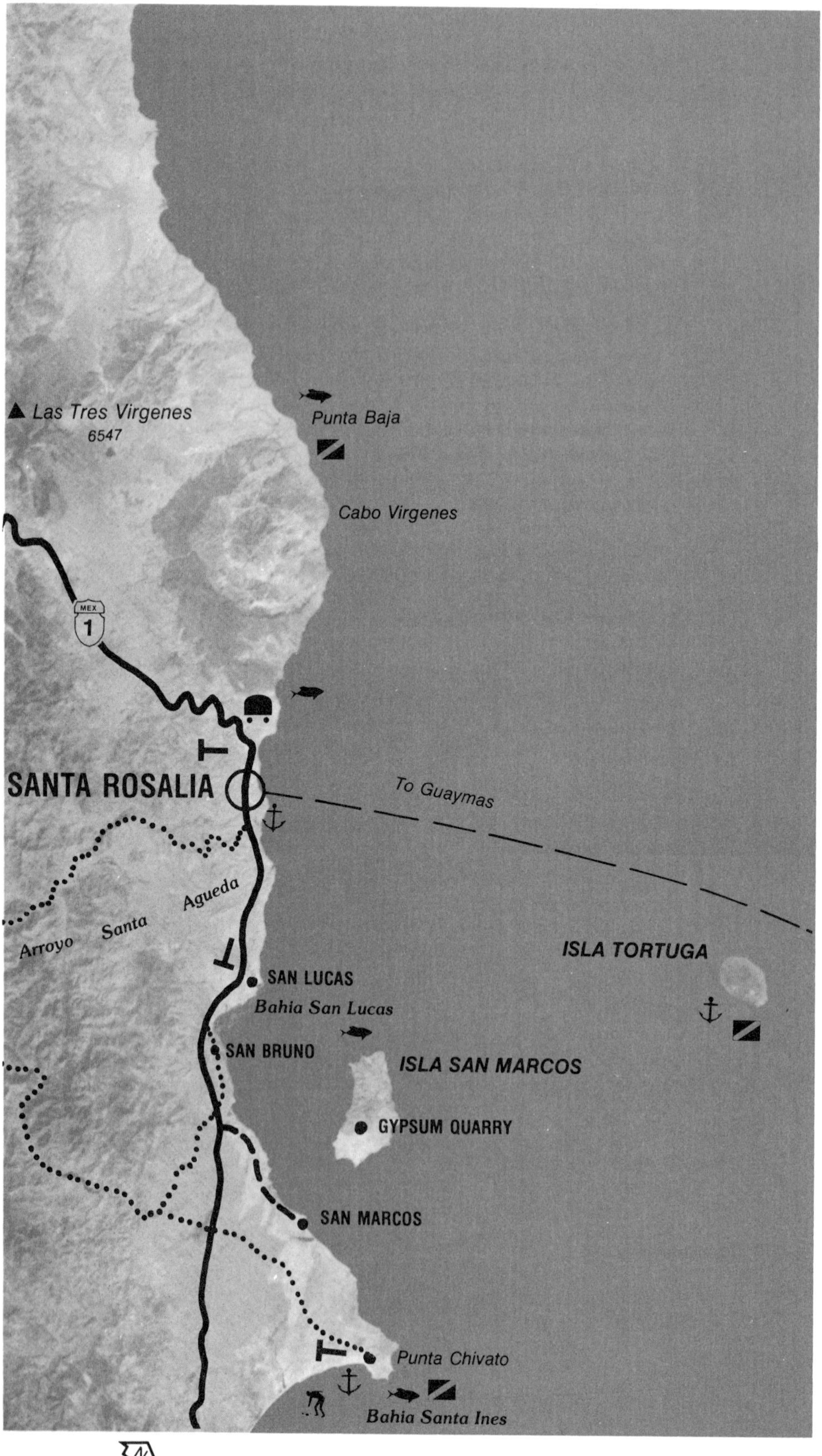
Las Tres Virgenes
6547
Punta Baja
Cabo Virgenes
MEX
1
SANTA ROSALIA
To Guaymas
Arroyo Santa Agueda
ISLA TORTUGA
SAN LUCAS
Bahia San Lucas
SAN BRUNO
ISLA SAN MARCOS
GYPSUM QUARRY
SAN MARCOS
Punta Chivato
Bahia Santa Ines
N

SEE PAGE 92

SEE PAGE 100

PARADOR SAN IGNACIO—SANTA ROSALIA

(continued from page 93)

Total Mileage	Running Mileage	
26	5	Small rancho with two windmills on left. Road continues to wind up and down through hills.
34	8	Here you have your first view of the Sea of Cortez. One-half mile further, begin descent from 1500′ to 300′ in less than 4 miles. Road is steep, narrow and twisting with no turnouts. Heavy rigs should be in low gear. Watch for slow vehicles ahead, 20-30 mph. Watch for over heating when coming from other direction.
38	4	A butane storage facility is to left in small arroyo.
40	2	Reach gulf shore and turn to south. Along here the yellowtail often come within range of shore casting during winter and spring. Watch for working fish and try white and chrome jigs.
41½	1½	Well travelled road to right leads to one of the copper mines.
44	2½	Pass by smelter and related equipment. Harbor is ahead and to left. Ice house is on left in back of large wooden building—Sign on end of building.
44½	½	Paved road right goes into Santa Rosalia. One-quarter mile further south is the modern ferry terminal. They serve very good meals Ticket office is located in building.

SANTA ROSALIA—LORETO

0	0	Leave ferry building and head south along Mexico 1.
1¼	1¼	Pass Hotel El Morro on left and wind through low hills. Speed 45-50 on most curves.
10½	9¼	Road left is to San Lucas, a beautiful palm shaded cove with sandy beach. A moderately priced resort hotel is scheduled to be built here.
15½	5	Pass small settlement of San Bruno.
20½	5	Road left is to Punta Chivato, 17 miles. Road is usually passable to passenger car. Inquire at San Bruno or Mulege.
21	½	Road right is to San Jose de Magdalena. Highway ahead has several dips, watch if attempting to pass.
25	4	Road left to Ejido San Lucas.

(continued on page 101)

Isla San Marcos . . . is an important source of gypsum to mainland Mexico and users in the United States. There is an enormous deposit located on the south portion of the island. The operation is a joint venture between a Mexican corporation and Kaiser Gypsum Company of the United States, and supports about 700 people in a small village just south of the mine. When the Spaniards arrived, there was a small colony of Indians living on San Marcos, but they soon died after being removed to Mulege by the Jesuit missionaries.

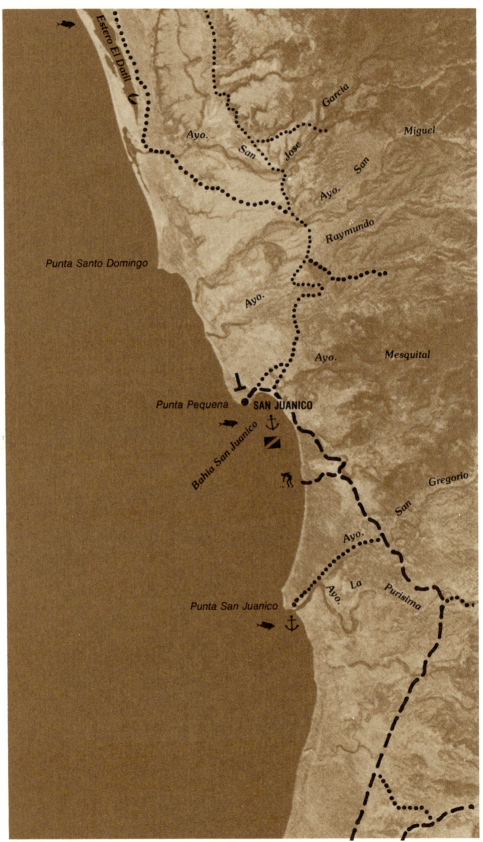

Estero El Datil

Garcia

Miguel

Ayo.

San

Jose

San

Ayo.

Raymundo

Punta Santo Domingo

Ayo.

Ayo.

Mesquital

Punta Pequena

SAN JUANICO

Bahia San Juanico

Gregorio

San

Ayo.

La

Purisima

Ayo.

Punta San Juanico

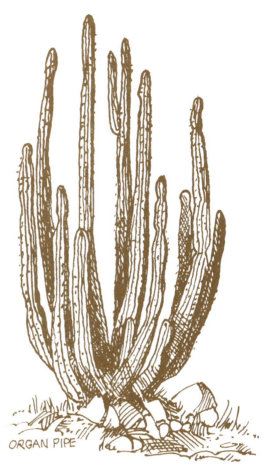

ORGAN PIPE

Isla Socorro . . . is part of the Revillagigedo group of islands scattered from 220 to 375 miles southwest of Cabo San Lucas. They are worthy of mention here because of the excellent fishing found in the region, particularly for wahoo and giant yellowfin tuna. Except for a small group of Mexican Navy men on Socorro, the group is uninhabited. Another of the group, Isla San Benedicto, was the scene of a volcanic eruption about 20 years ago. This isle is very isolated, but periodically visited by larger private and long-range sport boats.

THE 800 MILE CACTUS GARDEN

As the cirio might be considered the one plant that best symbolizes Baja California, the cactus family must be considered the group of plants that would best represent this strange peninsula.

Botanists have identified over one hundred species of cactus living in Baja California and fully three-quarters of these are found nowhere else in the world.

Baja is truly an 800-mile-long cactus garden that boasts the largest cactus in the world—the 80 ft. cardon—and also some of the smallest. There are several that barely reach an inch in height when fully grown.

SEE PAGE 92

SEE PAGE 96

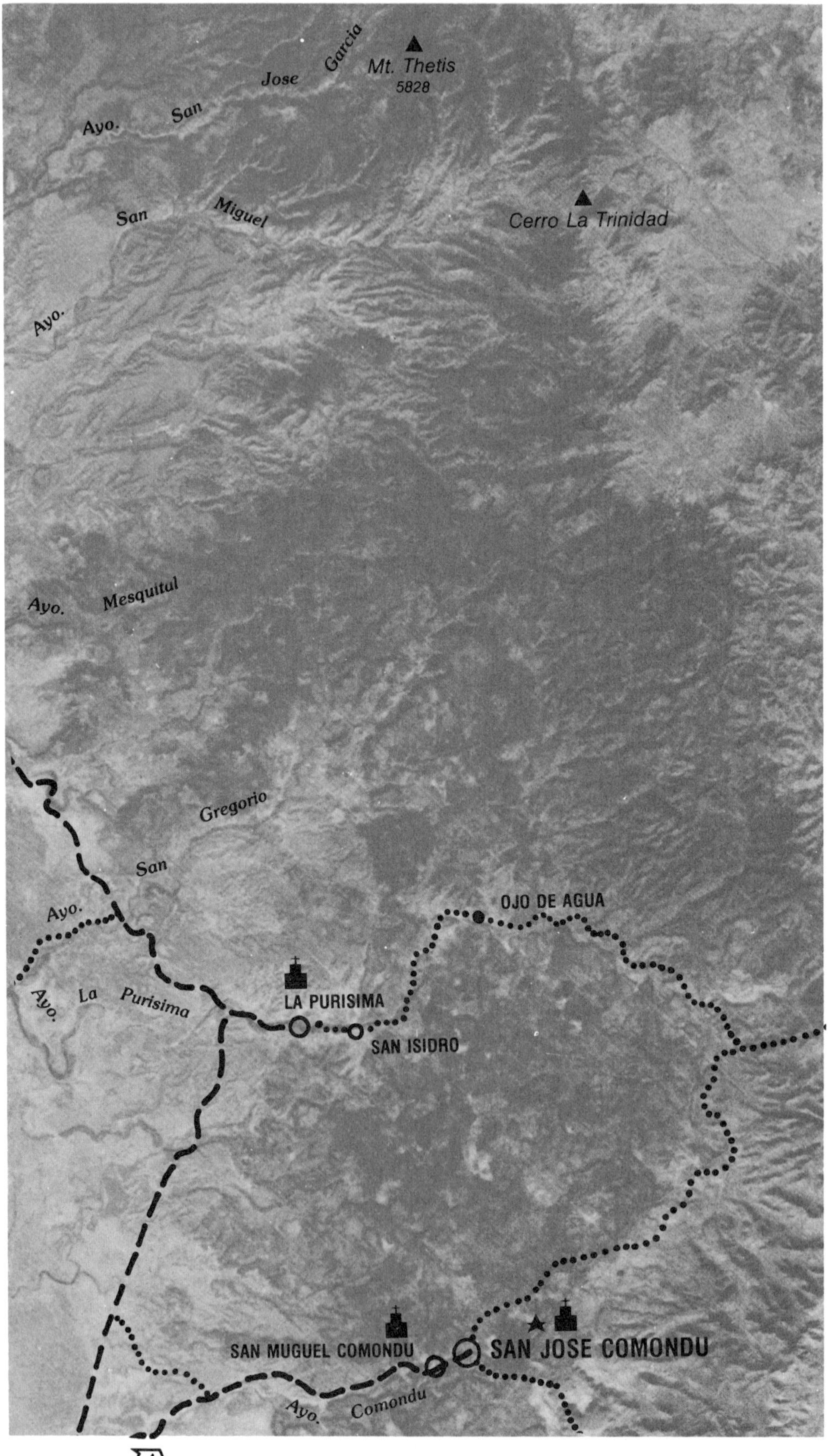
Mt. Thetis
5828
Ayo. San Jose Garcia
San Miguel
Cerro La Trinidad
Ayo.
Ayo. Mesquitul
Gregorio
San
Ayo.
OJO DE AGUA
LA PURISIMA
Ayo. La Purisima
SAN ISIDRO
SAN MUGUEL COMONDU
SAN JOSE COMONDU
Ayo. Comondu
N

SEE PAGE 100

SEE PAGE 106

A PONDEROUS PUZZLE

When the elephant tree was first seen by the exploring Spaniards, they must have wondered why such a short tree would have such a thick trunk and heavy limbs, yet be devoid of leaves for most of the year.

Some specimens have been described as having a trunk four feet in diameter, yet reaching a height of only ten feet. Their branches might extend only a few feet and measure 36 inches in diameter at the base.

The heavy trunk acts as a water reservoir for the months and sometimes years that pass without a drop of rain. Within days after a storm, the tree bursts forth with a mass of tiny green leaves. During the few weeks of greenery, the plant does all of its growing—until the next rain.

It usually blooms soon after the leaves fall off, creating a weird scene of pink blossoms on an otherwise dead-looking plant.

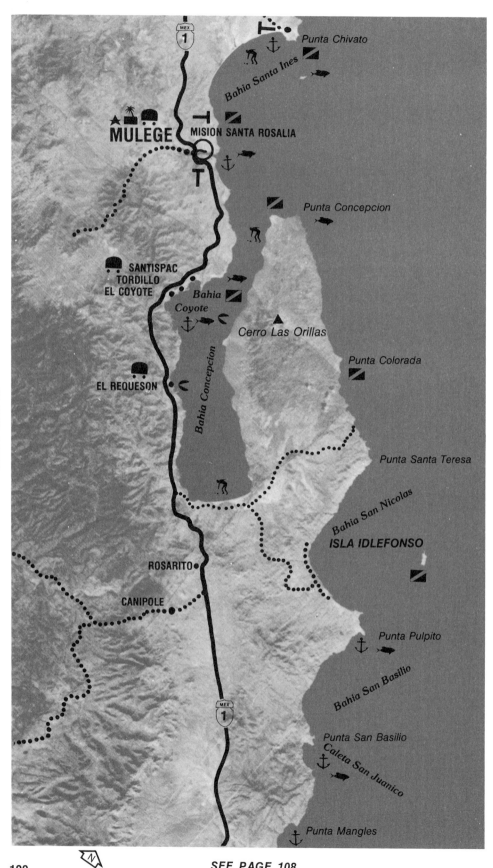

Punta Chivato

Bahia Santa Ines

MULEGE

MISION SANTA ROSALIA

Punta Concepcion

SANTISPAC
TORDILLO
EL COYOTE

Bahia
Coyote

Cerro Las Orillas

Punta Colorada

EL REQUESON

Bahia Concepcion

Punta Santa Teresa

Bahia San Nicolas

ISLA IDLEFONSO

ROSARITO

CANIPOLE

Punta Pulpito

Bahia San Basilio

Punta San Basilio

Caleta San Juanico

Punta Mangles

SEE PAGE 98

SEE PAGE 108

Total Mileage	Running Mileage	**SANTA ROSALIA—LORETO** (contd.from page 95)
33	8	Begin winding upgrade. Watch for slow traffic.
36	3	From top of grade, start winding downhill at 30-35 mph.
37	1	Reach bottom of grade. Mulege valley may be seen ahead.
37¾	¾	Road left into Mulege, north side of Rio Santa Rosalia and several resorts.
38	¼	Cross new bridge and continue south.
39	1	Road left to resorts along south side of river.
42½	3½	View of sand dunes and mouth of Bahia Concepcion.
47	4½	To left of highway is a large stone corral.
49	2	Begin descent toward Bahia Coyote. Watch curves.
50	1	Road left is to Playa Santispac. There are several primitive camping spots with moderate rates along a beautiful beach.
52	2	Left is Posada Concepcion on Bahia Tordillo. Probably the best trailer camp south of San Quintin.
54½	2½	Bahia Coyote. Beautiful public beach with some services.
64	9½	Road left is to Playa Requeson. Good clamming and snorkeling on sand bar and outside of island. Begin climbing over low hill shortly after passing turnoff. On left there are several views of the old road. (It doesn't take much to realize the challenge that the old road presented.) After climbing out of Concepcion basin you will wind up and down past many large cardon.
83	19	Small community of Rancho Rosarito is to right.
87	4	Road right is to Canipole (5 miles) and Pacific side through Comondu (47 miles) or La Purisima (46 miles). Continue winding south through cardons and other desert flora.

(continued on page 109)

Isla Coronado . . . located just north of Loreto, is only one and one-half miles from shore and is a terrific spot to spend a day lazing around on a white sand beach or gathering clams and catching fish for a beach barbeque. Fantastico!

Isla Carmen . . . is one of the largest islands in the Sea of Cortez and populated with several hundred workers in the solar salt works—which produce 50,000 tons of salt annually. The ponds are located in the northeasterly portion of the 17 mile long island. Carmen is only about seven miles offshore at Loreto, and provides good protection from all but the heaviest storms. The numerous coves and anchorages will certainly get a lot of play from those who trailer their boats down the new transpeninsula highway. Spectacular grottos, great fishing around the reefs and outside of Punta Lobos, and many miles of skin diving and swimming will lure visitors to this nearby island.

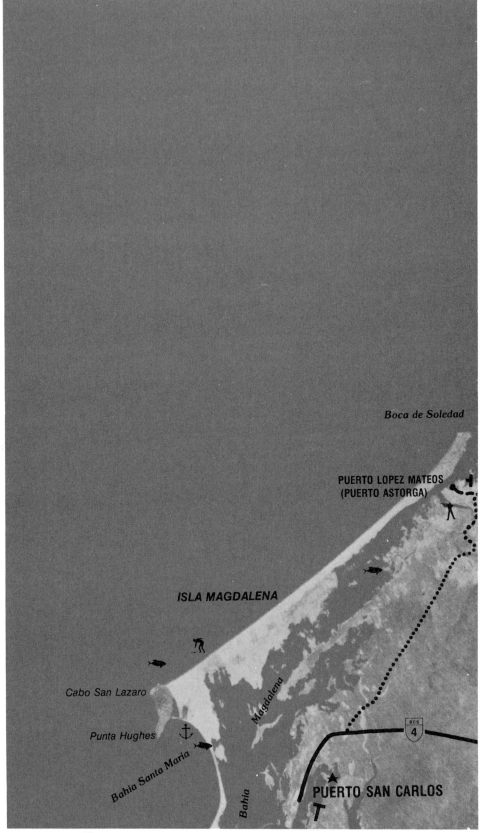

Boca de Soledad

PUERTO LOPEZ MATEOS
(PUERTO ASTORGA)

ISLA MAGDALENA

Cabo San Lazaro

Magdalena

Punta Hughes

BCS
4

Bahia Santa Maria

PUERTO SAN CARLOS

Bahia

102

N

SEE PAGE 110

BUSH PILOT AIRSTRIPS

Scattered throughout Baja California are numerous small clearings which are used by a certain breed of private pilot. These strips are located on ranches, by old mining claims and along remote beaches. They afford an opportunity to get away and "hide" for a few days for a surprising number of pilots and their families.

The condition of these strips must be observed very carefully before attempting a landing; but once down you are likely to be completely alone. Such ventures are not for the inexperiencd pilot nor should they be attempted without notifying the authorities where you plan to go.

EL COYOTE

He is everywhere . . . he can be heard at night almost anywhere in Baja . . . yet he is rarely seen. El Coyote is an everpresent shadow and companion to those who take to the backroads.

His adaptability to his environment is widely demonstrated in Baja. Some live along the coast and depend mainly on dead fish and seals to survive. Others take to the dunes in search of lizards, kangaroo mice and beetles. The high country is also full of their sign.

His average size and color varies with the region in which he lives. There is hardly a square mile of Baja that does not have its share of coyotes.

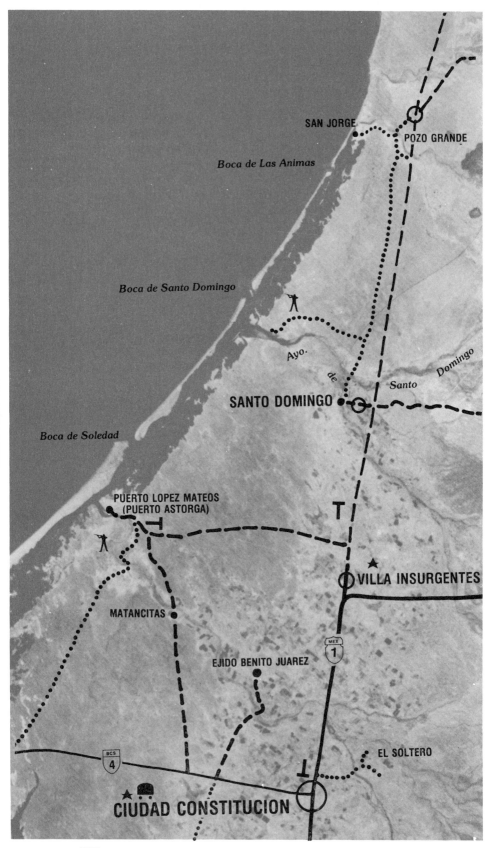

SEE PAGE 102

SEE PAGE 106

Boca de Las Animas

SAN JORGE

POZO GRANDE

Boca de Santo Domingo

Ayo.

de

Santo

Domingo

SANTO DOMINGO

Boca de Soledad

PUERTO LOPEZ MATEOS
(PUERTO ASTORGA)

T

VILLA INSURGENTES

MATANCITAS

MEX
1

EJIDO BENITO JUAREZ

EL SOLTERO

BCS
4

CIUDAD CONSTITUCION

LORETO—CIUDAD CONSTITUCION

(continued from page 107)

Total Mileage	Running Mileage	
69	2	Road to left is another road into Buenos Aires. Continue SE.
71	2	Approach intersection with road into Villa Insurgentes (1 mile right). Turn left and continue toward La Paz past numerous farms and small ejidos.
87	16	Pass large cotton gin on east side of road.
89	2	Enter Ciudad Constitucion. Small Tourism office is on left. Slightly ahead on right is paved road to Puerto San Carlos (35 miles).

BAKING OVEN

NEW FARMS FROM OLD WATER

A study of the Baja Spacemaps around Villa Insurgente, Ciudad Constitucion and Santa Rita show the many rectangular fields under cultivation.

Here, as in the Vizcaino Desert, "fossil water" is a primary source of that needed to make this rain-parched desert produce. It gives life to great quantities of cotton, grain, citrus, tomatoes and peppers. A number of cotton gins are seen as you drive through the countryside.

Through much of the year the climate is modified by an onshore flow of moist air from the adjacent Bahia Magdalena and Pacific Ocean. If camping in this region, do not be surprised at the amount of dew that collects on everything during the night.

Several fish canneries are located on Bahia Magdalena at Puerto Astorga and San Carlos. These are expected to eventually replace the cannery at San Lucas to the south.

The future for this portion of the Baja peninsula is indeed bright.

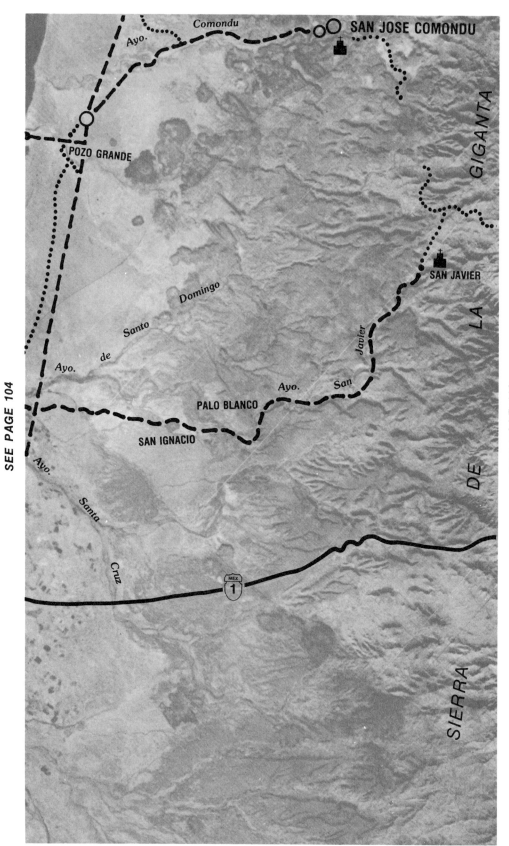

SEE PAGE 104

SEE PAGE 108

SAN JOSE COMONDU

GIGANTA

POZO GRANDE

Domingo

Santo

de

Ayo.

SAN JAVIER

LA

Ayo.   San

PALO BLANCO

SAN IGNACIO

Javier

Ayo.

DE

Santa

Cruz

MEX 1

SIERRA

N

SEE PAGES 112 & 114

LORETO—CIUDAD CONSTITUCION

(continued from page 109)

Total Mileage	Running Mileage	
30½	7	A tall peak is on the left as road continues to wind through narrow valleys. Numerous cattle graze here.
36	5½	Continue through a series of everwidening valleys on easily winding roadbed.
43	7	Leave mountains and follow straight path in SE direction across plateau. Countryside shows evidence of considerably less rain.
49½	6½	A deep canyon is on the left as road continues along the edge of the mesa. Descent becomes more rapid and road straightens as it passes several small clusters of houses.
67	17½	To the south is Buenos Aires, center of a newly developed cotton growing region. Alt. 250 ft.

(continued on page 105)

BATMAN COMES TO BAJA

As you drive south of San Ignacio on Mexico 1 watch for a series of tall steel towers perched atop a number of hills near the road. They are microwave relay stations, installed to bring telephone service to the southern portion of Baja.

Already partially in operation, they will soon bring the outside world to within milliseconds of such places as Mulege, Loreto, La Paz and San Jose del Cabo. They will make it easier to confirm reservations and communicate in emergencies, but it removes one more region from those few remaining places where you can get away from the phone. Another sobering thought . . . the relay stations can also be used for television transmission. Could it be that Batman will come to Baja?

SEE PAGE 100

SEE PAGE 106

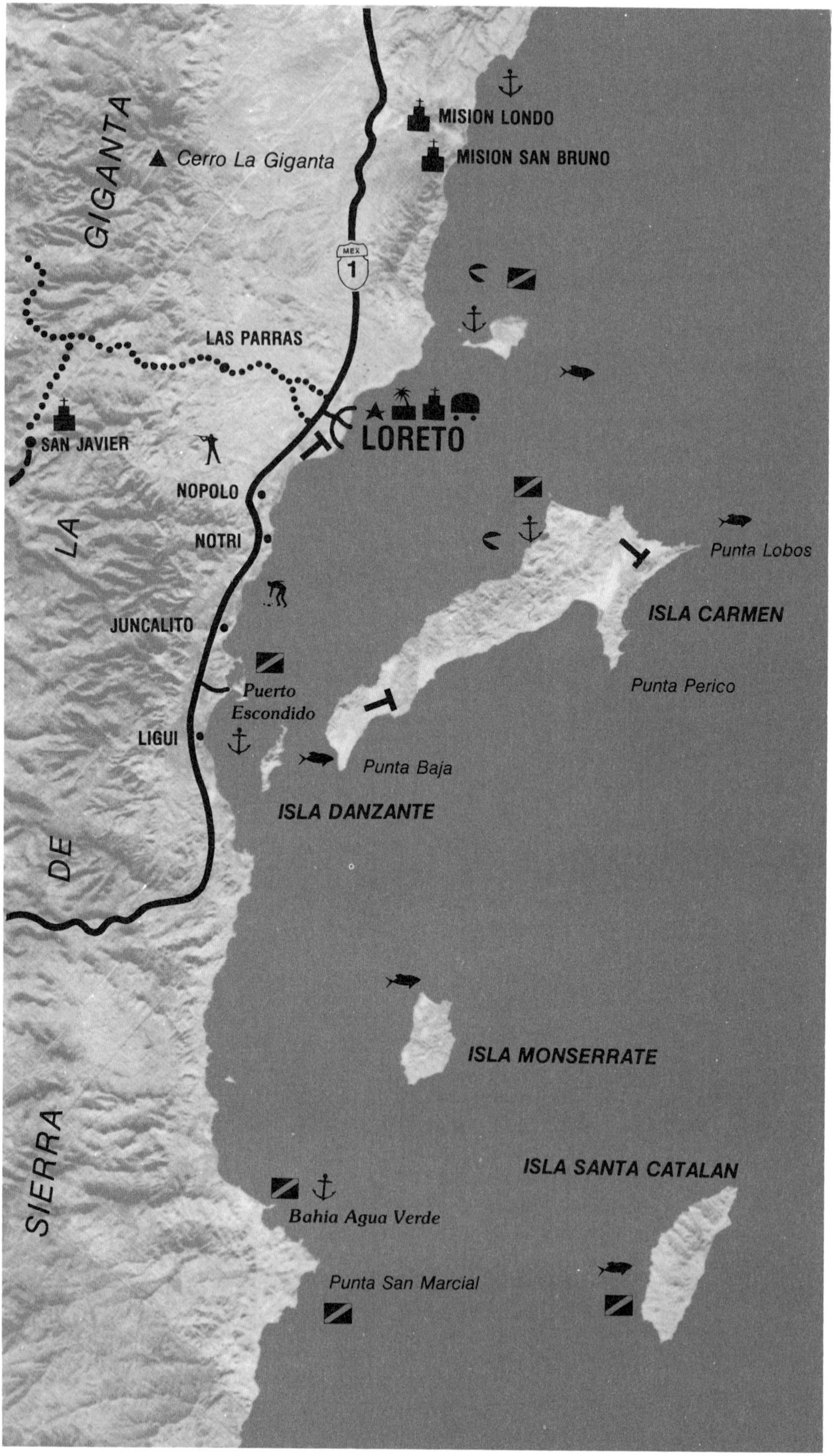
GIGANTA
Cerro La Giganta
MISION LONDO
MISION SAN BRUNO
MEX
1
LAS PARRAS
SAN JAVIER
LORETO
NOPOLO
NOTRI
LA
JUNCALITO
Puerto
Escondido
LIGUI
Punta Lobos
ISLA CARMEN
Punta Perico
Punta Baja
ISLA DANZANTE
DE
ISLA MONSERRATE
SIERRA
ISLA SANTA CATALAN
Bahia Agua Verde
Punta San Marcial
N

SEE PAGE 114

Total Mileage	Running Mileage	

SANTA ROSALIA—LORETO (contd.from page 101)

102	15	Road right goes into a beautiful little tree filled arroyo. Highway 1 climbs out of arroyo and onto plain.
109	7	Road becomes more winding. Watch speed and on-coming traffic.
117	8	You have a good view of Loreto about 5 miles distant before descending into valley.
121	4	Paved road to left into Loreto (2 miles). (See map page 137)

LORETO—CIUDAD CONSTITUCION

0	0	Leave intersection with Loreto in southerly direction on Mexico 1.
1	1	Road to right leads up through arroyo to Mision San Javier, 17 mi. past several picturesque ranchos. Road is supposed to be improved as part of mission restoration program. Inquire in Loreto before attempting in passenger car.
5	4	Nopolo Cove and Rancho. Scenic beach with some clams and tidepools. Good fishing in here at times. Some shelling.
8	3	Rancho Notri. Ranch house to right. To left is beach where many species of fish come quite close to shore. There is a large KOA campground planned for this region.
13	5	After winding up and down, begin another descent with view of small camp on beach. Named Juncalito, the best road in is at bottom of hill.
15	2	Paved road to left goes to Puerto Escondido (1½ miles). This is worth a visit as the region abounds with fish and other sea life. Boats for fishing may be rented. Eventually, there will be some tourist accommodations.
21	6	Ligui is a small group of houses several miles from the water.
22	1	Turn inland and up into pass through Sierra de La Giganta and onto Magdalena Plain.
23½	1½	Remains of old road may be seen to right. Watch the sharp turn ahead. Continue climbing with good views of deep arroyos and jagged peaks and more sharp turns with very few turnouts.

(continued on page 107)

Isla Monserrate . . . measures two by four miles in a north-south direction about halfway between Isla Santa Catalana and the mainland and is little visited except by birds and a few anglers.

Isla Danzante . . . provides good protection to Bahia Escondido two and one-half miles westward, as does Isla Carmen a few miles farther north. Danzante has long been a favorite of visitors to Loreto, who boat to the island for the plentiful fish or land at one of several coves to snorkel, beachcomb or to look for the Indian middens in the arroyos. It is uninhabited, except for an occasional visit from the Vagabundos during their migrations through the gulf.

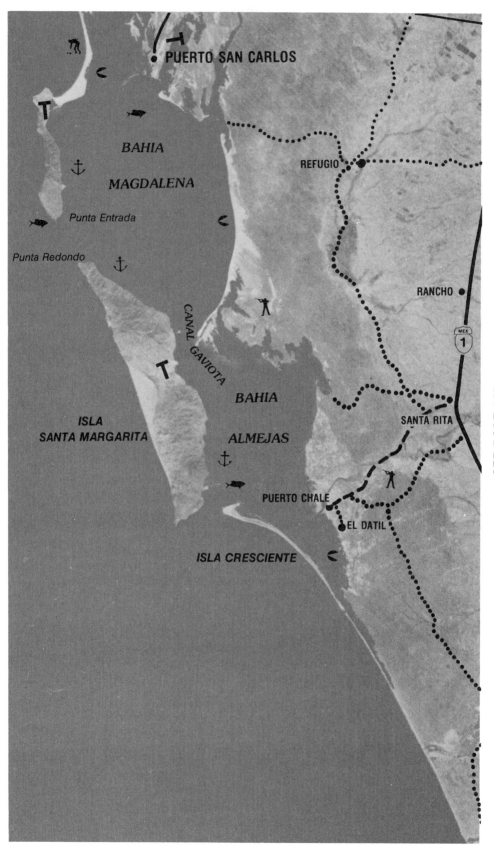

PUERTO SAN CARLOS

BAHIA

MAGDALENA

REFUGIO

Punta Entrada

Punta Redondo

RANCHO

MEX 1

CANAL GAVIOTA

BAHIA

ISLA
SANTA MARGARITA

ALMEJAS

SANTA RITA

PUERTO CHALE

EL DATIL

ISLA CRESCIENTE

SEE PAGE 112

N

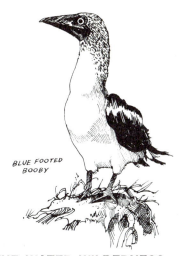

BLUE FOOTED BOOBY

THE WATER WILDERNESS

Bahia Magdalena and connecting waters to the north and south combine to form a protected inland waterway that extends for more than 150 miles behind numerous islands and sandspits.

Navigable its entire length with a shallow draft boat, it offers unlimited opportunities for exploration. The fish in the baylets, channels and around the Pacific entrances to the Magdalena waterway, are much the same as found offshore. In addition there are considerable populations of snook, croakers and corvinas that are found near the extensive mangrove swamps.

Clams and oysters have been taken commercially from this region for many years. Very fine scallops are brought into Puerto San Carlos. The many beaches and coves abound with shells of all descriptions.

Tremendous populations of resident and migrating waterfowl come from both north and south to winter or summer in this rich region. The miles of mangrove swamps are nesting places for numerous species of insect-eating songbirds. "Mag Bay" literally jumps with life—except there are few people to enjoy it.

The small colony at San Carlos and a few scattered fish camps and ranchos total only a few thousand residents. Access, too, is limited to the paved road from Ciudad Constitucion and a few scattered dirt trails that sometimes are not passable.

Nights along the Magdalena waterway are often damp with fogs that soak everything not protected. Bugs too, can be pesky around the mangroves, but a good repellent seems to work.

The possibilities for the small boater in this immense waterway system are almost unlimited, with hundreds of miles of shoreline to follow and explore. Watch for a series of launching ramps and small marinas to be established in this region in the next 3 or 4 years.

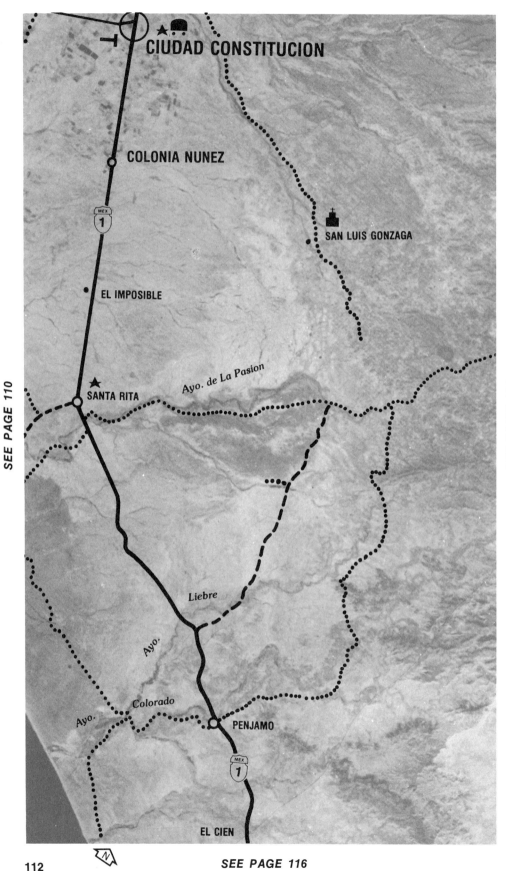

SEE PAGE 110

SEE PAGE 114

CIUDAD CONSTITUCION

COLONIA NUNEZ

MEX 1

SAN LUIS GONZAGA

EL IMPOSIBLE

Ayo. de La Pasion

SANTA RITA

Liebre

Ayo.

Colorado

Ayo.

Ayo.

PENJAMO

MEX 1

EL CIEN

Total Mileage	Running Mileage	

CIUDAD CONSTITUCION—LA PAZ

0	0	Leave intersection with San Carlos road and continue straight south through town and past radio transmitter tower on left at 2 miles.
12	12	Colonia Nunez is a group of homes in center of many cultivated fields. Road continues straight in SSE direction.
18	6	Pass Rancho El Imposible and Rancho San Martin, another 1½ miles south. Soon road will turn slightly to east.
33	15	Dirt road on right goes to Puerto Chale and El Datil. 100 yards further is restaurant "Santa Rita." Landscape is very dry as only 1 to 2 inches of rain fall in this region. Through here is a variety of ocotillo that is native to Baja. The road continues in long straight sections while slowly entering area of low hills.
67	34	Shortly after entering foothills you pass El Cien which is 100 km or 62 miles from La Paz. Road then climbs and for the next 20 miles meanders through increasingly heavy vegetation.

(continued on page 117)

VULTURE

CARDON

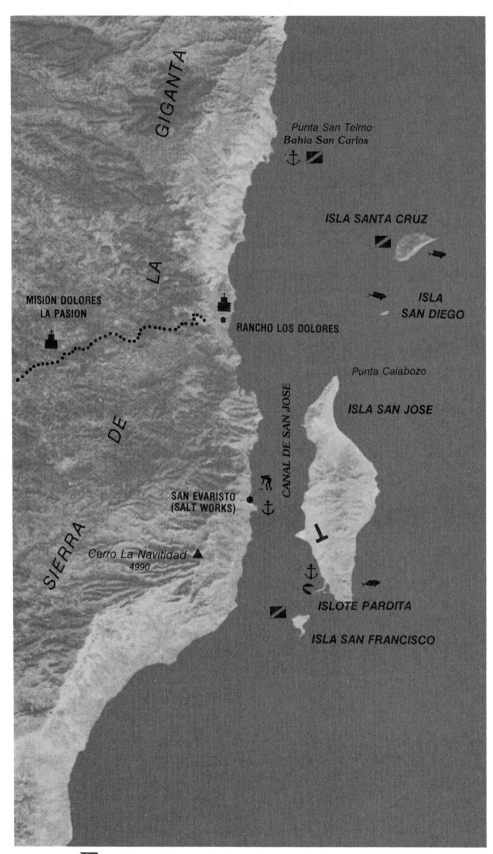

GIGANTA

Punta San Telmo
Bahia San Carlos

ISLA SANTA CRUZ

ISLA
SAN DIEGO

LA

MISION DOLORES
LA PASION

RANCHO LOS DOLORES

Punta Calabozo

ISLA SAN JOSE

CANAL DE SAN JOSE

DE

SAN EVARISTO
(SALT WORKS)

SIERRA

Cerro La Navitidad ▲
4990

ISLOTE PARDITA

ISLA SAN FRANCISCO

114

Isla Santa Cruz ... located about four miles north of Isla San Diego, it is a steep mass of rock, with only one small rocky landing located near the southwestern end. It is one of the most barren of the islands in the Sea of Cortez.

Isla San Diego ... is a narrow mile-long island that juts to 722 feet above sea level. Its abundant fish population is contrasted by numerous lizards, scorpions and rodents.

Isla San Jose ... lies parallel to the mainland and forms the eastern edge of the five to seven mile wide San Jose Channel. With a 16 mile length and four mile average width, it is one of the most fertile of the islands in the Mar de Cortez and harbors a good variety of plants and cacti—plus many birds, coyotes, rodents, and even a few deer. There are several families who work a small evaporative salt works towards the southwest end. Bahia Amortajada, it's beach and the nearby lagoon and mangrove swamp, provide just about everything needed for a weeklong stay. There are clams in the shallows south of the mangroves, calm, crystal clear water and plenty of fish to watch or catch. One more thing that is found on most outings is here—at times with a vengeance. The Mexicans call them **jejenes** or **bobos.** We would call them noseeums or gnats. When the wind dies down, the jejenes come winging in, armed to the teeth, so to speak. Their bites are usually not noticed until a half hour or so after they get to you—and they do itch. Fortunately, most of the first aid sprays take the sting out and the repellent sprays do a good job. The little varmints are often found in the vicinity of the mangroves, so let it be a warning.

Islote Pardita ... would not be worth mentioning if you were to consider only its size (an acre or two)—if it were not for the fact that about 40 people live on it! Located a few miles south of Isla San Jose, it has half a dozen buildings and sheds perched on its steep lee side looking out on a small rocky baylet and the Baja mainland. The entire group of inhabitants is apparently part of a family that came here to store and process the sharks caught in the nearby waters. All supplies, including water, are brought in from the mainland. They hosted a number of us one evening to a great turtle (cahuama) stew, complete with tortillas and limes. Occasionally live bait (goatfish) may be obtained from the bait receiver in front of the camp. They even had a garden ... one scrawny tomato plant well protected from kids, chickens and a couple of dogs. Considering that all of the water is imported, that tomato patch was a showplace.

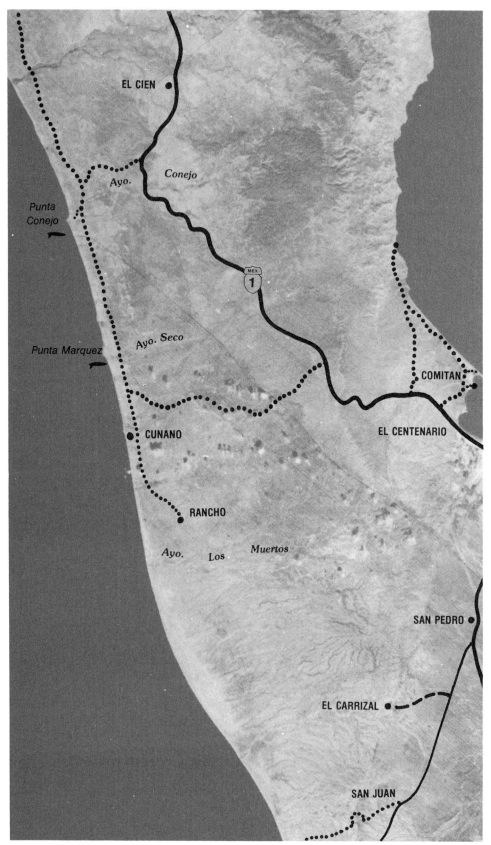

EL CIEN

Conejo

Ayo.

Punta
Conejo

MEX
1

Ayo. Seco

Punta Marquez

COMITAN

CUNANO

EL CENTENARIO

RANCHO

Ayo.   Los   Muertos

SAN PEDRO

EL CARRIZAL

SAN JUAN

N

CIUDAD CONSTITUCION—LA PAZ

(continued from page 113)

Total Mileage	Running Mileage	
91	24	On the right is a strange whitewashed cactus-shaped shrine.
93¼	2¼	Dirt road right goes to El Provencia. Continue through cattle grazing area.
104½	11¼	Road on right is to El Represso.
107½	3	Take road right to El Satisfacto. Just ahead begin a downgrade into La Paz valley. There is a good view of La Paz and the Sea of Cortez in the distance from here. To the west from here the Pacific is also visible. Watch the sharp curves and expect to slow to 25-30 mph on some turns.
110	2½	Road straightens at bottom of grade and heads directly for La Paz past many cardons, pitihaya and tall brush.
119	9	Road to left is marked "Comitan."

(continued on page 119)

Isla Santa Catalana . . . is an island of great interest to the naturalist. It is the home of the rattleless rattlesnake and the largest **biznaga** (barrel cactus) plants in the gulf islands. It also has a number of other plants that through centuries of isolation have changed their form slightly to better adapt themselves to the harsh environment of the island. The island has long been a campground for the itinerant **vagabundos** of the Sea of Cortez. Evidence of their visits may be found near the southern end. No permanent residents live on this seven and one-half by two mile island—the snakes and lizards pretty well have it to themselves. The Mexican government is endeavoring to preserve Catalana as a sanctuary for study by naturalists. (see page 108)

Isla Espiritu Santo . . . protects Bahia de la Paz from the east and along with its close neighbor, **Isla Partida**, provides many beautiful coves for swimming, diving, camping and so on. Their combined 12 by five mile terrain is of volcanic origin. Both were long ago uptilted to the east and show beautiful layers of red, pink, ochre, white and black on the tall cliffs along the east side. The sandy beaches are incredibly white and clean. Like most of their fellow islands further up the gulf, they harbor great numbers of fish, clams and other examples of a fertile marine environment. (see page 118)

Isla San Francisco . . . is popular with visiting yachtsmen and anglers and has several good anchorages. About one mile square with a hook-like arm on the south end, it has sparse vegetation and pools of brackfish water for some time following the rainy season. Occasionally worked by pearlers, it was the site of a one-man gold rush in the 1880's when a German uncovered enough metal to keep him busy for about five years. (see page 114)

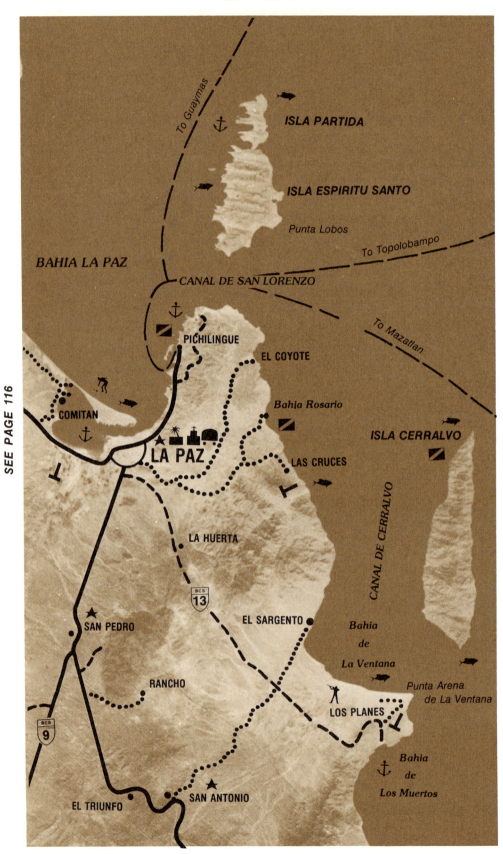

ISLA PARTIDA

ISLA ESPIRITU SANTO

Punta Lobos

To Guaymas

To Topolobampo

BAHIA LA PAZ

CANAL DE SAN LORENZO

To Mazatlan

PICHILINGUE

EL COYOTE

Bahia Rosario

ISLA CERRALVO

COMITAN

LA PAZ

LAS CRUCES

LA HUERTA

CANAL DE CERRALVO

BCS 13

EL SARGENTO

Bahia
de
La Ventana

SAN PEDRO

Punta Arena
de La Ventana

RANCHO

LOS PLANES

BCS 9

Bahia
de
Los Muertos

EL TRIUNFO

SAN ANTONIO

N

(continued from page 117)

Total Mileage	Running Mileage	
123½	4½	Paved road to right is to new La Paz International Airport. Continue past increasing numbers of homes and businesses.
127	3½	Arrive in downtown La Paz. (See map page 138)

LA PAZ TO BUENA VISTA

0	0	Take street southeast away from Malecon 1 mile to main street (Av. Isabel la Catolica). Turn right past Palacio Gobierno (on left)and supermarket (on right), bearing south after ¾ mile. (See La Paz map)
3	3	Road left to Los Planes (30 miles) and Bahia de Los Muertos (40 miles). There is an interesting beach here, facing to the south, where good fishing from shore is found, particularly at dawn and dusk. Vegetation typical of region—cacti and tall brush.
4	1	Ahead on hill to left is large shrine overlooking valley of La Paz. Continue past small ranchos.
16	12	Enter small community of San Pedro. To left is ranch that is using growing cardon cactus as a fence. Shrine at south end of town.
18	2	Road left to Ejido Alvardo Obregon, 3 km.
19	1	Paved road to right leads to Todos Santos and Pescadero. Rarely visited by tourists. An interesting farming and fishing region, but few facilities.
21	2	On left, another road to Ejido Alvardo Obregon, 3 km.
21½	½	Road right to Algodones.
25	3½	Rancho Santa Rita on right.
27½	2½	You are now at 1300 feet; begin downgrade, watch speed.
29½	2	Road right to El Rosario, 4 miles and beyond to other small farms.
31	1½	Top of grade, excellent view of El Triunfo.
32	1	Enter El Triunfo. Just across the bridge on right is a little handcraft shop selling clever items made from palm leaves. Well worth a stop.

(continued on page 125)

Isla de Cerralvo . . . is the southernmost island in the Sea of Cortez. Sixteen miles by about four in a north-south direction, it forms the eastern boundary of the Cerralvo Channel and is uninhabited. Cerralvo may be a bit short on vegetation, but its waters teem with fish, clams and scallops. It was a main source for the Baja pearls, almost since its discovery in 1533. Here, as elsewhere in the gulf, pearling came to a virtual halt in the 1940's when a mysterious disease wiped out most of the oysters.

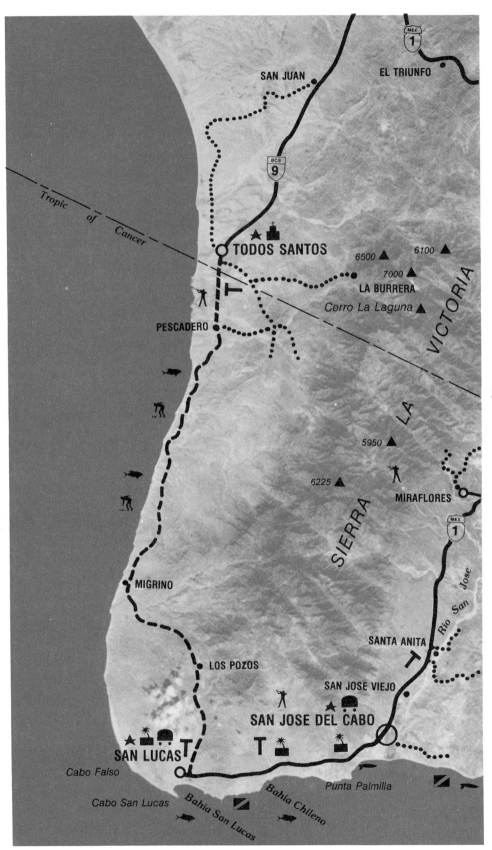

SAN JUAN

EL TRIUNFO

MEX 1

BCS 9

Tropic of Cancer

TODOS SANTOS

6500 ▲   6100 ▲

7000 ▲

LA BURRERA

Cerro La Laguna ▲

PESCADERO

5950 ▲

6225 ▲

MIRAFLORES

MEX 1

SIERRA   LA   VICTORIA

MIGRINO

Rio San   Jose

SANTA ANITA

LOS POZOS

SAN JOSE VIEJO

SAN JOSE DEL CABO

SAN LUCAS

Cabo Falso

Cabo San Lucas

Bahia San Lucas

Bahia Chileno

Punta Palmilla

SEE PAGE 124

N

SAN LUCAS—LA PAZ VIA TODOS SANTOS

NOTE: This roadlog digresses from our pattern of recording travel from north to south because at the present time this journey is much easier going from south to north.

Total Mileage	Running Mileage	
0	0	Turn north off of Mexico 1 a mile east of Pemex station and wind uphill past a number of small houses.
2	2	On left, Rancho Santa Fe. Roadbed sandy, but passable.
4	2	Fork in road. Left to airport (1 mile), right to Todos Santos.
4½	½	Another fork, stay to left.
7¾	3¼	Road to right, keep left. The sandy areas can easily be negotiated if you don't stop. Keep a steady, moderate speed.
10	2¼	Los Pozos, several small houses, corral. Curve left, continue up easy grade. El Saucito is ½ mile further. Road to right (from Saucito) to La Candalaria.
11	1	Top of grade, 1300′ alt. Heavy underbrush of cactus, palo blanco and numerous shrubs. First view of Pacific Ocean. Begin descent.
15	4	Rancho Buena Vista. Truly a beautiful view of Pacific Ocean. Cross arroyo and proceed toward ocean.
20½	5½	Top of gentle ridge. Panoramic view of Pacific Ocean.
21¼	¾	Road left to beach. (If you are driving a standard type car, check out the side roads thoroughly before attempting to drive them. It's no fun to get stuck anywhere, and it could be dangerous in remote desert regions.)
22	¾	Rancho El Migrino to left near mouth of Arroyo Candelaria. Road continues north parallel to ocean, but several miles inland, in and out of numerous small arroyos. Rainy weather on this stretch could be trouble until paving is completed.
29½	7½	Road left to beach, sandy, but not for standard cars.
30½	1	Beautiful beach near road. Many beautiful shells. Heavy surf and steep dropoff. Dangerous swimming but good fishing. Cast lures past breaker line or use bait near rocks to north.
32	1½	Rancho Piedrita on left. An old abandoned house in front of a newer one. A beautiful view of ocean and beaches. There are several roads to beach in this region. Check with people at ranchos for permission to camp.
33½	1½	Colonia Frutal is in arroyo with many palms, beach is to west. Very lovely. Continue past rich farmland and a succession of beautiful beaches.
40½	7	To the left is a fresh water lagoon separated from ocean by dunes.
44	3½	Small group of houses on right. Road left is to Playa Los Cerritos. This is southern end of farming town of Pescadero. Continue north and slightly inland past more farms and several roads west toward beaches, and east to foothills of Sierra de La Victoria.

(continued on page 123)

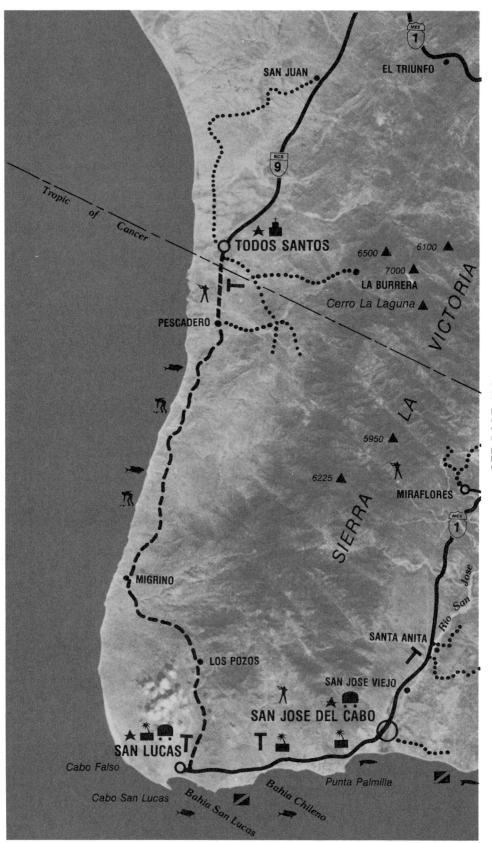

SAN JUAN

EL TRIUNFO

MEX 1

BCS 9

Tropic *of* *Cancer*

★ ☗ **TODOS SANTOS**

6500 ▲   6100 ▲

7000 ▲
LA BURRERA

Cerro La Laguna ▲

PESCADERO ●

VICTORIA

5950 ▲

6225 ▲

LA

MIRAFLORES

MEX 1

SIERRA

MIGRINO

Rio San Jose

SANTA ANITA

LOS POZOS

SAN JOSE VIEJO

★ ☗
SAN JOSE DEL CABO

★ 🌴☗☗ T
SAN LUCAS

T 🌴☗   🌴☗

Cabo Falso

Punta Palmilla

Cabo San Lucas   *Bahia San Lucas*   *Bahia Chileno*

122   ◈N

SAN LUCAS—LA PAZ VIA TODOS SANTOS

(continued from page 121)

Total Mileage	Running Mileage	
51	7	Enter Todos Santos and proceed north, turning right past Plaza. Scattered stores and Pemex station provide services, Follow road as it bears right, then left out of town to paving.
62	11	Road winds in and out of arroyos through brushy country. Road then straightens and goes north onto eastern portion of Llano Carrizal, a newly developed agricultural region.
72½	10½	First of several roads left to Ejido El Carrizal. There is supposed to be good duck hunting southwest of there at Boca de Palmarito (15 miles). Main road continues almost due north in straight line through heavy underbrush.
83	10½	Back at intersection with Mexico 1, right to El Triunfo, left to La Paz, 19 miles.
102	19	La Paz.

BUENA VISTA—SAN LUCAS

(continued from page 125

36	6	Entering Santa Anita. Thatched roof church on left.
37½	1½	Paved road west to new airport designed to bring jet service to region.
40	2½	San Jose Viejo, a long-established farming area. South are many fan palms, a few date palms and a number of fertile farms.
44	4	Fork left to San Jose del Cabo. Pemex station at intersection. Mexico 1 continues toward ocean.
46	2	Gov't trailer park on beautiful beach that offers good surfing during summer storm season. (July. August, September).
48	2	Turn left to Hotel Palmilla. (see Resort Roundup).
50	2	Camping beach with thatched ramadas.
55½	5½	Entrance, left, to Hotel Cabo San Lucas. Currently the largest hotel in area. (see Resort Roundup).
61	5½	Entrance to new Hyatt Cabo San Lucas and Cabo Bello resort development. Just beyond is excellent view of rocky tip of Baja.
62½	1½	Road right to Pacific side of peninsula and La Paz via Todos Santos.
63½	1	Pemex station.
64½	1	Left to Hacienda Hotel.
65	½	Enter town of San Lucas. To left are hotels and ferry building.

**Congratulations, Amigo . . .
you have reached Land's End!**

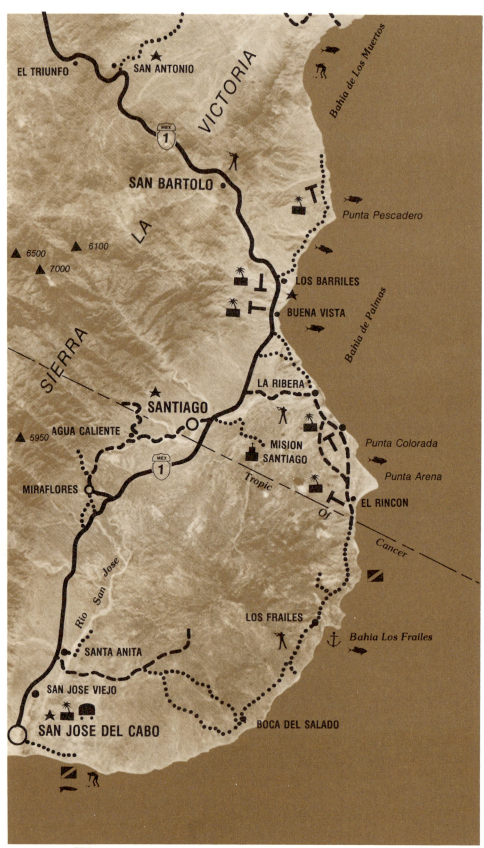

SEE PAGES 120 & 122

EL TRIUNFO

SAN ANTONIO

VICTORIA

Bahia de Los Muertos

MEX 1

SAN BARTOLO

LA

Punta Pescadero

▲ 6500   ▲ 6100

▲ 7000

LOS BARRILES

BUENA VISTA

Bahia de Palmas

SIERRA

LA RIBERA

SANTIAGO

Punta Colorada

▲ 5950   AGUA CALIENTE

MISION
SANTIAGO

Punta Arena

MEX 1

Tropic

EL RINCON

MIRAFLORES

Of

Cancer

Rio San Jose

LOS FRAILES

⚓ Bahia Los Frailes

SANTA ANITA

SAN JOSE VIEJO

SAN JOSE DEL CABO

BOCA DEL SALADO

N

LA PAZ TO BUENA VISTA

(continued from page 119)

Total Mileage	Running Mileage	
34½	2½	After winding ascent, reach top of ridge and drop into San Antonio Valley. Many curves through here; suggest 30 mph.
36	1½	San Antonio is on right. A number of mango trees and date palms are visible in canyon. Begin climbing out of canyon almost immediately. Road winds sharply in places (30-35 mph). Shortly, you will have views of Sea of Cortez as you pass through area of many flowers (following rainy season).
40½	4½	Road to left to Los Planes and Bahia de la Ventana, approx. 18 miles.
41¼	¾	Start down hill into arroyo.
53	11¾	Entering San Bartolo. Gentle decline, winding road, excellent view of the valley below. The narrow town has many picturesque little houses with thatched roofs nestled along sides of arroyo. Long famous as a garden spot. Many, many dove through this region.
64	11	Road left to Hotel Palmas de Cortez (was Bahia de Palmas until 1973). (see Resort Roundup). Pemex station on right 1 mile further south.
66	2	Road right to El Coro, 6 miles.
66½	½	Road left to Rancho Buena Vista resort about ½ mile. (see Resort Roundup).

BUENA VISTA—SAN LUCAS

0	0	Return to Mexico 1 at Buena Vista and continue south through cacti, small trees and shrubs. To left is new gringo residential development.
8	8	Road right is to Las Cuevas, a small community named for caves in cliff. It is reported that there are Indian pictographs in one of the caves.
		Road left is to La Ribera (8 miles). Several small stores and Pemex station ¾ mile south of town. Road continues south and east past Hotel Punta Colorada, 13 miles, El Rincon and Laguna Guest House, 21 miles, El Pulmo and on to Los Frailes at 31 miles. A bad road continues around past several beaches and finally joins Mexico 1 just north of San Jose del Cabo. The hurricane of October, 1976 did much damage to the roads in this area so enquire locally before proceeding too far.
13	5	Road right to Santiago. Paved road winds sharply down into Arroyo de Santiago and across to town. There is a large stand of fan palms along west side of arroyo.
		Santiago, on mesa above has a nice plaza surrounded by stores and cantina. Beautiful church is located ½ mile south of plaza.
15	2	Monument in form of large cement sphere marks Tropic of Cancer.
21	6	Road right to Miraflores (1¼ mi.).
24	3	Road right to Caduano, an agricultural ejido.
30	6	Top of grade. Road proceeds straight in SSE direction. Ahead to right is 6,250 foot high Cerro Santa Genoviva.

(continued on page 123)

TOWNS OF BAJA

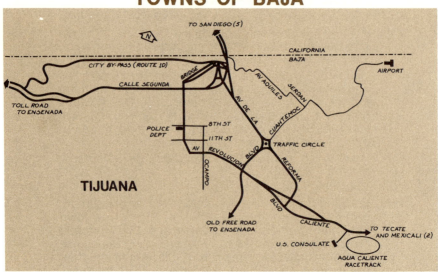

TIJUANA (Tee-WHAH-nah) The prohibition era of the 20's and the wide-open gambling that survived well after repeal in 1933 spurred the growth of Tijuana, formerly called Tia Juana, or Aunt Jane. Once a sleepy village of 600, it is now a sometimes-dazzling mixture of over 400,000 people, who derive most of their income from the Norteamericano.

Thousands of Mexicans daily cross the border to work in the fields, homes and factories around San Diego Bay. Many U. S. businesses have opened assembly plants in Tijuana to take advantage of favorable wage structures and a low duty rate. The electronic and clothing industries especially have tapped the great labor reservoir only a few miles south of San Diego.

Wares seen by the millions of **touristas** as they walk through jangled collections of stores or in the arms of hawkers working the lines of cars waiting to recross the border are produced locally—especially for the tourist. Side streets will often be crowded with the white, naked, plaster-of-paris replicas of everything from "The Last Supper" to "Snoopy" and "Charlie Brown".

The large stacks of empty Tecate beer cans seen as you skirt the northern edge of town on the way to the Ensenada toll road are snipped, bent, hammered and painted into lamps, candle holders, bird cages and wall dcorations found in the little stalls along Avenida Mexico and similar tourist shops throughout all border towns. Onyx elephants, chess sets, ashtrays and statues are cut, ground, smoothed and polished in hundreds of small plants throughout the city. In the outskirts, red clay pots are fashioned to the shape of the moment and often decorated with everything from so-called authentic Oaxacan designs to the faces of the latest rock stars.

Some of the more furtive and talented craftsmen are busy chipping "genuine" carved statues out of stone brought from central Mexico. Upon completion, they are buried for several days in the back yard, resurrected and clandestinely palmed off on those visitors who, with a touch of larceny themselves, smuggle the "ancient" artifacts into the U.S.A.

The border crossing between Tijuana and San Ysidro on the U. S. side is the busiest in the world, with more than ten million people passing through customs annually. At times, lines of cars extend well back toward San Diego and south along Avenida de la Reforma.

A large percentage of visitors to Baja California see little more than the shops, bars and restaurants within a mile or two of customs. Some will attend the Jai Alai games at the Fronton Palacio on Avenue Revolucion, or the horse and dog races at the newly-rebuilt Agua Caliente Race Track. Others find to their liking the bull fights at the Plaza de Toros, toward the race track, or at the Plaza Monumental (second largest ring in the world) overlooking the ocean west of town, and considerably cooler on a Sunday afternoon.

The tremendous number of dollars spent by Norteamericanos has attracted settlers from all over Mexico to the city, and this onrush of humanity has presented problems to Tijuana's city fathers that have defied solution. However, during the last few years, a great effort has been made to bring adequate water, power and other services to Tijuana citizens. Housing projects such as the Playa de Tijuana are being built. Health care facilities are expanding into many sections of the city. Numerous streets have been paved and trees planted. Civic pride is evident.

Tijuana will continue to depend upon the visitor from the north, but in the future, local industrial development in the fields of furniture, pharmaceuticals, electronics, paints, foods and others will assist in broadening the economic base. And don't forget those seat covers— tucked and rolled, as only the "TJ" vinyl artisans can tuck and roll. This is the place to come for custom upholstery.

And where else than in the largest Woolworth's extant can you buy Chanel No. 5 duty-free . . . or chile rellenos and cerveza on the blue plate special?

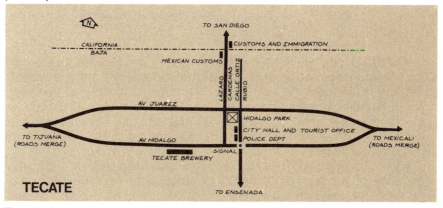

Tecate (Tay-CA-tay) A growing farming community near the U.S. border at 1600 feet elevation, surrounded by ever-increasing acreages of grapes, olives and grain. A town not highly oriented to tourism, it has been designated as part of the special industrial zone which offers advantages to United States industry. The climate is warm in summer, cool in winter.

With a population of 19,000, it is the home of Tecate and Carta Blanca beers, brewed in large modern facilities and considered by many to be better than beer brewed north of the border. German-Mexican brew-meisters are no doubt responsible. The proof is in the drinking. Rancho La Puerta, a noted health spa, is located on a hilltop overlooking the town.

La Rumerosa (La Roo-ma-RO-sa) . . . Perched at an elevation of 4,370 feet atop the pass through the Sierra Juarez, La Rumerosa is a favorite summer resort for Mexicali residents. A relatively new "ejido" colony is located here.

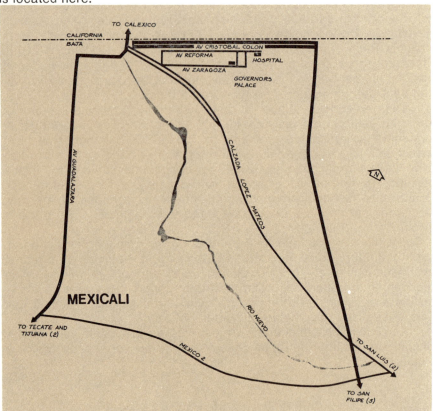

MEXICALI (Me-hi-CA-li) Capital of the State of Baja California. If you were to have visited the lower end of California's Imperial Valley at the turn of the century, you would have found a hostile, wind-swept desert inhabited by a few dozen disgruntled miners from El Alamo, a gold rush town set in the mountains east of Ensenada. They brought the name along with them, identifying themselves as being residents of La Laguna del Alamo.

Their precarious existence was eased considerably in 1902 with completion of the Imperial Canal, funneling water from the Colorado River to irrigate the rich but parched soil. The name was soon changed to Mexicali (a contraction of Mexico-California), and its eventful growth began.

Within a few years, it became a wild frontier town harboring various segments of the lawless bands that were rapidly being squeezed from other parts of California and Arizona with the coming of law and order. In 1911, during the Mexican Revolution, Mexicali was occupied by a band of soldiers of fortune who had designs on capturing portions of Mexico for their own gain. Order was reestablished in 1915 when Colonel Esteban Cantu became governor of the Northern District of Mexico. His rule of the region was very firm and practically independent of what was going on in the rest of Mexico.

Agriculture continued to be dominant throughout the valley, mostly under the ownership of the Colorado Land Company, an American enterprise engaged in raising cotton and other crops.

Immigrants to the area included thousands of Chinese laborers—until they were halted by 1919 restrictions. The slack was taken up by steadily growing numbers of Mexican farmers from central Mexico. In the middle 30's, nationalization of property ownership took place, forcing the Colorado River Land Company to sell its properties to Mexican interests, who formed a number of cooperative farming colonies called "ejidos."

Assurance of adequate water supplies, long a point of concern to the Mexicans, was apparently settled in 1954 when a treaty with the United States was signed guaranteeing Mexico a minimum 1,500,000-acre-foot share of Colorado River water. This treaty has not completely served its intended purpose, however, due to the practice, in some regions, of American farmers taking the water destined for Mexico and using it to leach the salts out of their own land. Thus, much of the water flowing across the border has such a high salt content that it has destroyed the usefulness of large tracts of land. Efforts are still being made by the government of Mexico to have this practice halted. Headway has been made through direct dialog between the Presidents of the two countries and hopes run high that the problem will soon be resolved.

Prohibition in the United States served as an encouragement to Mexicali to run "wide open", with gambling, prostitution and drugs. These practices were given legal status through taxing of such activities by the government in order to finance construction of roads and other material improvements. Pleasure-seeking Americans by the thousands daily streamed across the border to seek their particular brand of pleasure. The first automobile road connecting Mexicali and Tijuana was financed in this manner.

Gambling and other practices were driven out of business or went underground in 1935 with enforcement of the new Mexican national laws. Today, there is only a shadow of that part of Mexicali's bawdy past remaining in the numerous bars and nightclubs within walking distance of the border.

Agriculture is still the main source of income in this part of Baja California, followed by tourism and, to an ever growing extent, industrial employment centered about the establishment of assembly plants by large American corporations. The many activities in Baja California's capital city have fostered a phenomenal growth that has seen an increase of almost 100 percent, to about 400,000 inhabitants, between the 1960 and 1970 census.

American sportsmen have long known Mexicali as the "Gateway to the Sea of Cortez," with San Felipe only 125 miles to the south over an excellent paved road. Here the first rendezvous with this wondrous sea begins. There are numerous hotels and restaurants in Mexicali, somewhat similar to those found in such resort communities as Ensenada, Tijuana or La Paz.

The climate is typical of that in the lower desert regions of the Southwest. Daytime temperatures during the winter months are usually pleasant, with chilly nights and occasional winds. The summers (June to September) are hot, tempered by occasional thunderstorms. Extreme temperatures in the summer will sometimes push the mercury above the 120 degree mark. Average rainfall for the year is about three inches.

Guadalupe (Gua-da-LU-pay) In 1905, members of a religious sect called Molokans fled Russia to settle in Guadalupe. They were excellent farmers who raised grain, olives and grapes on the fertile land. The early colony was characterized by beautiful blond women and bearded men. Russian was the language spoken in their church.

Recent years have seen the young people drift away to the cities, until the town is gradually becoming like most small Mexican towns. Some of the old steambath houses still line the main street. The Guadalupe mission was erected near the east end of the village.

Rosarito (Rosa-REE-toe) . . . In the dim past, the local Rosarito Beach Hotel was a famous gambling casino that operated beyond the law for a number of years after it was made illegal in Baja California. There were quite a few Americans who spent time in the local "pokey" when Federal Officers finally raided the place. The beaches are very broad and the riding of rented hroses over the sand is popular with guests.

El Sauzal (El Sow-ZAL) . . . is the site of the largest fish cannery in Baja. Roll up your windows when passing, as the odor can knock you out. Natives do, however, put up some excellent products, including canned abalone. Several hundred people live and work in El Sauzal.

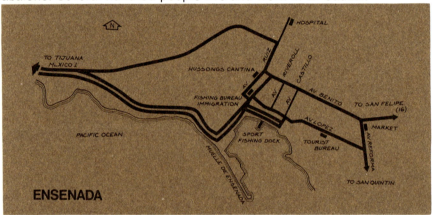

ENSENADA

Ensenada (Ensen-AH-da) is the third largest city on the peninsula, with a population of over 80,000. The climate is similar to San Diego's—two hours drive to the north. Ensenada for many years has been the deepest point of penetration into Mexico for most North American tourists. But while Ensenada derives much of its income from the visitor, it does not resemble Tijuana in mood or appearance.

Ensenada is also a busy seaport and the commercial hub for the outlying ranches, wineries and farms. Its beautiful beaches, hotels and active sportfishing fleet draw hundreds of thousands of visitors annually. Shopping in the duty-free stores will turn up many bargains in watches, cameras, English woolens, and other imports. Remember, all of Baja is a duty-free zone. Custom-crafted wrought iron, furniture, leather items, and other native products of excellent quality may be purchased here.

The large well-protected bay was first discovered in 1542 by Juan Cabrillo, who named it San Mateo. His description of the bay was somewhat limited, and when Vizcaino charted the coast in 1602, he renamed it Bahia de Todos Santos. There is no evidence of any early native settlements, probably due to lack of water, although it was apparently visited by inland tribes for the fishing and clamming to be found in the area.

During the 18th Century, the bay was used as a supply point for the inland missions. But it did not become a permanent settlement until after several gold strikes were made at Real del Castillo in 1870. Some of the buildings from before the turn of the century are still being used, the most famous of which is Hussong's Cantina. A landmark for over 80 years, Hussong's still serves the best Margaritas in Ensenada and is the first (and oftimes last) stop in town for many of the old timers. However, little by little, it is becoming a hangout for the college crowd.

Fishing provides many jobs for residents. There are several canneries and fish reduction plants that process the local catches and those made down the Pacific Coast as far away as South America. Sportfishing, too, is an important industry, with about 25 open party and charter boats operating. Once famous for its seemingly inexhaustible supply of yellowtail, halibut and white seabass, the local fishing grounds have suffered greatly from the lack of controls placed on commercial harvesting of the resources.

Ensenada has almost every item that might be needed for the traveller who plans to proceed on down the peninsula. This is a good place to stock up, as the selection—and supply—gets smaller as you head on down. The Limon Market on Avenida Internacional toward the south end of town offers almost everything that you would find in a stateside super market, and at comparable prices.

Quickest way to reach Ensenada is via the toll road from Tijuana. Tolls are paid at three stations en route along the beautiful, largely-untouched coastline, and total $1.70 for autos, a little more for trailers and trucks. There is also the old road, if you don't mind a narrow curving route that wanders miles inland at times. It's free, as is all the new Highway 1 south of Ensenada.

Maneadero (MAHN-a-ah-DER-o) is a rapidly growing farm community serving the Maneadero Valley. Population here is approaching 10,000. The town has several plants for processing chiles and other produce.

Punta Banda (POON-ta BAHN-da) . . . West of Maneadero lies a series of campgrounds and homesites for Americans. The paved road continues 12½ miles to La Bufadora, a spectacular 50 foot column of spray formed by wave action forcing air into a tidal cave and through a vent in the top. Many beautiful coves are found in this scenic area. A rumor of long standing names Punta Banda as the future site of a large hotel.

Santo Tomas (SAN-toe To-MAS) is an old agricultural community dating back to mission times. This was the original site for the famous Santo Tomas Winery that has since been relocated in Ensenada. Some grapes are still grown here, along with many acres of recently planted olives. La Palomar Resort offers trailer sites, swimming pool and a store with limited supplies of groceries and curios.

El Alamo (El AL-amo) . . . In 1889, El Alamo became a booming city of up to 8,000 people as the placer gold strikes in the nearby arroyos drew miners from all over the West. Within a few months, they began to drift away and most operations halted before 1910. Today, El Alamo is practically deserted, but there are many old buildings and remnants of mine machinery to be seen. Gold is still being mined on a very small scale, and several nearby ranches raise cattle.

Real del Castillo (Ray-AL del Cas-TEE-yo) . . . A gold mining center from 1870 into the 20th century. From 1870 to 1882, Real del Castillo was the seat of government for the northern portion of Baja. Eventually, the governing body was moved to Ensenada and ultimately to Mexicali.

La Bocana-Puerto Santo Tomas (LA Bo-CA-na PUER-toe SAN-toe Toe-MAS) . . . La Bocana is the location for a number of American vacation homes, including Los Angeles Times columnist Jack Smith, whose entertaining experiences have been followed by hundreds of thousands of readers.

A few miles to the north is Puerto Santo Tomas, where boats may be rented. The water is very clear and cold from a current upwelling that effects coastal water temperatures from Punta Banda south for about 200 miles. Bottom fishing is good, with occasional runs of yellowtail, barracuda, white seabass and bonito. The area has many coves reminiscent of the Monterey Peninsula region of California.

Ejido Erendira (A-HI-do Er-en-DIR-a) . . . 11 miles west of the highway is a farming community of about 150 people. One and one-half miles farther is San Isidro. To the north are cabin and trailer sites. The region offers fine surf fishing from rocky or sandy beaches, plus considerable commercial fishing (rockcod) and diving (abalone, seaweed for Japan, and sea urchins, also for Japan).

Skiffs are used in a busy sportfishing enterprise at Castro's Camp, which is productive for rockcod. It is not unusual to catch over 100 pounds of excellent-eating fish in a short time. Usually in the fall and winter, large schools of yellowtail, white seabass and barracuda move in here. Senor Castro has cabins for rent, but no restaurant.

Punta Cabra (POON-ta CA-bra) is five miles north and offers good surf fishing, camp sites and very limited supplies. Occasionally a skiff is available for fishing. Just before entering **Ejido Erendira**, is a road paralleling the beach for about six miles. Many camping, surfing and fishing spots are located along here.

San Vicente (SAN Vi-CEN-tay) . . . Elevation 300 feet, with a population of 1,200. San Vicente is an important agricultural valley for grapes, olives, chiles and barley. The site of the San Vicente mission, started by the Dominicans in 1780, is here. After the collapse of the mission and withdrawal of the military garrison in 1849, the valley was virtually deserted until the 1940's, when several agricultural colonies (ejidos) were started.

Colonet (Col-o-NET) . . . a number of homes along road and the site of a small hospital started by the Flying Samaritans, a group of doctors from the United States who at one time provided the only medical services south of Ensenada. Just past the town on the right is a road leading to a fishing camp at Punta Colonet (7.5 miles).

San Telmo (San TEL-mo) . . . The main part of the village is six miles to the left of the road. San Telmo is on the way to the Meling Ranch and the new National Observatory at the 9200-foot level of the Sierra San Pedro Martir. Nearby **Camalu** is a tomato growing area.

San Jose (Meling Ranch) (San Ho-ZAY) . . . Road to the left leads up into the foothills of Sierra San Pedro Martir. After 32 miles, you come to the famous Meling Ranch. A working cattle operation, it accommodates about a dozen guests at a time. From here, pack trips may be arranged into the high (8000 foot) meadows of the Martirs where deer and trout (see page 146) may be found among tall stands of yellow pine.

The casual air of the Meling Ranch might be best illustrated with the following story: Some years ago, Francisco Delegado, personal pilot of the governor of the State of Baja California, came to Meling Ranch with his wife and another couple. The help had just quit, so the guests were pitching in. Francisco and his friend took on kitchen duties and Aida Meling kept them busy. After everyone was fed and the dishes washed, the volunteer help virtually collapsed in Aida's office for a well-earned rest. By way of making conversation, Aida asked Francisco's companion what kind of work he usually did. He said, "Senora, I am your Governor." (See Resort Roundup)

Colonia Guerrero (Co-LON-ia Goo-RARE-oh) is the center of an ever-growing agricultural district. Here is raised much of the cauliflower and brussels sprouts found on the American market, plus tomatoes, chiles, potatoes and grain. The road to the west of the center of town leads 4.5 miles to San Ramon Beach.

San Ramon Beach (San Ra-MON) is one giant pismo clam bed. Good to excellent perch fishing any time of the year may be found along all of the 15 miles of beach between here and Bahia San Quintin. A great area for dune buggies. Many high dunes separate the beach from the road, which is sandy in places but passable, and extends south toward Cabo San Quintin. The nearest supplies are in Colonia Guerrero.

Bahia San Quintin (Ba-HE-a San Kin-TEEN) is a growing resort area that many believe will someday be a major American center for weekend and retirement homes. The region has most of the requirements; large bay with great populations of ducks and black brant during winter, miles of clam-filled tidal flats, moderate climate, excellent fishing in the bay and along the shore to the south and west, plus surface and bottom fish in the outer bay and around Isla San Martin. Pismo clams are abundant for miles in each direction along the ocean on minus tides. (See Resort Roundup)

El Rosario (El Ro-SAR-eo) is a fishing and agricultural village that formerly was the last outpost of civilization before the adventurous plunged into the desolate central portion of Baja. For years, Anita Espinosa's place was the last chance to fill up on gas, food and cerveza and a checkpoint for the **BAJA 1000.** Ask her about the Mickey Thompson and Parnelli Jones tacos.

The new highway is, of course, making many changes. A modern gas station has been completed. An abalone cannery is operating a few miles down the arroyo and lobsters taken here are trucked back to Ensenada. The climate is similar to Ensenada, though a bit windier and with about half the rainfall. In 1967, the town was partially destroyed by the same hurricane that hit San Felipe, and its recovery is a tribute to the hard-working people of this valley.

San Felipe (San Fay-LI-pe) . . . A few shacks were put up here in the middle of the 1800's, but there were no permanent residents until about 1920. Following the completion of a graded road (built by the U.S. Government to service a radar station during World War II), the town has engaged in large scale commercial fishing and shrimping.

In the late 40's, American sportfishermen discovered the excellent totuava fishery. The town experienced a welcome burst of prosperity. In the late 60's, totuava practically disappeared, due to commercial over-fishing and the loss of fresh water that formerly came from the Colorado River.

In September, 1967, a rare hurricane nearly leveled San Felipe. With help from many sources, the inhabitants rebuilt the town, greatly improving the quality of the housing.

Tourists have since discovered the warm, sunny winter and spring weather and have surpassed the economic contribution formerly made by totuava anglers. There is still a spring run of white seabass in the vicinity of Consag Rock and small corvina may be caught from the shore. Good clamming abounds both north and south of town. The current population of San Felipe is about 4,500.

A new breakwater and resort facilities will bring many visitors to the area. A paved road to Bahia Gonzaga and back to Mexico 1 is planned for some years in the future.

Puertecitos (Puer-ta-SEE-toes) . . . A private camp that is popular with Americans who like this picturesque site to place trailers or build homes as a vacation retreat. Boats can be launched in the shallow bay, with good fishing within a few miles of shore. Toward the point is a series of warm spring-fed pools that afford comfortable bathing if the tide is not too high. Weather is hot in the summer, but pleasant at other times. Rainfall here is practically nil.

Bahia San Luis Gonzaga (Ba-E-a San Loo-EES Gon-ZAH-ga) . . . Here and at **Ensenada de San Francisquito**, there are a number of fishing and trailer camps—with more planned. The region is rich in sea life from the tidal flats to the offshore islands. Winds can be nasty and care should be taken in venturing from shore. Spring tides to 20 feet set up strong currents and leave boats far from the water. Scenery is very beautiful and the area's popularity is growing. There are boats available to rent at most of the resorts. Shelling and clamming are also attractions. (See Resort Roundup)

Santa Ines (SAN-ta I-NES) . . . In the days of the old road, Santa Ines was one of the primitive way-stations where a meal, bed and sometimes gasoline could be obtained from the drums laboriously hauled over more than 150 miles of bad road between Santa Ines and Ensenada. It was necessary to filter all fuel through a chamois to remove dirt and water that accumulated in the drums. It was in Santa Ines that adventuresome groups going north and south would exchange stories about road conditions and as to where they might camp the next night. Mechanical problems were also discussed. Sometimes, parts were adapted or fabricated by the talented "mecanicos" who worked on the ranch.

Today, Santa Ines has a stock of tourist supplies, a gas station, garage and a new 28-room motel, El Presidente Catavina, on the bluff overlooking the palm-lined arroyo. The original Rancho is located several miles east on the south side of the arroyo and still displays the great Baja hospitality.

About 14 miles farther east over a poor jeep road lies the ruins of Mision Santa Maria (See Mission Section). There is talk of the government paving a road from here past the mission to intersect the proposed highway south of Gonzaga Bay at Punta Final. (See Resort Roundup)

Laguna Chapala (La-GOO-na Sha-PA-la) is a large and very dusty lake bed to the east of the highway . . . well remembered by everyone who attempted to conquer the Baja road in the days before pavement. If you were able to avoid getting the inside of your vehicle knee-deep in dust up to this point, your efforts were in vain. The depth and fineness of the "tereno" or "polvo" just north of the lake bed is unbelievable.

Rancho Laguna Chapala (RAHN-cho La-GOO-na Sha-PA-la) is owned by Sr. Grosso, brother of Anita Espinosa in El Rosario. His hospitality and sprightly manner in a region where one cow would be hard pressed to survive on five square miles has made him one of the legendary figures that made the old Baja run such a memorable experience. He used to challenge anyone who came by to a foot race—he had few takers, even though he was in his sixties. There will soon be a new Pemex station near here.

Parador Punta Prieta (PAR-a-dor POON-ta Pre-A-ta) . . . located about 8 miles north of the town of Punta Prieta at turnoff to Bahia de Los Angeles. Facilities include gas, travel supplies, restaurant and tourist information and trailer camp. Check here for road conditions into Mision San Borja, a worthwhile side trip if time and conditions will permit.

Bahia de Los Angeles (Ba-E-a day Los-AN-hay-lace) . . . see page 75

San Borja (San BOR-ha) . . . is a tiny, but charming, community of about a half dozen families gathered around the Mision San Francisco de Borja. They raise a few dates, olives, pomegranates and vegetables. Water is from several small springs and a well.

Punta Prieta (POON-ta Pre-A-ta) . . . a bleak-looking collection of old adobe homes contrasting with the new buildings to the west of the community which have been built for road maintenance crews. Northeast of town there is an enormous paved air strip. This is an alternate landing field for jets when main field at Guerrero Negro is weathered in.

El Rosarito (El Rosa-REE-toe) . . . Small group of houses and ranchitos. Just south of town at Nuevo Rosarita a man named Gomez has a tiny gas station with the usual refrescos.

Paralelo 28 (Pa-ra-LAY-lo VAIN-tee O-cho) . . . a newly constructed tourism complex located 2½ miles north of the Guerrero Negro intersection. Here the Mexican government has built a 24-room hotel, a parador and facilities for 50 trailers. Just to the north is a large airfield to refuel jets, but it is not yet operational. At the center of the complex is a giant 135 foot high Aguila (eagle) monument, the symbol of Mexico, marking the border between the states of Baja California and Baja California Sur.

Guerrero Negro (Goo-RARE-ro NAY-gro) . . . Here salt is the main commodity. Most of the 4300 residents live in the company town, owned by Exportadora de Sal. The vast regions of tidal flats of Scammon Lagoon provide over 3,000,000 tons of salt each year for use in chemical processing throughout the world. Giant trucks shuttle the salt from the evaporating pens to the dock at Puerto V. Carranza, to be loaded into barges for the trip to Isla Cedros for trans-shipment to Long Beach and other ports. Services in town include a Pemex station, the Los Pollos and Malarrimo restaurants (both owned by Enrique Achoy, who speaks English and can aid in arranging whale watching trips) and two motels. The weather is often windy and foggy, especially during spring and early summer. (See page 69)

Ejido Vizcaino (A-HEE-do Vees-KAEE-no) . . . a relatively new colony of about 2,000 and site of an agricultural experiment station where research into desert cultivation crops is made.

El Arco (EL AR-co) . . . was once the center of considerable mining activity; then it became a major way-station for those hardy souls who were driving the old road to Mulege and points south. The new highway by-passes El Arco and it has resumed its quiet ways.

Abreojos (A-bray-O-hos) . . see page 89

San Ignacio (San Ig-NA-seo) . . . is acclaimed by almost everyone who visits this palm-studded oasis as one of the beauty spots of Baja California. Here the Arroyo San Ignacio brings its underground water to the surface and supports 80,000 date palms, many citrus and fig trees, vinyards and flowers and gardens galore. Nearly 4000 lucky people call San Ignacio and adjoining San Lino home. It has a beauty and charm that is bound to make it one of the most popular places on the Trans-peninsula Highway.

The reconstruction of Mision San Ignacio was essentially completed during 1976. Its chapel and outbuildings, overlooking the cool plaza lined with giant Indian laurel trees, provide one of the most worthwhile stops in all of Baja. Nestled among the date palms as you enter town is the beautiful El Presidente Hotel.

This town has the potential of becoming a very popular resort. The small reservoir to the north of town is said to contain fish and turtles. The Sea of Cortez is only an hour away; Mulege just two hours. Closer, there are many Indian caves, hidden valleys and abundant varieties of cactus.

The late Frank Fischer was for years the salvation to many Baja travellers. His ability to repair anything mechanical is one of the legends of Baja. His son Oscar maintains the garage and has added a small motel and restaurant—Posada San Ignacio. Sr. Fischer will make arrangements for guided trips into the back country (See Resort Roundup.)

Santa Rosalia (SAN-ta Ro-sa-LI-ah) . . . came into existence when copper was discovered in the nearby hills during the 1870's. In 1885, all interests were consolidated under a French company, Boleo Mining Company, and a large smelter began producing copper for Europe and the United States. Yaqui Indians were brought from Sonora to work in the mines and engineers from France supervised the mining and smelting operations.

Once the ores were depleted Boleo ceased operations in 1953. Later, the Mexican government reopened the mines and smelter. Today, most of the ore is brought in from China and Chile. The town of 12,000 appears much as it must have fifty or more years ago, with stereotyped houses lined up one after another along both sides of the arroyo.

Vestiges of the original French company still remain in the architecture, an excellent bakery and in a very picturesque church. The church (currently undergoing restoration) is made from large galvanized iron sheets that were brought in from France in the 1880's.

The terminus for the ferry to Guaymas is in Santa Rosalia. This modern air-conditioned buliding looks somewhat out of place among the older structures and the great sheds of the antiquated smelter. The town offers many subjects for the dedicated camera bug.

Summers in Santa Rosalia can be oppressive, as it is sheltered from the cooling breezes, yet it is open to strong winds during the winter. There are few tourist accomodations; however, one, the new El Morro Hotel a few miles south of town is nicely situated on a rocky bluff. (See Resort Roundup).

Punta Chivato (POON-ta Chi-VA-toe) . . . 17 miles east of highway on point north of entrance into Bahia Concepcion. The beaches near here are especially abundant with shells of many varieties. The shallow rocky reefs are excellent for snorkeling and provide good fishing. The closed Hotel Punta Chivato stands on the rocky point. The best shelling is on the beach west of the landing strip.

Mulege (Moo-la-HAY) . . . The population of 3,200 is sure to increase rapidly with the opening of the new road, as Mulege is one of the more beautiful of Baja's resort areas. Site of Mision Santa Rosalia de Mulege (under reconstruction) and the unique territorial prison, the town extends along the banks of the Rio Santa Rosalia, one of the few rivers in Baja California, and its only navigable one. Thousands of palm trees and many flowering shrubs provide a tropical oasis atmosphere that is almost unreal compared to the brown dusty desert to the north and south. The entrance to the harbor is guarded by a cone-shaped hill named El Sombrerito. July and August are very hot here when the usual breezes fail. Good fishing and several comfortable resorts are to be found. (See Resort Roundup).

Comondu (Co-mun-DU) . . . refers to two small settlements of nearly 1000 residents located only two miles apart. Both mission sites, (see Mission Section) San Juan Comondu and San Miguel Comondu are presently served by a difficult road that was the old highway across the peninsula. The towns offer only limited supplies of fuel and groceries, but expected road work will change this.

La Purisima (La Poo-RI-si-ma) . . . is one of the better irrigated valleys of the region, with fields of grapes, corn, tomatoes, citrus and dates much in evidence. Its climate is tempered by the sea breezes—cool in winter and pleasant during summer months with less than 2 inches of rainfall annually, usually in August and September. Several thousand people live here and in adjacent Colonia San Isidro.

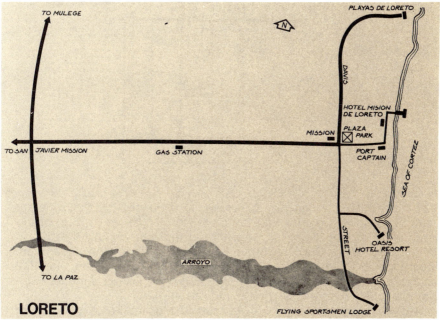

LORETO

Loreto (Lo-RAY-toe) . . . This is the oldest settlement in Baja California and was the capitol of the original California—which included present day California as far north as San Francisco—from its founding in 1697 until a hurricane virtually destroyed the town in 1829. The so-called "Mother of the Missions", Mision de Nuestra Senora de Loreto, has been restored and is well worth a visit. The resorts here all offer good accommodations and some of the best sportfishing north of La Paz. (See Resort Roundup).

Supplies are still limited but adequate for its 5000 residents. A number of new projects encompassing more camping and hotel facilities are due to start shortly. The town has been subjected to various disasters over the nearly three centuries of its existence, including several floods and a great earthquake . . . each time struggling to its feet, only to be flattened again. Today, construction projects to contain the torrents from rare chubascos protect Loreto.

Villa Insurgente (VEE-ah In-sur-HEN-tay) . . . has boomed in the last few years to a modern town of nearly 10,000, with the agricultural development of the broad Magdalena Plain. It has a variety of stores and at least one modern gas station—a short distance north of the junction of the main road from Loreto.

Ciudad Constitucion (Cee-OO-dod CONS-tee-too-see-OWN) . . . is the commercial hub of the Magdalena Plain farming operations and many of the nearly 20,000 residents are shopkeepers employed in services for the surrounding farms. Some 34 miles to the west is the shipping port of Puerto San Carlos, where much of the cotton and grain of the region is shipped to ports on the Mexican mainland. There are many stores and several Pemex stations to choose from . . . a local hotel, Las Conchitas, is adequate, at best.

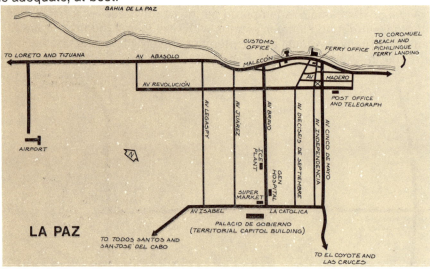

La Paz (La Pause) . . . Contrary to its name (The Peace), Las Paz's history is one of the most violent of all the cities on the peninsula. Site of the first Spanish attempt to settle what was at that time believed to be an island called Santa Cruz, it began with the captain of the expedition, Diego Becerra, being murdered by his crew in 1533 just before a landfall was made. Shortly after landing, the new leader, Fortun Jimenez, and 22 of his soldiers were slain by the Indians.

Two years later, Hernan Cortez himself led another expedition of soldiers and colonists to La Paz. The group that remained was unable to survive when political turmoil on the mainland caused a cessation of supplies.

Just prior to the 1600's another attempt was made, only to end when a fire destroyed most of the supplies and buildings. The year 1683 saw another colony fail when rebellion by the Indians followed the murder of several of their number—after being invited to a banquet by the Spaniards.

Later, still another attempt ended in disaster when the southern portion of the peninsula erupted in the rebellion of the Indians against their masters in 1734. The colony was restocked, only to collapse again when epidemics swept the Indian population in 1749.

The area saw no permanent residents until 1811, following a land grant to a retired soldier, Juan Jose Espinoza. The town slowly grew and was named the capitol of the Southern Territory in 1829 after the virtual annihilation of Loreto by a fierce storm. During the war between Mexico and the United States in 1847, La Paz was occupied by American troops and a number of skirmishes resulted. The soldiers withdrew after the treaty of Guadalupe Hidalgo returned Baja California to Mexico.

Violence again visited La Paz when the self-styled American adventurer William Walker, made a brief stand before being driven out.

The prime lure of the colonists were the rich pearl oyster beds in the nearby gulf. In the 18th Century, many of the finest pearls of the royal treasury in Spain came from La Paz. Pearling continued until the pearl supply disappeared in the early 1940's after a mysterious disease destroyed almost all of the oyster beds in the Sea of Cortez.

In the 1950's, sportfishermen from the United States discovered the rich bounty of gamefish abounding in nearby waters and to the south. La Paz quickly acquired the reputation of being one of the billfishing centers of the world. Countless articles in publications throughout America assured a steady stream of visitors, and numerous fishing resorts were established.

Improvements in transportation has also encouraged agricultural activities in the region and the nearly 40,000 people of La Paz are among the better fed and housed in Baja California. (See Resort Roundup).

El Triunfo (El Tree-OON-foe) . . . came into existence with the discovery of silver in 1862. Within a few years the mines, stamping mills and smelter provided livelihood for nearly 10,000, before playing out. Situated in the mountains, 600 inhabitants today live in a cooler wetter climate than La Paz. The ruins around the old smelter (look for tall chimney) are interesting.

San Antonio (San An-to-NE-oh) . . . had its beginnings in 1756 when Gaspar Pison opened a silver mine. Its nearly 1000 residents now engage in agriculture.

San Bartolo (San Bar-TOE-lo) . . . Strung out along a narrow canyon, the area has many small farms that raise sugar cane, mangoes and citrus.

Santiago (San-ti-AH-go) . . . Grew up around the mission and presently accommodates over 1000 people who farm several thousand acres nearby. The town has a new plaza surrounded by various stores and a small restaurant.

Miraflores (Me-ra-FLOOR-ace) . . . Farming and cattle center where fine leatherwork may sometimes be purchased. Several backpacking guides into Sierra La Victoria live here.

San Jose del Cabo (San Jose del CA-bo) . . . Once a supply station for the Manila galleons and mission site, this town is now a farming and tourism center. A beautiful town of many trees, San Jose del Cabo is tempered by ocean breezes and enjoys a mild climate. A large international airport is under construction 6 miles north of town.

San Lucas (San LU-cas) . . . Often miscalled Cabo San Lucas (which is the name of the rocky ridge extending south into the ocean), the town is rapidly growing and will undoubtedly double in size within a few years. A number of hotels are situated along the beaches to the south and east. The region is justly famous for the excellent fishing in nearby waters. There are many beautiful beaches in this area. A new marina and ferry terminal (San Lucas to Puerto Vallarta—see Cortez Circuit, Page 26) is located in newly dredged harbor. A cannery is located here and employs many of the townspeople. (See Resort Roundup).

El Pescadero (El Pes-ca-DARE-oh) . . . A farming community of about 2000 located a short distance from the Pacific. There is good hunting for dove and duck in vicinity. The beaches west of here have fine fishing and are accessible over sometimes rough local roads.

Todos Santos (TOE-dose SAN-tose) . . . Began as a farm and mission visiting station in the early 1700's and finally gained mission status in 1734. Today, it is a busy sugarcane raising center with its own mills. During harvest time, January and February, the mills make a delicious dark sugar candy called panocha. Mangoes too are a major crop. Some good beaches are reached by roads west of town. Most services are available here. It would be expected that there will be future resort development near here, in spite of considerable foggy weather during spring and early summer. Fishing is excellent offshore.

LAND'S END – CABO SAN LUCAS

BLUE PALM

BAJA'S PALM CANYONS

The road south across the Laguna Salada leads to a series of palm-studded canyons that descend sharply from the eastern side of the Sierra Juarez. A number of these canyons have small streams fed by winter snows and summer thunderstorms. The water disappears before reaching the dry lake bed, but its presence in the narrow canyons has created beautiful oases of palms, flowers, ferns and the many forms of animal life that thrive in such an environment. Even the desert bighorn and deer will visit these islands of life in an otherwise hostile country.

Generally, the road is passable for a standard automobile to both Cantu Palms, 19 miles from Mexico Highway 2, and to Canon de Guadalupe 16 miles further on. Access to the others, such as Santa Isabel and Palomar, is much more difficult and should not be attempted except with specialized equipment, and then in pairs.

Cantu was once a gathering place for the Cocopah Indians, as evidenced by the petroglyphs and mortars for grinding seeds to be found on a number of the rocks. Miners also visited here in times past, along with woodcutters, and evidence of their presence still exist. The beauty of the canyon undoubtedly will lead to some sort of development in the future.

Canon de Guadalupe already has a small commercial development to take advantage of the hot springs and the cool sparkling stream that tumbles from the 6,000 foot high mountains immediately to the west. Here again, palms line the floor of the arroyo with hundreds of species of plants and animals crowded into a stretch of only a few miles. Waterfalls and pools are in the upper portions of the canyon, and some evidence of the Indian's visits may be found.

There is room for about thirty campers at a time and rates for the use of the facilities, including the swimming pool and hot springs, are very reasonable. The region is thoroughly interesting and is best visited in the spring when the flowers are at their peak and the weather has not gotten too hot.

BEACHCOMBING

If you are the type that goes for a walk along the ocean shore . . . inspecting what has been washed above the water line and maybe collecting a few of the more interesting specimens of shells, driftwood and other debris . . . you can spend a lifetime along the nearly 3,000 miles of coast line encompassing Baja California and Baja California Sur.

Shell collectors will find hundreds of varieties from which to choose, sometimes in incredible numbers. Wide windrows occur along several beaches west of Punta Chivato, north of Scammon Lagoon and east of Ei Golfo de Santa Clara. The urge to load up the car with colorful conch, clam, oyster and abalone shells is almost irresistible and each succeeding beach visited will seem to have even more to offer.

The beaches along Baja's Pacific side collect flotsam from the entire northern Pacific Ocean. It is possible to find giant redwood logs from the northwest United States, white cedar stumps from Canada and Alaska, hatch covers from the ships of the world, bottles—old and new. Occasionally, a glass net float will survive the journey from the Japanese fishing grounds. Here, too, is evidence of man's carelessness in the many plastic cups, bags and egg cartons scattered about.

The beaches on the Cortez side yield copious selections of intricately sculptured driftwood—bleached almost white by the sun and torn from some distant canyon by an infrequent deluge of rain. The skeletal remains of seabirds, fish, whales and seals are scattered throughout the coves and rocky headlands that comprises much of the shoreline.

Eventually, all but the most remote shores will be picked clean of their treasures. But, by taking only a few rememberances for the bookshelf back home, the supply may last long enough for many to experience the exhilaration of a valuable "discovery".

MINI-TRIPS: TAKE YOUR PICK

Though driving Mexico 1 may be the most popular way to go to Baja, there are an increasing number of special fishing package tours or others of special interest.

Air Cortez is a growing airline which offers a variety of tours to Mulege, Loreto and Guaymas/San Carlos from Ontario International Airport. Write them at 422 S. Walker Ave., Ontario, CA 91761 phone (714) 988-7703.

Mexico Air Service (MAS) flies charters into all parts of Mexico from Santa Monica. Write or call: MAS, 3000 Airport Ave., Santa Monica, CA 90405, (213) 391-6355.

A unique trip for the private pilot into one of Baja's most beautiful and remote shores is offered by Punta San Francisquito resort. Write to them at 2004 Newton Ave., San Diego, CA 92113, (714) 239-8872.

Three organizations which provide a variety of package fishing tours to Baja are: Baja Fishing Adventures, Box 4012, Downey, CA 90241, (213) 923-2233; Pescadero Travel Tours, Box 1408, Santa Maria, CA 93454, (805) 928-2308; and Ken's Tours, 2308 Welby Way, Canoga Park, CA 91307, (213) 348-0641. All are recommended for individual or group travel.

For those with a deeper interest in the natural history of Baja California and the Sea of Cortez the following are among those offering excellent programs of study in the area:

Baja Expeditions, Inc., Box 3725, San Diego, CA 92103, (714) 297-0506. Boat trips guided by Tim Means and his staff spotlight the Cortez and Bahia Magdalena, a major calving ground for the California gray whale.

Pacific Adventures Cooperative (PAC), Box 5041, Riverside, CA 92507, (714) 684-1227. Alan Erghott has pioneered a number of adventure trips, particularly to study the ancient and mysterious cave paintings of central Baja. They are popular with the young naturalist.

Often local colleges and universities offer credit courses which include trips to Baja. A check of their schedules might turn up a unique destination.

WHY NOT HOP A BUS?

At least three buses depart daily from Tijuana for La Paz. The Tres Estrellas de Oro buses are modern, some even having bathrooms. There are also a variety of local buses which may be taken for shorter trips, and although all are not "scenicruisers" they go almost anywhere at little cost.

One-way fares currently are around $23 to La Paz on a first-come basis. The entire trip takes about 21 hours, with brief food stops. Tickets may also be purchased for intermediate destinations such as Mulege ($15) but you cannot get off and resume your trip later on the same through-ticket as you can in the U.S.

Busing through Baja could be considered a bit rugged by tourists, but is a hit with the sleeping bag set—at the right price.

IF YOU WANT TO FLY

If time is at a premium, or you wish to meet someone who is already in Baja, there are several airlines which can take you into the more populous regions. La Paz and the East Cape/Cabo areas, Loreto, Mulege, San Felipe, Tijuana and Mexicali are on the schedules of one or more of the following airlines:

Aeromexico has regular nonstop jets from Los Angeles into La Paz and Los Cabos for around $220 round trip. They also have two flights daily from Tijuana to La Paz. These are popular as they offer savings of about $70 over an LAX departure.

Mexicana flies daily LAX to Cabo and from Tijuana to La Paz. The prices are comparable to those noted above. All of the flights on these two airlines are popular and it is wise to reserve well in advance.

The Midwest is served by connecting flights into El Paso where Continental Airlines schedules flights into both Los Cabos and La Paz. Continental offers attractive advance-purchase discounts on these flights—ask for them when booking.

There are several Baja-oriented charter services and air taxis that can take you to almost any one of the hundreds of dirt strips in the peninsula: Mexico Air Service was mentioned on Page 143. Another is Jimsair Aviation, Inc., 2904 Pacific Hwy., San Diego, CA 92101, (714) 298-7704.

BAJA'S NUMERO UNO PILOT

Few people become legends in their own time, but Francisco Munoz became one nearly 30 years ago—yet he is still blazing new trails through the skies of Baja California.

Hundreds of dirt strips and some of the paved landing fields of Baja would probably not exist had it not been for this amazing man. His expertise led to the story that Captain Munoz can make a wheelbarrow fly and he can land a DC-6 in a sand trap, but his true exploits in supplying the remote ranchos and fishing villages and his work in countless search and rescue missions are legion.

Today, Captain Francisco Munoz works for the evaporative salt works, Exportadora de Sal, at Guerrero Negro as their chief pilot. Between flights he still has time to make census reports for scientists studying the California gray whale's calving and mating behaviors in the Baja lagoons of Guerrero Negro, Scammon, San Ignacio and Magdalena.

He and his wife Lysl have also established themselves as experts on the nearby early Indian settlements. And their interests in everything from glass floats to relics from old sailing ships has turned their home into a fascinating display of what Baja's beaches hold for the inveterate beachcomber.

THE LONG RANGE BOATS

Most of the October-April activity at the San Diego sportfishing docks is centered around the eight to 10 large deluxe sportfishing boats that specialize in fishing the waters along Baja's Pacific coast. Ranging as much as one thousand miles south of their home port, they offer some of the world's finest fishing in an atmosphere of luxurious comfort.

Private or semi-private staterooms, air conditioning, stereo music, great food and efficient crews, added to the quality fishing, brings people back time and time again.

Popular too are the January to March trips into such wildlife sanctuaries as Scammon's Lagoon and Laguna San Ignacio where the life cycle of the California gray whale may be studied along with other marine mammals and a wide variety of bird and sealife.

Reservations are a must on any of the above trips. Rates run $100-120 per day, plus possible fuel surcharge. Contact:

Lee Palm's Sportfishing, Foot of Emerson St., San Diego, CA 92106, (714) 224-3857.

Fisherman's Landing, 2838 Garrison St., San Diego, CA 92106, (714) 222-0931.

H & M Sportfishers, 2803 Emerson St., San Diego, CA 92106, (714) 222-1144.

Point Loma Sportfishing Assoc., 1403 Scott St., San Diego, CA 92106, (714) 223-1627.

FIRST TASTE OF THE CORTEZ

My first romance with the Sea of Cortez came as a result of an article by Ray Cannon in the early 1950's. He wrote glowingly of the great size of the totuava and described how the fish would migrate past San Felipe on their journey to deposit millions of eggs in the brackish water of the Colorado River delta to the north. Cannon had worked out their timetable so that one could take advantage of their ravenous nature following the spawn.

In 1953, I ventured into that primitive gulf port as he directed. The first fish was the largest I had ever taken—about 75 pounds. The weight turned out to be unimportant a short while later when the second totuava topped a hundred pounds. I was hooked on the Cortez.

— From Tom Miller

CAGUAMA
GREEN SEA TURTLES

FISHING BAJA—NO FISH STORY

The first thought that most people have about Baja California is of its reputation for being a giant fishing platform from which are tapped the great riches of the Sea of Cortez and the Pacific Ocean. And this is most certainly true, with Baja's boundless sea bounty consistently providing more than just "fish stories."

The waters surrounding the Baja peninsula vary from cool upwelling regions, that offer shallow depth rock fishing similar to that found off central California, to tropical climes where sea temperatures rarely drop below the 70 degree mark and will top 90 in the late summer.

The great tidal movements of the middle and upper gulf cause a continuous upwelling of cool nutrientladen water into the warmer surface water, bringing about conditions that nurture incomparable concentrations of sea life. Dozens of major species of fish have their beginnings in these regions.

Although known primarily for its saltwater fishing, Baja, through its eons of isolation, has produced an indigenous fresh water trout very much like the world renowned rainbow, but more brightly colored. They inhabit several streams in the shadow of the Picacho del Diablo east of the Meling Ranch, where you can fish in quiet surroundings without finding another angler behind every bush.

But it is the hundreds of species of saltwater fish that really put meat on the table and money in the pockets of those who live and work along the coasts of Baja.

An incredible mixture of species in every life stage creates a great smorgasbord for millions of living things, each feeding on one or more of his neighbors. For man to reap the benefits of the many life sources around Baja California, he needs little more than a willingness to exercise a bit of patience.

The results, assuming the fish are in a cooperating mood, are astounding in the varieties which may be taken both on the Pacific Ocean side of the peninsula and in the Sea of Cortez.

Beginning on the northern Pacific side of the peninsula, here is what you might expect to find with exact locations noted in the map text and on the maps.

Tijuana to Abreojos . . . Those inshore species of rock and surf fish found around Southern California (perch, croaker, corbina, opaleye, etc.) are generally more plentiful in Baja than in the States. Surf rigs with clams or mussels usually do the job. Offshore fishing boats from San Diego, Ensenada and San Quintin, plus scattered skiff operations, offer varying degrees of comfort while garnering catches of yellowtail, white seabass, rock cod, black sea bass and bonito. Unless you depart from San Diego or Ensenada, plan to use your own jigs and feathers— plus whatever dead gait (carnada) your guide may have. With the help of local fishermen, the bays (esteros) at San Quintin and Guerrero Negro produce plenty of sport, or you can fish from shore on the high tides.

Abreojos through Magdalena to Puerto Chale . . .The many lagoons and warmer waters of this region bring about a mixing of the northern species with those that thrive in a more tropical habitat. Croakers and corbina are joined by the triggerfish, corvinas, snook and others that take clams, cut bait and lures on many of the beaches and in the lagoons.

The Magdalena complex of bays has hardly been touched by the sport angler; over 150 miles of inland waterway and hundreds of baylets and estuaries have yet to be tested. Resident and migrating populations of watrfowl make this region one of great interest to the naturalist. A fall or winter trip to this area produces a potpourri of fishing, exploring, and clamming.

The only organized access to offshore waters at the present comes from the dozen or so long-range San Diego-based sportfishing boats. (See list on page 145) The area around the mouth of Bahia Magdalena and numerous offshore reefs yield good catches of the same fish taken to the north, plus yellow fin tuna, wahoo, dorado (dolphin fish) and billfish. Small boats are best suited for inside the bays, as treacherous curents and windy seas often prevail on the outside, where the Pacific not always lives up to its name.

Below Magdalena to Cabo San Lucas . . . The many sandy beaches and pounding waves throughout most of this distance hold many of the species also found in the lower portions of the gulf. Lures cast past the surfline could connect with roosterfish, toro (jack creralle), pompano or any of dozens of other roving varieties. Baits also prove productive for a number of species. Remember to use enough weight to keep drifting to a minimum.

Here too, the San Diego boats provide the main offshore fishing access, due to so few good anchorages or launching areas. Fish taken are the same as noted in the Magdalena region.

Many fish caught in the shallows will be the immature versions of the larger ones found in deeper water. Occasionally, however, a 50-pound roosterfish or a 20-pound toro will come almost onto the beach to grab your lure.

Cabo San Lucas to Las Paz . . . Here, the true character of the storied Sea of Cortez begins to unfold—calm seas and sheltered coves afford bases of operation for the many fishing fleets of the Baja resorts. The bays, islands, reefs and channels are within range of the visiting angler. Here visitors have the choice, most any time of year, of trying to catch a marlin, sailfish, wahoo, dolphinfish, tuna, roosterfish, amber-jack, pargo or yellowtail. There are also sierra, barilette, pompano, cabrillo, bonito, corvina, shark and hundreds of other species that join their larger cousins in accommodating the angler, whether he walks the surfline or uses a boat. It is rare when some type of fish cannot be taken by any sportfisherman somewhere along this section of Baja.

La Paz to the Midriff Islands . . . The smorgasbord continues—although the migrations of the greater fish bring a more seasonal aspect to fishing. These regions are visited by schools of billfish, dolphinfish and tuna during the summer months (wahoo are rarely found this far north), then are quickly replaced by ravaging schools of yellowtail and sierra. The cabrilla, pargo and grouper, often neglected during the summer, also move in to fill the void. Many of the inshore species are on a continual rampage and the trick is to locate where they are at any particular time.

Bays and shallow reefs around the islands and along the coast are places of fascination for anyone with a love of the water and an interest in its inhabitants. Months could be spent exploring Bahia Concepcion alone. The narrow entrances to bays such as Puerto Escondido and the lagoon at the south end of Isla San Jose often contain enough varieties of brightly colored fish to stock any major metropolitan aquarium.

The region north of La Paz tosses in a teaser which has been frustrating avid anglers for years and will likely continue to do so. The brackish waters of the Rio Santa Rosalia at Mulege reportedly contain black snook (robalo) that would break all existing fishing records for that species. They are most often taken by the local residents by spearing, but they elude all but the astute angler by either not biting or taking off for the mangrove roots as soon as they feel the hook. Smaller ones are caught occasionally on feathers, but those of record proportions demand live bait.

The Midriff . . . Its narrow width, plus the numerous islands between the Mexican mainland on one side and Baja on the other, generates great surges of tidal movement that creates a unique environment. Cool waters from the deep subsurface canyons mix with oxygen-rich warmer surface waters, causing a "bloom" of microscopic plankton. This is devoured by the tiny fish, who are in turn eaten by their larger companions, who fall prey to their even larger neighbors. At times, great hordes of birds and fish, and small groups of anglers, arrive at the same place at the same time. It is difficult to maintain your perspective when witnessing such an event . . . you are torn between getting away for fear of being overwhelmed, or wading in and filling the boat with limitless numbers of frenzied fish.

Yellowtail, particularly, consider the Midriff their domain. They are year-around residents of this region, and often their migrating schools will extend for many miles. This, too, is the home of a large portion of the gulf's population of white seabass. Cabrilla, grouper and black sea bass also find the cooler waters and abundant food supply to their liking, and they range throughout the Midriff. The region also abounds with sea lions. There are several large pods of the baleen (plankton eating) type whales that call the Midriff home, having forsaken their normal migration routes into arctic seas.

Above Midriff to Colorado River . . . Once again the sea warms up, heated by the blistering winds of the desert. The higher temperatures (into the 90's during the summer) acts as a barricade for some species and a playground for others. Sharks and corvina thrive, but many other species retreat into the cooler waters of the Midriff. The upper gulf offers seasonal appearances of white seabass (winter and spring), sierra (fall and spring) and the yellowtail (spring and early summer south of Puerte citos).

Today, the visitor to San Felipe will rarely see the once abundant totuava. Long the main attraction of the northern Gulf, the loss of suitable spawning areas and overharvesting by commercial netters has reduced this giant (to 300 pounds) cousin of the white seabass to the brink of extinction.

Tackle . . . Any size of rod, reel and line that you might take will be right for some of the fishing to be had, wrong for the rest. It doesn't make sense to try for the big ones with a 4-pound test outfit, unless you are an expert and are willing to lose a lot of fish. But that same trout-type tackle will provide great sport around the rocks, using small lures or tiny pieces of bait.

A good versatile combination would be a two-piece 9-foot rod capable of casting 4 to 6 ounces of weight, either conventional or spinning reel, with several extra spools loaded with 15 to 30 pound test line. This will handle any but the roughest of customers. A rig suited for 8 to 12 pound line will provide even more sport and will work quite well.

Should you decide to try billfishing, it is not necessary to take heavy marlin tackle with you, as it is standard equipment on the resort boats. This gear is a lot better than it was years ago, but if you are a serious billfisherman, you'll want to brink your own outfits, with fresh line and a smooth-working drag.

Lures... With few exceptions, live bait is unavaliable in Baja, and lures play a big part in fishing the gulf. Clams, shrimp and chunks of fish do well as attractors for some species, but often the action is found by casting or trolling the artificial lure.

Feather lures—such as the leadhead type that slides up the leader —in whites, yellows and greens are effective trolled over rocky structures and in the offshore migration routes. Sometimes, it pays to string 2, 3 or 4 feathers together on one leader, giving a longer target to the attacking fish. One speciality type of trolling feather that has proven deadly for wahoo is manufactured by Spoofer Lure and Tackle Company. Called the "V.I.P.", it incorporates a heavy chromed 9 ounce keel with long dark colored hackles and a fluorescent plastic skirt. It is best used at a fast (8 to 10 knot) troll. The same enticer has taken marlin, dolphin-fish and tuna, but it seems to especially attract the wahoo. Sevenstrand's Psychobead lures are likewise good gamefish getters.

A most effective family of jigs are those shaped like a candy bar. Flat on one side with curved top and tapered side, they do a good job of simulating the action of live bait. Although they are sometimes trolled, a fast retrieve near the surface or angled up from a greater depth will give the best results. For some species, a heavy jig bounced, or "yo-yo'd", near the bottom will prove irresistible. Names of typical proven jigs of this type include Salas, Hacker, Straggler and Maverick, but there are dozens available.

Slow retrieves are sometimes more effective when a spoon-shaped wobbling type lure is used. Such product names as Krocodile, Hot Shot, Spoofer, Hoodwink and Tady have shown themselves as effective. Slow to moderate retrieval speeds often better suit the mood of the fish. If you are unable to score with the candy bar type, give these a try.

Another class of effective lures are those that more closely resemble the actual shape of a fish. These Rebel or Rapala types often prove deadly when no others will work, but their light weight makes casting difficult and so they are generally trolled at relatively slow speeds. It is well to take a few along in the 4½ and 7 inch lengths.

The light tackle buff who enjoys being on the beach at first light will find many places where he can cast small spinners into marauding schools of fish as they feed on the young **sardinas** in the shallows. Later in the day, sporadic action may be found on the tidal changes around the mouths of the esteros and rocky points—wherever the current movement stirs up the morsels of food that triggers the "eat and be eaten" cycle of the ocean. Small lures such as the Roostertail and Abu Reflexe, and their larger ¾ to 1 ounce versions, will produce lots of action. Copper, gold and silver spinners too, work well, especially if the trailing streamers are white or yellow.

It is imperative to have an extra supply of line available—plus extra lures, sinkers and hooks—because the loss of these essentials will really put you out of business in Baja. There is not one well-stocked tackle store in the whole peninsula, yet.

Another item that would be wise to include is a big supply of wire-leadered hooks and short wire leaders for use with jigs. Many fish of the gulf are toothy and will slash monofilament to pieces.

You are likely to come up with many types of fish that you have never seen before, plus a few of the more familiar spcies. Following are some fish that might be taken or seen, plus some hints on turning them into delicious eating.

FOOD FOR THOUGHT

The Sea of Cortez abounds with creatures that may become part of a meal and they needn't always be the highly-prized dorado, cabrilla or grouper. Many species, with very little effort, can be a main dish to savor.

TRIGGERFISH

The trigger fish is easily caught almost anywhere in the Cortez where there are rocks. He takes both lures and bait (use wire leaders as their teeth are sharp) and will put up a stiff fight. His armor-like hide can discourage, but once the fillet is removed, it is great when fried or steamed.

Fried Triggerfish: Brush meat with soya sauce and let stand for about ½ hour. Pat dry, dredge in seasoned flour and fry in oil.

Steamed Triggerfish: Steamed, or poached, this fish makes into a delicious seafood cocktail, which resembles crab or lobster. Simmer fillets in or over water containing boiling spices (allspice, peppercorn, several small dry chiles, bayleaf and the rinds of one or two limes). Cook until tender, cool and break into bite-size pieces. Add these to a spicy seafood cocktail sauce and get ready for a stampede.

COCKTAIL SAUCE

½ cup chili sauce	Tabasco sauce to taste
4 Tbsp lime juice	½ tsp celery salt
1 Tbsp horseradish	2 Tbsp onion, finely chopped

Salt and pepper to taste. Blend all ingredients and chill. Serves 6.

MARINE MARINADE

This marinade works well on bonito, yellowtail, sierra and many other species where the fish can be quarter-filleted and the dark meat removed.

> 1 cup Italian Dressing
> Juice of 6-8 limes (or 2-3 lemons)
> ¼ cup dry white wine
> ½ to 1 onion, thinly sliced
> parsley or cilantro to taste

Marinate fillets in mixture for 1-3 hrs. in refrigerator or a cool place, turning occasionally. Lay directly on grill over hot coals. Turn once when lightly browned. Cage-like hamburger or hot dog grills work well here.

USE THAT BARBEQUE

In addition to fixing fish, a bed of hot coals will do wonders for clams, lobster and shrimp.

Lobsters, when available, are delicious when basted with lime juice and garlic butter and sprinkled with paprika. Split the tails and start with shell side up, turning once.

Both coasts of Baja offer a number of species of clams or cockles (2-3 inches in diameter) that, after being allowed to cleanse themselves in sea water for several hours, are ready to be put directly on the grill and heated just until they open or start to drip juices. Remove and serve with garlic butter and lime juice or hot sauce.

Shrimp may be skewered, brushed with a small amount of butter or bacon grease and lime juice, then cooked until barely done. Scallops, too, respond well to this treatment.

SAN QUINTIN STEW

This was invented out of necessity one evening while camped on a clam beach west of San Quintin, when a number of hungry people arrived with only a few miscellaneous canned goods left over from several days of camping. Carlton Bishop and I tossed in what we had, as did two Japanese anglers who came over the dunes. We gathered a big bucket of pismo clams to fill out the meal. All cans were the 1 lb. size, except at noted.

> 2 cans each potatoes and tomatoes
> 1 can pork and beans (large)
> 1 can each creamed corn, regular corn, kidney
>   beans
> 2 onions chopped
> 1 large can condensed milk
> 1½ dozen pismo clams, cleaned and cut into
>   bite sized pieces. (Put round, reddish
>   muscles or "buttons" aside.)
> Salt and pepper to taste

Open all cans, put everything but clams into a big pot and cook until onions are done and mixture thickens. Add clam pieces and bring back to barely boiling. Remove from heat and serve. It fed the four fishermen (Bishop, Miller and the two Japanese), a young couple who were lost(showing up as we started to eat) and a family of three who had spent all day trying to repair a loose gas tank. We've fixed San Quintin Stew a number of times since.

COOKING WITHOUT HEAT

A way to beat the energy shortage is to get the cebiche habit.

Cebiche, or seviche, is a dish consisting of certain mild flavored fish and shellfish marinated in a mixture of lime juice, tomatoes, onions and chiles. It requires no heat. In fact it may be refrigerated before serving.

1 pound of sierra fillets	1 small onion
Juice of about a dozen limes	¼ to ½ tsp oregano
(or enough to almost cover)	3 or 4 pieces cilantro
2 medium tomatoes	Pepper to taste
2 jalapeno chiles, pickled	

Cut the fish into small pieces, add lime juice and refrigerate for 3-4 hours, or until fish loses transparent look. Stir occasionally. Peel and chop tomatoes, removing seeds. Finely chop chiles after removing seeds. Thin slice onion and crumble oregano. Chop cilantro and combine all ingredients with fish and lime juice. Let stand for 1-2 more hours if you can. Serve with slices of avocado if available.

Pargo, wahoo, dorado and shellfish such as shrimp (peeled and deveined), scallops and lobster may be used in place of sierra.

EASY SHRIMP

2¼ pounds (1 kilo) medium shrimp
¼ lb butter or margarine (or ½ cup of cooking oil)
2 cloves garlic or ¼ tsp garlic powder.

Wash and drain shrimp well, leaving shells on. Heat oil and garlic in frying pan. Add shrimp and cook until they turn pinkish (3-5 min.). Remove from oil, drain and serve hot. Let guest remove shells and put in "bone dish". Messy, but great eating. Have plenty of paper towels handy.

SCALLOPS IN WINE

1 lb. scallops (½ kilo)
¼ cup chablis or other white wine
½ cube butter
Garlic salt to taste
¼ cup grated parmesan cheese

Marinate scallops in wine 1-2 hrs. Melt butter with garlic in frying pan and scallop-wine mixture. Simmer about 10 minutes. Drain and serve hot sprinkled with parmesan cheese. Great as a main dish or as hors d'oeuvres.

PISMO CLAM "BUTTONS"

Slice the "buttons" crosswise and cover with lime juice. Add a **little** cilantro, finely chopped and some very thinly sliced serrano chile, if desired. Marinate 1-2 hrs. in a cool place. Just before serving, add a teaspoon of soya sauce and stir. Drain and serve on crackers. Great!!

PISMO

COCKTAIL TIME

For many regular visitors to Baja, a cocktail made from Tequila, the beverage that has become synonymous with Mexico, is the only way to start the evening.

Made from the fermented and distilled juices of the heart of the maguey cactus, this fiery liquid is usually served in one of the following ways:

STRAIGHT

This way can be rather hazardous and is usually left to the old hands who have measured well their capacity.

Moisten the skin between the thumb and forefinger and sprinkle salt on the area. Holding a wedge of lime with the "salted" thumb and forefinger and the jigger in the other hand, lick the salt, down the tequila and suck the lime. Then take a deep breath—you may need it.

WITH SANGRITA

This method too is popular, and devastating if not careful.

Sangrita is a highly-spiced orange juice mixture which has been blended with one-eighth part lime juice and a little grenadine. To this add a little finely chopped onion and enough tabasco sauce to make it just a bit too spicy for comfort. Refrigerate for several hours and strain out the onion.

Use as a chaser for the tequila—or is it the tequila as a chaser for the sangrita? It's not too important with this one.

BAJA MARY

Variation on the Bloody Mary introduced to Baja resorts by EB nearly a decade ago, this is a much more benign libation. Lime and salt the rim of a tall glass, add a jigger or two of tequila and fill with tomato juice or your favorite bloody mary mix. Squeeze in half a lime, drop the peel, season with salt, pepper, Worchester and Tabasco. Ole!

BAJA MARGARITA

Perhaps the classic form of the now world-famous Margarita is made by most resorts in the Peninsula, the difference being that the Baja-produced liqueur Damiana is substituted for the usual Cointreau or Triple Sec. Like Tequila, Damiana is derived from a plant native to the region. Mixed together two-to-one with an equal amount of lime juice, they make up a variation unique to Baja California. Mix in a blender with plenty of crushed ice.

BAJA LOVE POTION

A Baja Margarita is often made with Damiana liqueur, rather than the Triple Sec used elsewhere. Damiana is flavored with the leaves of a shrub that grows only in the southern part of the peninsula. The Indians believed that the damiana plant contained a powerful aphrodisiac and many swore by its powers. The bottled liqueur likewise made these claims, until the government made them change their label. We can, however, vouch for the fact that it does make an excellent Margarita.

AGAVE

RESORT ROUNDUP

Lodging between the border cities of Tijuana, Mexicali and Ensenada and the region to the south—La Paz, the East Cape and Cabo San Lucas—is still not plentiful but is adequate to handle all but the most crowded holiday times. Accommodations range from modest to luxurious, as found in the Mexican government's El Presidente Hotel chain.

It is rarely necessary to have reservations and as so many Baja visitors travel by camper, trailer or motorhome, a hotel room is often only for that occasional time when a thorough "sprucing-up" is in order.

Telephones now reach almost all populated portions of central Baja except Guerrero Negro. Where phones are lacking, there is often a government radio station which may be used for emergency messages. All of the El Presidente Hotels are connected by radio to the main office in Ensenada, and may be used in emergencies.

In all that 400-mile mid-Baja wilderness, which has for centuries separated the north from south, we counted less than 200 rooms at printing time. Most are in the deluxe category, and priced accordingly. There are also modern trailer camp accommodations for some 200 units in that region. If you were to drive from sunup to sunset, you could barely cross those 400 miles in daylight, so plan an overnight stop somewhere along the way.

The main roads of Baja are patroled during the day by Mexico's famed Green Angels (see page 19) who are equipped to do minor repairs on the spot and to help stranded motorists on their way.

Plan your trip so that you will be checked into a room or camped well before dark. It is definitely **dangerous** to drive at night in Baja. Livestock on the highway and narrow roadbeds combine to create a great hazard.

Once on the Sea of Cortez at Santa Rosalia, with the Vizcaino behind you, accommodations are easier to find. A number of fishing resorts and motels are located along the bays and beaches.

Prices shown are given in U.S. Dollars, and must be considered indicative rather than firm due to inflation. The resorts and restaurants are arranged roughly north-south by regions.

The following is a list of hotels and trailer parks in Baja California and along the west coast of Mexico. An asterisk (*) indicates hotels and trailer parks that offer 10-20% discounts on their prices to members of the Mexico West Travel Club, Inc. (See page 183 for information on membership.)

Where to Stop or Stay

TIJUANA

Palacio Azteca—90 rooms. Pool, Excellent Restaurant. P.O. Box 40-A, San Ysidro, CA 92073. Phone (706) 686-5301.

* **El Presidente**—200 rooms. On Agua Caliente Blvd. near racetrack. Air, Pool, Dining room. P.O. Box 1588, San Ysidro, CA 92073. Phone (706) 686-5000.

Hotel Lucerna—130 rooms, Air, Suites, Pool, Restaurant. P.O. Box 4471, San Ysidro, CA 92073. Phone (706) 686-4801.

ROSARITO BEACH

Quinta del Mar Hotel—71 rooms. Pool, Restaurant, Tennis. P.O. Box 4243, San Ysidro, CA 92073. Phone (706) 612-1300.

Rosarito Beach Hotel—73 rooms, Two Pools, Tennis. P.O. Box 145, San Ysidro, CA 92073. Phone in Rosarito, (706) 612-1106

KOA Trailer Park—(San Antonio Exit) 200 RV sites. P.O. Box 2082, Tijuana, Baja Calif., Mexico. Phone (706) 686-1412.

El Manana Trailer Park—93 sites with hookups. Pool, Showers, 2½ miles south of Rosarito.

Puerto Nuevo. A group of restaurants located about 10 miles south of Rosarito. Specialize in lobster dinners, top establishment is Oretega's.

ENSENADA

San Miguel Village—45 RV sites, 50 + Tent area. Toilets, Showers, Groceries, Propane, Restaurant. P.O. Box 55, El Sauzal, Baja Calif., Mexico.

Granada Cove Motel and Trailer Park—40 rooms moderately priced. Good restaurant. Write: Granada Cove Motel, Ensenada, B.C. Mexico.

* **Ensenada TraveLodge**—41 rooms. Pool, Color TV. U.S. Reservations Agent: TraveLodge Reservations Systems (800) 255-3050.

* **San Nicolas Hotel**—120 rooms. Pool, Dining and Coffee Shop, Bar and Disco. Apartado Postal 19, Ensenada, B.C., Mexico. Phone (706) 676-1901.

El Cid Motor Hotel—36 rooms. Pool, Air, Restaurant. Write: Apartado 1431, Ensenada, B.C., Mexico. Phone (706) 678-2401.

* **Hotel La Pinta**—52 rooms. Pool, Restaurant. Reservations: Mexican Hotels, Inc., 7488 La Jolla Blvd., La Jolla, CA 92037. Phone CA Toll Free (800) 542-6028 or elswhere (800) 854-2027.

Villa Marina—Older well-kept motel in center of town. Reasonably priced. P.O. Box 28, Ensenada, B.C., Mexico. Phone (706) 678-3321.

Corona Beach Trailer Park—8 miles south of town off road to Estero Beach—60 spaces with water and electricity. Cold water showers, good beach for swimming and fishing.

Estero Beach Trailer Park and Resort Hotel—87 rooms. 8 miles south of Ensenada and 2 miles west, Bayfront, Boat Ramp, Restaurant, 75 RV sites. Write: Apartado Postal 86, Ensenada, B.C., Mexico. Phone (706) 679-1001.

Hussong's Cantina—Popular spot for atmosphere and the best "Margaritas" in the world. Don't let the outside scare you away. Downtown Ensenada on Ruiz St.

El Rey Sol—Outstanding and popular restaurant featuring French cuisine.

Casa Mar and Casa Mar II Restaurants—on waterfront streets. Excellent fish and seafood dishes moderately priced.

La Cueva de los Tigres—South of town on water. Very good food, excellent view of bay, famous for abalone.

SANTO TOMAS

El Palomar Hotel and Trailer Park—5 rooms. 20 RV sites with hookups, Pool, Showers, Groceries. Apartado Postal 595, Ensenada, B.C. Mexico.

COLONIA GUERRERO
*Posada Don Diego Trailer Park—100 spaces with hookups, Showers, Restaurant. Write: Apdo. Postal 7, Colonia Guerrero, Valle de San Quintin, B.C. Mexico.
Motel Sanchez—16 small clean rooms. Emergency.

SAN PEDRO MARTIR MTNS.
Mike's Sky Rancho—American Plan, Camping, Pool, Hiking. Hunting. Write 874 Hollister, Sp. 48, San Diego, CA 92154. Phone: (714) 423-2934.

SAN QUINTIN
*Hotel La Pinta San Quintin—60 rooms. Restaurant and Bar, On Beach. Contact: Mexican Hotels, Inc. Toll Free CA (800) 542-6028 or Toll Free elsewhere (800) 854-2027.
Molino Viejo Motel (Old Mill)—12 rooms, some with kitchenettes, Fishing and Hunting, Airstrip (2000 ft.) Write Molino Viejo, Apartado Postal 90, Valle de San Quintin, Baja Calif. Mexico.
Cielito Lindo Motel—24 rooms. Restaurant, Trailer Park with limited facilities. Write Santa Maria, Valle de San Quintin, B.C., Mexico.
Ernesto's Motel—12 rooms. Hunting, Fishing, Restaurant. Next to Old Mill. Not always open.

EL ROSARIO
Espinosa's—Rustic accommodations available. Anita Espinosa's lobster tacos are the best in the world.

MEXICALI
Hotel Lucerna—200 rooms. Two pools, Restaurant and Night Club. Air cond. Blvd. Benito Juarez 2151. Write P.O. Box 1479, Calexico, CA 92231 or phone: (706) 564-1000.
Holiday Inn—125 rooms. Air-Cond., Pool, Restaurant and Bar. P.O. Box 5497, Calexico, CA 92231 or phone: (706) 568-1300 or Holiday Inn Reservations (800) 238-8000.
Campo Rio Hardy—10 rooms. Boat Ramp, Fishing, Hunting. Cafe and Store. Write P.O. Box 43, Calexico, CA 92231.
El Mayor—Camping and trailer sites. Fishing and Boating.

SAN FELIPE AREA
Campo Kingfish, Campo San Jose, Rancho Ponderosa, Pete's El Paraiso, Campo Hawaii, Campo El En Canto, Playa del Sol and Campo Pee Wee offer showers, flush toilets and water for washing only. All reasonably priced and located north of San Felipe on Highway 5.
Playa Blanca Mar de Cortez—4 miles north on Highway 5. Open on beach. Campsites, RV hookups. Flush toilets and showers. Beautiful beach.

SAN FELIPE
Playa de Laura Trailer Park—61 spaces with hookups. In town on water. Showers and flush toilets.
Ruben's Trailer Park—One mile north on main street. 50 spaces with hookups. Flush toilets, showers, boat ramp, restaurant. For reservations phone San Felipe 7-10-91.
Club de Pesca—150 spaces with hookups. Boat Ramp, Recreation Hall, Laundry. Phone 7-11-80 for reservations.
*Hotel Castel San Felipe—120 rooms. Modern hotel on water. Air Cond., Restaurant, Pool, Disco. Reservations: Mexican Hotels, Inc., 7488 La Jolla Blvd., La Jolla, CA 92037 or phone Toll Free CA (800) 542-6028 and Toll Free (800) 854-2027.
Hotel Riviera—44 rooms. Air Cond., Pool, Restaurant and Bar. Write: Apdo. Postal 102, San Felipe, B.C., Mexico or phone San Felipe 7-11-86.
El Cortez Motel—40 rooms on beach. Air-Cond., Pool, Restaurant. Write: P.O. Box 1227, Calexico, CA 92231 or telephone San Felipe 7-10-55.
Hotel Viva San Felipe—140 rooms. 12 miles south of town. Two Pools, Restaurant and four bars. Reservations to: Hotel Viva San Felipe, Ave. Reformas 1200, Mexicali, B.C., Mexico or phone (706) 564-0393 or (706) 564-0394.
El Faro Beach Trailer Park—12 miles south of town, 150 RV sites most with hookups. Showers, toilets, groceries, ice, restaurant, bar. Write: Apdo. Postal 107, San Felipe, B.C. Mexico or P.O. Box 5925, Calexico, CA 92231.

SAN FELIPE TO PUERTECITOS AND BAHIA DE LUIS GONZAGA

Bahia Santa Maria—21 miles south of San Felipe. Campsites.

Nuevo Mazatlan—Campground with toilet facilities and water.

Aqua Azul de Acapulco Beach—Outdoor toilets, fishing, refreshments.

Coloradito Sportfishing Resort—Surf fishing, outdoor toilets.

Speedy's Camp—2 miles north of Puertecitos, campground with cafe and outdoor toilets.

La Costa Campground—5 miles south of Puertecitos, surf fishing, food.

Campo Salvatierra (Mateo's Place)—14 miles north of Gonzaga Bay.

Papa Fernandez' on the Bay—Cabins, refreshments, boats and airstrip (1885 ft.).

Alfonsina's—A tourist camp with fishing and airstrip (2375 ft.). Restaurant.

TECATE

Rancho La Puerta—An original "fat farm." Vegetarian food served in ranch like atmosphere. 125 rooms with weekly rates. On road from Tijuana just out of Tecate. Write Rancho La Puerta, Tecate, CA 92080 or Phone (714) 478-5341.

El Dorado Motel—41 rooms. Air-cond. with pool on Avenida Juarez 1100. Write P.O. Box 7, Tecate, B.C., Mexico

SANTA INES

***Hotel La Pinta Catavina**—28 rooms. Pool, Restaurant and Bar. Write: Mexican Hotels, 7488 La Jolla Blvd., La Jolla, CA 92037. Phone Toll Free CA (800) 542-6028 or Toll Free elsewhere (800) 854-2027.

Rancho Santa Ines—located just off highway ¼ mi. south of hotel. Bunkhouse style accommodations, good food and friendly atmosphere.

BAHIA DE LOS ANGELES

Casa Diaz—26 rooms. Hunting and Fishing. Boats and Boat Ramp. Write Antero Diaz, P.O. Box 579, Ensenada, B.C., Mexico.

***Villa Vitta Motel**—30 + rooms. Modern with air-conditioning, pool, jacuzzi, restaurant and bar. Fishing. Write Jimsair, 2904 Pacific Hwy., San Diego, CA 92101 or phone (714) 298-7704.

PARALLELO 28/GUERRERO NEGRO

***Hotel La Pinta Guerrero Negro**—24 rooms. Air cond. Restaurant and Bar. Phone: Mexican Hotels, Inc., Toll Free CA (800) 542-6028 or Toll Free elsewhere (800) 854-2027.

Parador Parallelo 28 Trailer Park—60 spaces with hookups. Toilets and showers. Sometimes somewhat run down.

Baja Sur Motel—180 rooms. Write Apdo. Postal 6, Guerrero Negro, B.C.S. Mexico.

Dunas Motel—36 rooms. One mile west of town. Adequate. Write: Dunas, Guerrero Negro, B.C.S., Mexico.

Malarrimo Restaurant—Fine food. Located one mile from town. Also limited accommodations for trailers.

PUNTA SAN FRANCISQUITO

***Punta San Francisquito Resort**—10 Cabanas, Restaurant and Bar with boats. Airstrip (3000 ft.). Write: Jim Irwin, P.O. Box 424, Fullerton, CA 92632 or phone (714) 870-7551.

SAN IGANCIO

***Hotel La Pinta San Ignacio**—28 rooms. Air-cond., Pool, Restaurant and Bar. Reservations: Mexican Hotels, La Jolla, CA or phone Toll Free CA (800) 542-6028.

La Posada Motel—6 very modest rooms. Clean and cheap. Good restaurant. Write: La Posada, San Ignacio, B.C.S. Mexico.

SANTA ROSALIA

Hotel El Morro—20 rooms. Air cond., Cocktails and Dining Room. For reservations write: Apdo. Postal 76, Santa Rosalia, B.C.S. Mexico. Phone (706) 852-0414.

Hotel Punta Chivato—Should be mentioned although it is not open at present. Beautiful beach and good camping area. South of Santa Rosalia by about 14 miles and then about 14 miles off highway.

MULEGE

***Hotel Las Casitas**—6 rooms. Small and clean, good restaurant, reasonably priced in center of town. Write: Las Casitas, Mulege, B.C.S. Mexico or phone (706) 853-0019

Hotel Mulege—22 rooms. Closed at this time.

*****Hotel Serenidad**—35 rooms. Fishing, hunting, beach, air-cond., airstrip (4100 ft.), RVs welcome but no hookups. Write: Serenidad, Mulege, B.C.S. Mexico. Phone: (706) 853-0111

Hotel Terrazas—20 rooms. Air-cond., clean, in town.

Oasis Rio Baja Trailer Park—2 miles south of town on river. Mostly permanent trailers. Boat ramp and Scuba dive shop.

BAHIA CONCEPCION

Posada Concepcion—20 trailer spaces with hookups. Toilets, showers, on beach, tennis. One of the nicest trailer parks in Baja.

Playa Santispac—(A public beach), 13½ miles south of Mulege. Popular spot in cove with pit toilets and palapas for shade.

Playa El Coyote and **El Requeson**—Public beaches with limited facilities located 16 and 27 miles south of Mulege.

LORETO

*****Hotel El Presidente/Nopopo**—250 luxury rooms. 8½ miles south via Hwy. 1. Air-cond., 2 pools, tennis, restaurant and coffee shop, bar. Reservations: Mexican Hotels, Inc., 7488 La Jolla Blvd., La Jolla, CA 92037 or phone Toll Free CA (800) 542-6028, Toll Free elsewhere (800) 854-2027.

*****Hotel Oasis**—33 rooms. Amer. Plan, Air-cond., Pool, Fishing, Restaurant and Bar. Write: Hotel Oasis, Loreto, B.C.S. Mexico. Phone: (706) 833-0112.

*****Mision Loreto**—32+ rooms. Pool, Fishing, Restaurant and Bar. Write: Box 49, Loreto, B.C.S. Mexico. Phone: (706) 833-0048.

Hotel Villa del Mar—about 100 rooms. Excellent bargain hotel featuring Pool, Restaurant and Bar. Built from prefab trailer units. On beach.

CUIDAD CONSTITUCION

Hotel Casino—36 rooms. Dining Room and Bar. Write: Casino, Guadalupe Victoria, Ciudad Consticucion, B.C.S. Mexico or phone: (706) 832-0004.

Hotel Maribel—39 rooms. Dining Room, Air-Cond. Write: Maribel, Guadalupe Victoria 156, Ciudad Constitucion, B.C.S. Mexico or phone: (706) 832-0155.

Campestre La Pila—About 20 spaces with hookups, toilets, showers. 2 miles south of town.

LA PAZ

Hotel Los Arcos—130 rooms. Pool, on waterfront, Air-cond., Restaurant and Bar, Fishing available. Phone: (706) 822-2792. Write: Baja Hotel Reservations, 10941 Bloomfield St., Los Alamitos, CA 90720 Toll Free CA (800) 352-2579 or elsewhere (800) 421-3772. **Cabanas de Los Arcos**—52 rooms. Air-Cond., Pool. Reservations: see Hotel Los Arcos above.

*****Castel Palmira**—120 rooms. Air-Cond., Pool, Dining Room, Tennis, Bar and Disco. Write: Mexican Hotels, 7488 La Jolla Blvd., La Jolla, CA 92037. Phone: Toll Free CA (800) 542-6028 or Toll Free elsewhere (800) 854-2027.

La Posada—25 rooms. Next door to Gran Baja, Air-Cond., Heated Pool, Restaurant and Bar. Reservations: Apartado Postal 152, La Paz, B.C.S. Mexico. Phone: (706) 822-0663.

*****Las Misiones**—On Mogote across from La Posada. Secluded beautiful setting with Pool, Restaurant and Bar with entertainment. Reservations through La Posada (see above).

*****El Presidente Sur**—109 rooms. 3 miles northeast of town, Air-Cond., Pool, Restaurant and Bar, on beach. Reservations through Mexican Hotels (see above).

Gran Hotel Baja—250 rooms. High-rise on beach. Pool, Tennis, Restaurant, Bar, Disco and entertainment. Write: Gran Hotel Baja, Apartado Postal 223, La Paz, B.C.S Mexico or phone: (706) 822-3844 or Toll Free (800) 325-3535.

Hotel Gardenias—56 rooms. Air-Cond., Pool, Restaurant, clean and very nice. Located in residential area of town with good parking for travelers towing boats and trailers. Write: Apartado Postal 197, La Paz, B.C.S. Mexico or phone (706) 822-3088.

Motel Calafia—28 rooms. Air-Cond., Pool. Adequate. Write: Apartado Postal 21, La Paz, B.C.S. Mexico or phone (706) 822-1139.

El Cardon Trailer Park—90 spaces with hookups. Toilets and Showers, Laundry, Pool. Write: P.O. Box 104, La Paz, B.C.S. Mexico. Phone: (706) 822-1261 or (706) 822-0078.

Puerto Balandra and Playa Tecolote are public beaches with minimal facilities located 4 to 6 miles north of ferry terminal at Pichilingue.

EAST CAPE

*Hotel Las Arenas—40 rooms. Luxury hotel, Amer. Plan, Fans (air not really needed). Sportfishing fleet, Airstrip (4200 ft.), Restaurant and Bar. Reservations: P.O. Box 3766, Santa Fe Springs, CA 90670. Phone: (213) 949-0201 or Toll Free in CA (800) 352-4334.

Hotel Punta Pescadero—Fly-in resort with 20 rooms. Airstrip (4000 ft.). Pool, Restaurant and Bar and Sportsfishing fleet. Reservations: P.O. Box 1044, Los Altos, CA 94022 or phone: (415) 948-5505.

*Hotel Palmas de Cortez—32 rooms. Air-Cond., on white sandy beach, Sportfishing fleet, 65 miles south of La Paz, Airstrip (3000 ft.). Write: P.O. Box 1284, Canoga Park, CA 91304 or phone: (213) 887-7001.

*Hotel Playa Hermosa—12 rooms. On beach north of Palmas de Cortez, Dining Room and Bar. Fishing cruisers available; also 15 trailer park spots with showers Write: P.O. Box 1284, Canoga Park, CA 91304 or phone: (213) 883-2049.

Rancho Buena Vista Resort—45 rooms. Amer. Plan. Beach plus pool. Fishing fleet. Hunting, Air-Cond., Diving, Tennis and lighted airstrip (3000 ft.). Write: P.O. Box 673, Monrovia, CA 91016 or phone: (213) 303-1517.

*Hotel Club Spa Buena Vista—13 rooms. Amer. Plan, converted mansion, Pool and hot mineral baths, Restaurant and Bar. Write: P.O. Box 2573, Winnetka, CA 91306 or phone: (213) 703-0930.

*Hotel Punta Colorada—31 rooms. 13 miles east of highway on unpaved road. Airstrip (3200 ft.). Private beach, Air-Cond., Restaurant and Bar, Sportfishing fleet. Write: P.O. Box 2573, Winnetka, CA 91306 or phone: (213) 703-1002.

Vista del Mar Trailer Park—Mostly permanent. Self-contained vehicle parking available. Boat ramp. Located just south of Buena Vista.

La Capilla Trailer Park—Just south of Hotel Spa Buena Vista, entrance is from Mexico 1. Some hookups, fine beach.

SAN JOSE DEL CABO

Hotel Palmilla—40 rooms. Amer. Plan, Pool, Horses, Tennis, Fishing fleet, Driving Range and Putting Green, Air-Cond., Restaurant and Bar. Write: P.O. Box 1775, La Jolla, CA 92038 or phone: (714) 454-0600.

*El Presidente—240 rooms. Luxury first class hotel. Reservations through Mexican Hotels, Inc., 7488 La Jolla Blvd., La Jolla, CA 92037. Toll Free in CA (800) 542-6028 or Toll Free elsewhere (800) 854-2027.

Nuevo Sol—Excellent bargain hotel featuring Pool, Restaurant and Bar. Built from prefab trailer units. On beach just west of town.

*Brisa del Mar Trailer Park—80 spaces with hookups. Motel, Laundry, Store, Pool, Tennis, Toilets and Showers. One of nicest in Baja. Write: Apdo. Postal 45, San Jose del Cabo, B.C.S. Mexico.

CABO SAN LUCAS

Twin Dolphin Hotel—50 luxury class rooms. Amer. Plan, Pool, Tennis, Horses, Beach, Air-Cond., Sportfishing. Write: 1730 W. Olympic Blvd., Suite 402, Los Angeles, Ca 90015 or phone: (213) 386-3940.

Hotel Cabo San Lucas—75 rooms. Amer. Plan, Pool, Air-Cond., Championship Tennis Courts, Beach, Diving, Fishing Fleet, Horses, Airstrip (3600 ft.). Beautiful location overlooking Sea of Cortez. Write: P.O. Box 48088, Bicentennial Station, Los Angeles, CA 90048. Phone: (213) 655-4760; or Toll Free (800) 282-4809.

Hotel Cabo Baja—125 rooms. Pool, Air-Cond., Beach, Reservations: Mexican Hotels, CA Toll Free (800) 542-6028 or Toll Free elsewhere (800) 854-2027.

Hacienda Hotel—100 + rooms. Pool, Air-Cond., Beach, Tennis, Fishing, U.S. Reservations: See Hotel Cabo San Lucas.

*Hotel Finisterra—58 rooms. Pool, high above beach, Fishing Fleet, Restaurant and Bar, Air-Cond. Write: 10941 Bloomfield St., Los Alamitos, CA 90720. Phone: (213) 583-3393, (714) 827-3933 or Toll Free (800) 352-2579.

*Hotel Solmar—61 rooms. Pool, Fishing Fleet, Restaurant and Bar, on beach at southernmost tip of the peninsula. Write: P.O. Box 383, Pacific Palisades, CA 90272. Phone: (213) 459-3336.

*Hotel Mar de Cortez—70 + rooms. Some air, some fans. Restaurant, Pool, reasonably priced units. Write: Apdo. Postal 11, Cabo San Lucas, B.C.S. Mexico. Also: P.O. Box 342, Monterey, CA 93940 or phone: (408) 373-7925.

GOING HOME VIA MEXICO'S WEST COAST

The use of the ferry system between the Baja California peninsula and the West Coast of Mexico gives one an opportunity to visit yet another portion of Mexico for hardly more than the expense of the ferry passage as outlined in the Cortez Circuit, page 26.

Once on the mainland side there is an excellent highway that will take you back to the border. Mexico 15 is spotted with numerous hotels and resorts where the traveler may relax.

Recreational pursuits in this portion of Mexico are centered on the water-oriented activities found at San Blas, Mazatlan, the Topolobampo region, Guaymas and around Bahia Kino. In addition, excellent bird shooting is found around the rich farming communities of Culiacan, Los Mochis, Ciudad Obregon and Navajoa. The irrigation dams above these regions offer largemouth bass fishing that borders on the unbelievable, with experienced anglers taking literally hundreds of two to five pound fish in a single trip.

There are several side trips toward the east that are also rewarding. Briefly they are: 20 miles east of Mazatlan is the furniture town of Concordia where beautiful handcrafted tables, etc. may be purchased at bargain prices. Out of Navajoa 34 miles is Alamos where the architecture of the early Spanish period is beautifully preserved. The states of Sonora and Sinaloa are undergoing a rapid expansion of their paved highway system and many more areas of interest are expected to be opened to visitors in the near future.

We have listed below only a very few of the many fine resorts on this portion of Mexico's west coast as space will not allow us to list all of them.

PUERTO VALLARTA

* **Posada Vallarta Hotel**—Large attractive hotel on beach, Pool, Air-Cond. Write: Posada Vallarta Hotel, Puerto Vallarta, Jalisco, Mexico, or Loew's Representation Intl., 666 Fifth Ave., New York, N.Y. 10103.

MAZATLAN

* **Hotel Playa Mazatlan**—242 rooms. Pool, Air-Cond., on beach. Write: P.O. Box 207, Mazatlan, Sin., Mexico or phone: (706) 823-4455 or 823-1120.
* **El Cid Resort Hotel**—200 + room resort, Pool, Air-Cond., on beach. Write: P.O. Box 813, Mazatlan, Sin., Mexico or phone: (706) 822-5199. U.S. Office: 5475 Leetsdale, Denver, CO 80224, phone: (303) 320-6771.
* **Oceano Palace**—On beach, Pool, Air-Cond. Write: P.O. Box 411, Mazatlan, Sin., Mexico. Phone: (706) 822-3111.
* **Playa Escondida Trailer Park**—Write: P.O. Box 202, Mazatlan, Sin. Mexico. Phone: (706) 783-2578.
* **San Bartolo Trailer Park**—Write: P.O. Box 480, Mazatlan, Sin. Mexico. Phone: (706) 783-5755.

* **Sabalo Beach Trailer Park**—Write: P.O. Box 480, Mazatlan, Sin. Mexico. Phone: (706) 783-5755.

LOS MOCHIS

* **Hotel Santa Anita**—136 rooms, in town, Air-Cond., Pool. Write: Roberto Baldamara, Apdo. Postal 159, Los Mochis, Sin., Mexico or phone: (706) 812-0046.

GUAYMAS

* **Nueva Posada de San Carlos**—Air-Cond., Pool, on beach, Tennis, Boat Dock. Write: P.O. Box 57, Guaymas, Son., Mexico. Phone: (706) 226-0122.
  Hotel Playa de Cortez—72 rooms. Pool, Air-Cond., Beach. Write: P.O. Box 66, Guaymas, Son., Mexico.

HERMOSILLO

  Motel Valle Grande—102 rooms. Pool, Air-Cond. Write: P.O. Box 988, Hermosillo, Son., Mexico
* **Teta Kawi Trailer Park**—Write: P.O. Box 671, Guaymas, Son., Mexico or phone: (706) 226-783-0220.

SANTA MARIA 1823

MISSIONS . . . INTRODUCTION

The 16th Century, known as "the century of discovery," was the period when Catholic missionaries fanned out into the New World putting forth zealous efforts to convert the millions of inhabitants. At this time, the Spaniards had not only acquired most of the land, but they also represented the majority of church delegates sent to establish profitable missions throughout the New World.

Church activities on the mainland of Mexico kept the Padres busy well into the 17th Century, with only a few cursory attempts to establish a beachhead in Baja. Finally in 1696, the Jesuits, led by Padre Juan Maria Salvatierra and his party of nine men, made a landfall at the mouth of a palm-lined arroyo. Thus began the arduous task of the building of Mision Nuestra Senora de Loreto, mother of the missions in Baja California.

The Jesuits had an exclusive mandate to "civilize" the natives and to exploit the riches of the western lands for the benefit of the Spanish crown and the church. But the following 150 years of painstaking effort by the Jesuits, and later the Franciscans and the Dominicans, proved unrewarding to their sponsors and disasterous to the inhabitants.

The five major groups of Indians — Diegueno and Cocopah in the north, Cochimi in the central portion, and the Guaycura and Pericue to the south — totaled an estimated 50,000 when the white man first set foot in their lands. By 1845, there were estimated to be less than 6,000 left with the original blood lines. Only a few small colonies remained.

Despite the difficulties, the mission system was the key to the opening of the Baja peninsula. Restoration of some of the missions (San Borja and south) is being undertaken by the Mexican government. See pages 163-170.

In the north, a group of private citizens headed by Sr. Tom Robertson of San Miguel Village, is endeavoring to restore several of the missions north of Mision San Borja. Another group, headed by the owner of the mission site, Sra. Josephina Zuniga, is planning to restore the picturesque Mision Santa Maria de Los Angeles. Nestled in a remote canyon east of the Santa Ines Ranch, Santa Maria should be one of the most interesting of the mission restorations, as the area has not changed since Father Victoriano Arnes first visited the site in 1767.

SANTA MARIA
1973

The **Mision Santa Clara** (Me-see-OWN SAN-ta CLAR-a), or so the story goes, was erected about 1767 by a group of Jesuits who used the mission as a depository for the treasure they acquired while in Baja. The mission was supposedly located in the Sierra Pintadas near some placer gold deposits that were reported to have been worked during mission times. There is considerable doubt that any such treasures actually existed, but stories have it that when the Jesuits were warned that they were about to be dispossessed by the Franciscans, they secreted a vast hoard of gold, silver, pearls and other valuables for retrieval later.

The highly doubtful existence of the **Mision Santa Isabel** (SAN-ta E-SA-bell) is attributed to the possible caching of vestments and other valuables left from the era of the Dominican priests in Baja from 1773 until the complete collapse of the mission system in 1885. Fable has it that Santa Isabel was built along the upper Gulf Coast region, but numerous observations of the area by foot, dune buggy, airplane and even helicopter have failed to locate even one encouraging sign of its existence.

Mision Descanso (Des-CAHN-so) was established by the Dominicans in 1778. Nothing remains to indicate the exact site, but it is reported to have been located in a narrow valley extending into the foothills near the Halfway House Resort on the road from Tijuana to Ensenada. It is the nearest to the Border of seven northern missions scheduled for restoration.

Mision San Miguel Archangel (San ME-gell Arc-AN-hell) . . . The remains of the mission's adobe walls may still be seen on the left side of the old Tijuana-Ensenada road 3.5 miles after turning under the toll road at La Mision and heading inland. Founded by Father Luis Sales in 1787, this was the third site for this mission. Two previous sites had been abandoned, one for lack of enough water for crops, and the second to relocate close to a proposed road which would link Baja California missions with those in Alta California. Restoration is planned.

Mision Guadalupe del Norte (Gua-da-LU-pay del NOR-tay) was the last mission to be founded in Baja California. In 1833, Father Felix Caballero established the mission to serve the Indians working in the fertile Guadalupe valley between Ensenada and Tecate. The treatment of the Indians caused the Mision Guadalupe's demise in 1893, when they revolted, killing a number of its defenders. The present town of Guadalupe is 25 miles north of Ensenada, one mile west of the highway. The mission was located on a small knoll to the right of the road just before entering Guadalupe. A large thicket of tuna cactus that once grew along one of the walls is all that remains of the mission.

SAN JAVIER

Mision Santa Catarina de los Yumas (SAN-ta Cat-a-REE-na day lows U-mas), known in the beginning as **Mision Santa Catalina Virgin y Martir** (Cat-a-LEE-na VIR-hen y mar-TEER), was founded in 1797 by Father Jose Loriente to serve as the supply point for proposed settlements near the mouth of the Colorado River. This mission is located in the mountains about 70 miles southeast of Ensenada near the Ensenada-San Felipe highway (now under construction). Once again, harsh treatment of the Indians led to several uprisings, resulting in many deaths on both sides and causing the system to collapse in 1840. There are stories of the Dominicans taking considerable gold from the surrounding canyons and some evidence of earlier workings were found during the gold rush of 1871. Restoration is planned.

Mision Santo Tomas de Aquino (SAN-toe Toe-MAS day A-KEY-no) . . . 1791 marked the date that Father Jose Loriente established the Mision Santo Tomas, starting with a small structure just up the arroyo from Puerto Santo Tomas. Several years later, he moved the mission inland to a spot that may still be seen off to the right 3.5 miles from the main highway on the dirt road to Puerto Santo Tomas. Only low mounds of adobe attest to the once-proud mission site. Seven years later in 1801, the final move was completed and the ruins of some of the outbuildings are still evident by the side of the road near the north end of town. There are a few palm trees and a large grape vine, presumably planted near the site by the Padres. The Santo Tomas mission was one of the more prosperous of the Baja California missions, supporting about 1000 Indians, 1200 cattle and 2600 sheep during its heyday, plus supplying altar wines for many of the missions throughout Mexico from its lush vineyards. Epidemics finally depleted the Indians and the mission slipped from sight in 1849. Restoration is planned.

Mision San Vicente Ferrer (San Vi-CEN-tay Fair-RARE) . . . Begun in 1780, Mision San Vicente Ferrer floundered when attacked by roaming Yuma Indians on the warpath. This setback was quickly followed by a smallpox epidemic, but the mission was revived a year later by Father Luis Sales. San Vicente served as the capital of La Frontera and housed the main garrison of troops in northern Baja for 16 years after the mission closed in 1833. Extensive adobe ruins may be found a few miles down the arroyo that crosses the highway just above town. A large graveyard overlooking the north side of the stream is believed to contain graves from mission times. Restoration is planned.

LORETO

Mision San Pedro Martir de Verona (PAY-dro Mar-TEER day Ver-OWN-a . . . One of the least successful of the missions, it was built primarily as a base from which to graze cattle. It was established in a remote mile-high mountain valley deep in the Sierra. Extensive ruins of this mission, which lasted only until 1806, can be found on a long horseback ride southeast of the Meling Ranch. Restoration is planned.

Mision Santo Domingo (SAN-toe Do-MEEN-go) . . . A year after Mision El Rosario had been dedicated, it was decided that the distance between the new mission and San Vicente was too great to effectively convert the "heathens" who lived in the hills and along the beaches. Thus, in 1775, a site in an arroyo near what is now Colonia Guerrero was chosen for Santo Domingo. Finding water a problem, they picked up their belongings in 1782 and relocated several miles up the canyon, where an ample supply of water produced abundant crops over about 120 acres of fertile land. Due in part to a reported epidemic of syphillis, the population didn't keep pace with the crops, and as the supply of labor decreased, the mission slowly died out. The last inhabitants left about 1839. Stone foundations and crumbled adobe walls of the mission and a number of grave markers may still be seen by taking the side road to the east to the small farming community of Santo Domingo. Restoration is planned.

Mision Nuestra Senora del Rosario (New-ACE-tra Sen-YOR-a del Ro-SAR-eo) . . . like a number of the other missions established in Baja California, Rosario had several locations before settling two miles southwest of the center of presentday El Rosario. Many Indians were converted, worked and died here from the time of its inception in 1774 until it was abandoned in 1832.

SAN FERNANDO

Mision San Fernando de Velicata(Vel-e-CA-ta) . . . It is the only monument, though crumbling, to the work of the Franciscans during their short tenure in Baja California. Established in 1769 by Father Junipero Serra before he moved on to San Diego in Alta California, it became an important mission, caring for about 1500 Indians. A tragic epidemic during the years of 1777-80 destroyed its ability to function properly and it was deserted in 1818. The mission is about two miles down the arroyo west of El Progresso.

Mision Santa Maria de los Angeles(Ma-REE-a day-lows AN-hay-lace) . . . was founded in 1767 by the Jesuit Priest, Father Victoriano Arnes, only a year before the expulsion of the Jesuits from Baja California. The general terrain proved inhospitable for farming, in spite of adequate water, and the mission was abandoned by the Franciscans in favor of Mision San Fernando. The adobe walls of Mision Santa Maria are still in relatively good condition and it is slated to be restored and made into a tourist attraction in the future. Presently, it is reached over a 14-mile jeep trail up the arroyo from Santa Ines, which must be followed by a rugged two-mile walk.

Mision Calamajue (Cal-a-ma-WHEY) . . . Founded in 1766 by the Jesuit Fathers Victoriano Arnes and Juan Jose Diaz, who discovered—after completion of the mission buildings—that the water was so mineralized their crops could not grow. They left after only a few months. The faint remains of the foundations are still evident. The ruins can be found near the Bahia Gonzaga-Laguna Chapala road across from an abandoned gold ore mill about 15 miles to the north of the junction with the old transpeninsular road.

Mision San Francisco de Borja(BOR-ha) . . . If the name "Borja" or "Borgia" sounds familiar and conjures up impressions of poisonings and intrigue, you will be surprised to know that the Borja (Spanish spelling) family supplied the money to build this mission, and also those at Calamajue and Santa Maria. Specifically, it was Maria, Grand Duchess of Borja, who heard of the Baja mission projects from a servant who had lived in one of the missions. The Grand Duchess ultimately left a sizeable amount of her estate to the Jesuit Pious Fund. Within a few years after completion in 1762, it served nearly 3000 converted Indians living around the mission. Poor growing conditions forced the other missions to ship food into this spiritually-fertile region, and the success enjoyed by the Padres was dimmed by rampant "white man's" diseases. Less than 100 Indians remained when the Dominicans left in 1818. A rather poor dirt road from Rosarito goes about 20 miles northeast to San Borja. The present stone church was built in 1801 to replace several adobe structures that literally melted away from the rains. This mission is one of the best preserved and is being restored and the road improved by the Mexican Government.

SAN BORJA

Mision Santa Maria Magdalena (Mag-da-LAY-na) . . . Not until 1966 was the location of this mission known to modern Mexico. During one of the famous Erle Stanley Gardner explorations of Baja, his party came across what appeared to be the remnants of a dam in an arroyo. Further exploration turned up evidence of a building site. According to records, Santa Maria Magdalena was never completed. But the area was described so well that scholars believe that Gardner did, indeed, find one of the old mission sites. It is located in almost inaccessible terrain 40 miles south of Bahia de Los Angeles.

Mision Santa Gertrudis la Magna (Ger-TRUD-ess la MAG-na) . . . Seeing this mission site today, you would wonder how it was possible to use the mission as the spiritual center for over 3000 novitates into Christianity. Flash floods have removed most of the tillable land and a small white stone chapel is about all that remains of this once extensive mission. There are a few families who still use a portion of the two-century-old irrigation ditches and tend the few old grape vines, olive trees and date palms, along with their own crops. Located some 23 miles east of El Arco, it once served as the main mission for exploration to the north. It is presently undergoing restoration.

Mision Dolores del Norte (Dough-LOR-ace del-NOR-tay) . . . Only a few years ago there was much doubt about the actual existence of Mission Dolores. Records were questioned because they listed its location in a very inhospitable portion of the mountainous central section of Baja, and the names of the landmarks were lost in the memories of old-time residents. Then, by accident it was located by a party searching for a cave full of giant painted figures made by an unknown tribe of Indians long before Columbus. Started by Father Fernando Consag sometime before 1745, it was not very successful due to a lack of water and closed after about 20 years. It is rather unlikely that many tourists will visit Mision Dolores due to its inaccessibility. Consag Rock in the Sea of Cortez off San Felipe is named for this Padre.

Mision San Ignacio de Kadakaman (Cadacaaman) (Ig-NAS-eo de ka-da-KAHM-an) . . . 1728 was the year that the San Ignacio mission was dedicated by Padre Juan Bautista Luyando. A few years later, Luyando introduced the Arabian date palms to the region, and these dates are still the primary crop of San Ignacio. Blessed with a good water supply from an underground river that surfaces here, it proved to be one of the most successful of the Jesuit missions serving about 5000 Indians. Disease, however, reduced the number to 120 by the end of the 18th century. Mision San Ignacio is one of the best preserved of the mission buildings, due to its construction from cut lava rock four feet thick, and its continued residence. The mission is located in the center of the town of San Ignacio and its restoration is virtually complete.

SAN IGNACIO

Mission San Juan Bautista (San Wan Bau-TEES-ta) . . . The only record of this mission's existence comes from a Jesuit Journal designating its location to have been in the Santa Clara mountains west of San Ignacio. A truly lost mission.

Mision Nuestra Senora de Guadalupe (New-ESS-tra Sen-YOR-a de Gua-da-LU-pay) . . . Located about 25 air miles due west of Mulege, Guadalupe was far from a roaring success. It was founded in 1720 by Father Juan de Ugarte and struggled for existence. A rugged jeep ride and a number of hours atop a mule are necessary to view the unimpressive stone foundations of the church. Nearly a lost mission, or at least a lost cause.

Mision Santa Rosalia de Mulege (Rosa-LEE-a day Moo-lay-HAY) . . . The Jesuits founded the mission of Mulege in 1705 and it was well attended by the 2000 natives until a flood in 1770 leveled most buildings. Epidemics did their part to cut the population to less than 100 by 1782. The stone church is presently being restored and overlooks the town from a low bluff half a mile up the arroyo. The tropical atmosphere of Mulege gives it one of the most beautiful mission settings in Baja California. It is sure to be a favorite of visitors to Mulege when it is completely restored.

Mision Guadalupe de San Bruno (San-BREW-no) . . . In 1683, Jesuit Padres Copart, Kino and Gomi made the first of several unsuccessful attempts to establish this mission. Evidence of one of their efforts may supposedly be found on the shores of Bahia San Bruno, 13 miles north of Loreto.

Mision San Juan Bautista Londo (Bau-TEES-ta LOAN-dough) was another abortive attempt to bring Christianity to the primitive residents of Baja California. Several miles inland from where the attempt to establish Guadalupe de San Bruno was made, San Juan Bautista Londo started in 1687 and collapsed a year or two later.

MULEGE

Mision La Purisima Concepcion (Poor-E-si-ma Con-sep-si-OWN)
. . . In 1730, eleven years after its beginning, La Purisima was reported
to be the most successful of the missions thus far, as Padre Tamaral had
baptized 2000 Indians. The mission workers' efforts at road building
were widely admired throughout the adjoining missions until harsh
treatment at the hands of the Jesuits drove off most of the new recruits.
In spite of the fertile land and good water, it slowly dwindled to nothing
in 1822. Little remains of the mission today in the town of La Purisima.

Mision San Jose de Comondu (San Ho-SAY de Co-moan-DO) was
founded by Padre Mayorga in 1708, some 24 miles north of its final location. The town that grew up around the mission after the dissemination
of the Indians gradually swallowed the buildings and nothing remains of
the structures today. However, a replica is slated to be built on the
original site.

Mision San Miguel de Comondu (San ME-gell day Co-moan-DO) . . .
Founded in 1718 by Padre Ugarte, San Miguel was located 1.8 miles up
the arroyo from Mision San Jose de Comondu. It, too, did well for a short
period, but as the population dwindled, it was absorbed by Mision San
Jose. Principal crops were sugarcane, grapes and fruit.

Mision Nuestra Senora de Loreto (New-ESS-tra Sen-YOR-a day
Low-RAY-toe) . . . Loreto was chosen by Padre Juan Salvatierra in 1697
to be the capital of the mission system being built in the Californias. This
was the first of the 20 missions started by the Jesuits during their 70
years of control. The mission that governed the peninsula and ministered
to the spiritual needs of its residents was designated the capital city of
all the Californias. In 1829, a hurricane almost destroyed the town,
which was rebuilt several times following floods and earthquakes.
Loreto is being completely restored under a Mexican Government
mission rehabilitation project.

Mision San Francisco Javier de Vigge (HA-vee-air day VEEG-gay)
. . . Begun in 1699 by Padre Francisco Maria Piccolo, this mission was
moved five miles south to its present location in 1720. Completed in
1758, the stone church remains as the best preserved and most impressive of all of the buildings erected in Baja California during the mission
area. San Javier is probably the most rewarding of all the missions to
visit, as it is very much as it was over 200 years ago. It, too, is undergoing
reconstruction and the currently poor road into San Javier will be improved soon.

Mision San Luis Gonzaga (San Loo-EES Gon-ZAH-ga) . . . Located
about 25 miles east of Ciudad Constiution this mission was open only
about thirty years (1737-1768) before epidemics eliminated all but about
three hundred of the Indians. The present stone church was built by

Padre Juan Jacob Baegert in the 1750's. It is presently being restored by the government. Only a few families live near the church and raise some dates, figs, oranges and mangos, using water from a small spring above the mission.

Misiones Dolores de la Pasion and Nuestra Senora Los Dolores del Sur (Do-LOR-ace day la pa-si-OWN and New-ESS-tra Sen-YOR-a Los Do-LOR-ace del Sur) . . . In the region east of La Purisima, these two missions played hopscotch for about 30 years searching for locations which would support the converts recruited by the Jesuit Padres. Unfortunately, the Indians expired before sites could be found. The missions were abandoned and the survivors removed to other missions.

Mision Senora del Pilar de la Paz (Pea-LAR de la Pause) . . . Although the La Paz area was the first to be visited by the Spanish in Baja California, it was not until 185 years later that the Spaniards returned to establish permanent quarters. In 1720, Padres Jaime Bravo and Juan de Ugarte began the building of a fort and church, preparatory to baptizing the residents. Diseases took a tremendous toll on the local Indians by 1749. There were to be no more permanent residents until 1811, thus making La Paz one of the younger major towns on the peninsula. No evidence remains as to the exact location of the fort, but it is believed to have been very near the site of the old post office in downtown La Paz.

Mision Todos Santos de Santa Rosa (TOE-dose) . . . This mission was well named, as it was populated by Indians from a number of the other missions as they were phased out. Epidemics and a major rebellion assured a rapid turnover of inhabitants, in spite of plenty of fertile land and excellent water. Its 120 year existence ended in 1854 with the final expulsion of the Dominican Priests. The town of Todos Santos has continued to exist and is one of the most charming communities on the Peninsula. Little remains of the original dwellings, but the present church —built in 1840—is near the original site.

Mision Santiago de las Coras (San-tee-A-go day las CO-ras) . . . Established in 1724, it was here that the Pericu Indian revolt began in 1734 with the murder of Padre Cerranco. The revolt spread throughout the southern missions and by the time the Missionaries regained control several years later, many on both sides were killed. Soon after this, an epidemic practically eliminated the Santiago tribes, reducing their numbers from 1100 to only 40. The mission closed in 1795.

Mision San Jose del Cabo (San Ho-SAY del CA-bo) . . . Founded in 1730 by Padre Nicolas Tamaral, this most southerly of the missions served as a supply and refitting stop for the Manila galleons. The mission was not a healthy place for the Indians, and in 20 years, disease took all but 100 of the original population. The mission struggled on into the 19th century by importing mestizos from the mainland. Nothing remains of the original church, but the present church stands on the same site.

BELLS FROM
EL ROSARIO MISSION

WANT TO RETIRE IN BAJA ?

If you are American and at least 50 years of age, you may make application to retire in Mexico as an Inmigrante Rentista.

If single, you must prove that you have and will continue to have a guaranteed monthly income of at least $240 U.S. (that's 6000 Mexican pesos) for the next five years. If married, the couple must have a combined income in excess of $320 monthly (8000 pesos).

The document stating proof of such income must be notarized, and the signature of the Notary legalized by the Mexican Consul in the American city from which the applicant obtained the statement of income.

Inmigrante Rentistas may not legally work for pay in Mexico during the first five year period of residence, though there are exceptions to this rule. They may buy or lease a house, but not income-producing property.

If your income is partly from interest on investments, you might consider Mexican trust funds or other investments which yield considerably higher rates of return than similar investments in the U.S. Many of the 100,000 American retirees there have done so. Mexico has recently relaxed regulations on foreign investments. (See section on investments).

There are rather complex regulations regarding **inmigrante** applications, the importation of personal goods, automobiles, immigration forms, fees, etc. Visit your nearest Mexican Consulate for details.

A WORD ON LAND INVESTMENTS

A law enacted under former President Echeverria authorized the Foreign Affairs Ministry to extend permits to national credit institutions enabling them to hold or acquire in trust, real estate holdings destined to be used for tourism, personal use or industrial activities.

The system operates as follows: the Mexican owner of land in a restricted area may ask a credit institution to set up a trust to administer the property for a specific use, in this case, the creation of tourist centers or industrial zones. The credit institution then proceds to issue participation certificates which entile the holder to share in the profits derived from future exploitation of these ventures.

The land continues to be Mexican-owned while participation certificate holders have full use of the installations built for tourism purposes along the coasts and borders, or share in the profits earned in the exploitation of these installations. The same system operates in the case of industrial activities.

For the protection of all foreign investors who might not have access to reliable information, Mexican law specifies that only credit institutions may act as trustees to hold and administer property for the benefit of an individual or organization. This is an added guarantee for foreign investors. A further element of security is Mexican participation in investments and the Government's decision to facilitate capital investments in tourism and industrial activities in coastal and border zones.

To date, 430 projects have been authorized under this system. Of these, eleven are large tourism centers, such as San Quintin in the State of Baja California. Another seven are industrial projects, and the remainder are building programs for tourist and retirement centers.

It is important to note that upon the sale of lands held in trust, each participation-certificate holder receives an aliquot share of the value.

WHO TO WRITE

As the Tourist Cards and other permits are best obtained through agencies of the Mexican Government, we have compiled a directory of where to write or call for these services. They will be happy to answer any other specific questions about travel in any part of Mexico.

Mexican Consulates

Albuquerque, NM 87106 (505/217-2139)
1020 Tijeras Ave. NE

Austin, TX 02110 (512/426-4942)
716 Brazos

Brownsville, TX 78520 (512/524-4431)
1000 E. Elizabeth St.

Calexico, CA 92231 (714/357-3863)
Imperial Ave. & 7th

Chicago, IL 60606 (312/782-5888)
201 N. Wells St.

Corpus Christi, TX 78475 (512/882-2375)
148 Guaranty Place Bldg.

Del Rio, TX 78840 (512/775-2352)

Denver, CO 80202 (303/832-2621)
1050 17th St.

Detroit, MI 48226 (313/965-1869)
232 W. Grand River

Eagle Pass, TX 78852 (512/773-9287)
391 Main St.

El Paso, TX 79901 (915/553-3640)
416 N. Stanton

Fort Worth, TX 76106 (817/336-1023)
810 N. Houston

Fresno, CA 93721 (209/233-8714)
211 Tulare St.

Houston, TX 77002 (713/223-1700)
1520 Texas

Kansas City, MO 64106 (816/421-5956)
823 Walnut Ave.

Laredo, TX 78040 (512/723-6360)
1612 Farragut

Los Angeles, CA 90012 (213/624-3261)
125 Paseo de La Plaza

McAllen, TX 78501 (512/686-6631)
119 S. Broadway

Montreal, Que Can. (514/288-2502)
3450 Drummond Ave.

New Orleans, LA 70130 (318/522-3596)
1140 International Trade Bldg.

New York, NY 10017 (212/689-0456)
8 East 41st St.

Nogales, AZ 85621 (602/287-2521)
135 Terrace Ave.

Ottawa, Ont Can. (613/233-8988)
130 Albert Ave.

Philadelphia, PA (215/922-4262)
12 S. Twelfth St.

Sacramento, CA 95814 (916/446-4696)
809 Eighth St.

San Antonio, TX 78205 (512/227-9145)
127 Navarro Street

San Diego, CA 92101 (714/239-9483)
1007 15th Avenue

San Francisco, CA 94102 (415/392-5554)
870 Market Street

San Jose, CA 95113 (408/295-0290)
12 S. First St.

Seattle, WA 98101 (206/682-3634)
1402 Third Ave. #720

Washington, D.C. 20009 (202/234-0442)
2829 16th St.

Vancouver, B.C., Canada (604/684-3747)
625 Howe St. #310

Mexican National Tourist Council Offices

Atlanta, GA 30303 (404/659-2409)
Peachtree St. N.E. #1201

Beverly Hills, CA 90212 (213/274-6315)
9701 Wilshire Blvd. #1201

Chicago, IL 60611 (312/649-0090)
John Hancock Ctr. #3612

Dallas, TX 75219 (214/526-6950)
Two Turtle Creek Village #1230

Denver, CO 80202 (303/222-4501)
633 17th St. #2010

Houston, TX 77056 (713/840-8332)
C-E Lumis Tower, #1370

Miami, FL 33132 (305/371-8037)
100 N. Biscayne Blvd. #2804

Montreal, Que H3B 3M9, Can. (514/871-1052)
One Place Ville Mar, #2409

New Orleans, LA 70139 (504/525-1502)
One Shell Square Bldg. #1515

New York, NY 10022 (212/755-7212)
405 Park Ave. #1002

San Antonio, TX 78216 (512/341-6212)
800 N.W. Loop 410 #240

San Diego, CA 92101 (714/236-9314)
San Diego Federal Bldg. #1220

San Francisco, CA 94111 (415/986-0992)
50 California St. #2465

Toronto, Ont M5H 2E1, Can. (416/364-2455)
101 Richmond St. West #1212

Tucson, AZ 85711 (602/745-5055)
5151 E. Broadway

Vancouver, B.C. V7Y 1B6, Can.
(604/682-0551)
700 W. Georgia St.

Washington, D.C. 20005 (202/296-2594)
1156 15th St. N.W. #329

FIRST AID, BAJA STYLE
BE PREPARED, JUST IN CASE

SUN STROKE AND HEAT PROSTRATION . . . is definitely something to guard against in the sunny climes of Baja California. High temperatures or long exposure to the sun might bring these problems on. The excessive loss of body fluids and salt lowers the blood pressure and lessens the brain's blood supply.

Symptoms are flushed and clammy skin, and a rapid, weak pulse. Nausea, headache, cramps and blurred vision are often accompanying symptoms.

Have the victim lie down in a cool shaded place with the head slightly lower than the rest of the body. Any tight clothing should be loosened and the body sponged with cool water until the body temperature drops. Get to a doctor as soon as possible.

It is a good idea to wear a light colored, long sleeved shirt and a broad brimmed hat, at least during the hottest part of the day.

SNAKE AND SCORPION BITES . . . A scorpion bite, though not as dangerous as that of a rattlesnake, can be fatal and should be treated in a similar manner. If the snake is a non-poisonous variety, clean well with soap and water and guard against infection.

A bite from a rattler or scorpion should be treated with a snake-bite kit. Keep the tourniquet between the bite and the heart, two to four inches from the wound. Loosen the constricting band for a few seconds every 15 minutes. An ice pack placed on the bite is of great help. Have the victim move as little as possible, and keep the injured area below the level of the heart. Get to a doctor, as soon as possible.

Scorpions may be found under rocks and in dark corners of the tent or camp kitchen. Always check your clothes in the morning, especially shoes, to make sure that the little critters haven't joined you during the night.

TICKS are not common, but should be removed as quickly as possible, as they do carry several diseases that can be uncomfortable later on. A drop of oil or alcohol, like tequila, will cause the tick to let loose.

JELLYFISH . . .Their long stringers can be downright uncomfortable and are almost invisible. If you swim into one, you will feel a hot burning sensation. Rub the area well with beach sand, then apply ammonia to the affected surface. This should take out the sting in a short time.

CACTUS THORNS . . . Remove as many as possible by pulling gently back in direction they went in. Removal in the wrong direction will cause them to break off. If possible apply ice to area after removing all possible needles. Keep area clean and protect from bumping.

BOOKS ON BAJA

There have been several hundred books published on Baja California. Its people, history, climate, flora, fauna and the sealife of the surrounding waters have commanded the attention of many authors. Many are out of print and many others are generally inaccurate or poorly organized.

If a person wished to expand his knowledge of the subject by adding to his library, he would do well to consider four or five books that are available and have much to offer the reader.

CANNON, Ray, **The Sea of Cortez.** Lane Publishing Co., Menlo Park, California, or from author, 645 N. Serrano St., Hollywood, CA 90004. $14.75

The subject of several television features, the romance, the people and the fish of the Sea of Cortez has been captured in word and picture by this remarkable man. He spent more than 20 years travelling through this fantastic region, and obviously loved every minute of it.

LEWIS, Leland and EBELING, Peter, **Baja Sea Guide**, Sea Publications, Inc., Costa Mesa, CA. $29.95

The view of the yachtsman has been taken by the authors in this large well illustrated book. The research that went into this book must have been tremendous. Every anchorage on both the Pacific and Gulf sides have been photographed from the air and diagrammed. A beautiful book with many hours of excellent reading.

MC MAHAN, Mike, **There It Is: Baja!** McMahan Bros. Desk Co. 3131 So. Figueroa, Los Angeles, CA 90007. $6.95

A highly entertaining book by a man who obviously relishes the time he spends in Baja. His witty, informative and sometimes irreverent views of the country give a good "feel" for the back country of Baja. The book has no specific directions on how to get anywhere, but doesn't need them.

MILLER, Tom, **World of the California Gray Whale.** Baja Trail Publications, Inc., Huntington Beach, CA 92646. $4.00

An excellent field guide to the marine mammals of the Eastern Pacific.

WHEELOCK, Walt, and GULICK, Howard, **Baja California Guidebook**, Arthur H. Clark Co., Box 230, Glendale, CA 91209. $10.95

Early printings of this book were indespensible before the opening of Mexico 1. The logs of the side roads of this 1975 edition are still of great value.

Walt Wheelock is also the owner of La Siesta Press, Box 406, Glendale, CA 91209 and has written a number of small books on various Baja subjects. We suggest you write for a list of available books.

COYLE, Jeanette, and ROBERTS, Norman, **Field Guide to the Plants of Baja California.** Natural History Publishing Co., Box 962, La Jolla, CA 92037. $7.95

It should be in every Baja travel kit.

SENTERFITT, Arnold, **Airports of Baja California.** Box 81005 San Diego, CA 92138. $10.95

OTHER BOOKS ON BAJA

ASCHMANN, Homer, **The Central Desert of Baja California.** Mannessier Publishing Co., Riverside, CA (1967)

BAEGERT, Jacob, **Observations in Lower California.** Ibero-Americana, Los Angeles, CA (1955)

CROW, James, **Baja Handbook.** Available through Cepek Co., Southgate, CA. (1970)

GARDNER, Erle Stanley, **The Hidden Heart of Baja, Camp and Camino in Lower California, Hovering Over Baja, Hunting the Desert Whale,** and **Mexico's Magic Square.** All by William Morrow Co., New York, N.Y.

KRUTCH, Joseph Wood, **The Forgotten Peninsula.** William Morrow & Co., New York, N.Y. (1961)

MILLER, Max, **Land Where Time Stands Still.** Dodd, Mead, & Co., New York, N.Y. (1943)

ROBINSON, John, **Camping and Climbing in Baja.** La Siesta Press, Glendale, CA (1972)

SCAMMON, Charles, **The Marine Mammals of the Northwestern Coast of North America.** Dover Publications Inc. (1968)

WHEELOCK, Walt, **Beaches of Baja, Byroads of Baja.** La Siesta Press, Glendale, CA (1968 & 1971)

SAYING IT IN SPANISH

Spanish is the language of Mexico, though English is widely spoken, particularly by those with whom the traveler ordinarily may come in contact. You can enjoy the country more, however, if you learn even a few phrases of Spanish and use them.

Mexicans, unlike some other nationalities, are not scornful of mispronunciations and errors in grammar; rather, they welcome even the most halting attempts to use their language.

For an English-speaking person, it's easier to learn a smattering of Spanish than of any other language. Many words have the same source: family is **familia,** restaurant is **restaurante,** cathedral is **catedral.**

Spanish is an almost phoentic language. With a few exceptions, the consonants are pronounced as in English. The pronunciation of the exceptions, as well as the pronunciation of the vowels is given below:

A—as the a in father
E—as the e in they
I—as the i in machine
O—as the o in over
U—as the u in rude
Y—as the y in yes
G—with i or e as the h in home
G—with a, o, or u as the g in go
H—always silent
J—as the h in home

LL—as the y in yes, with a silght j to it (jyes)
N—as the ny in canyon
Q—as the c in come
R—has a single trill
RR—has a double-triple-quadruple trill
V—often pronouced b or a combination of b and V

An accent mark over a letter signifies the accent on that syllable. Esta is pronounced ES-tah. Esta is pronounced es-TAH.

Almost all words have the accent on the next to the last syllable.

(continued on page 176)

SAYING IT IN SPANISH

(continued from page 175)

Please—Por favor
Thank you—Gracias
Good morning—Buenos dias
Good afternoon—Buenas tardes
Good evening, good night—Buenas noches
Good-bye—Adiós
How are you?—Cómo está usted?
Excuse me—Perdóneme
Yes, No—Si, No
I don't speak Spanish—No hablo español
I don't understand—No Comprendo
I need—Necesito
You're welcome—De nada
I am sick—Estoy enfermo

We want to eat now—Ya queremos comer
I am thirsty—Tengo sed
Give me a beer—Déme una cerveza por favor
Give me a soft drink—Déme un refresco por favor
What is your name?—Cual es su nombre?
My name is—Mi nombre es
Let's go—Vamonos
What time is it?—Qué hora es?
Where is the road to . . . ?—Dónde está el camino a . . .
Is that road in good condition?—Está en buen estado aquel camino?

Numbers:

1. uno	11. once	21. veintiuno	
2. dos	12. doce	30. treinta	
3. tres	13. trece	40. cuarenta	
4. cuatro	14. catorce	50. cincuenta	
5. cinco	15. quince	60. sesenta	
6. seis	16. diez y seis	70. setenta	
7. siete	17. diez siete	80. ochenta	
8. ocho	18. diez y ocho	90. noventa	
9. nueve	19. diez y nueve	100. cien	
10. diez	20. veinte	200. doscientos	

Days:

Sunday—domingo
Monday—lunes
Tuesday—martes
Wednesday—miércoles
Thursday—jueves
Friday—viernes
Saturday—sábado

Directions:

right—la derecha
left—la izquierda
straight ahead—el derecho
road—el camino
north—el norte
south—el sur
east—el este
west—el oeste or oriente
street—la calle
highway—la carretera
avenue—la avenida
corner—la esquina
block—la cuadra
point—punta
river—rio
mountain range—sierra
valley—valle
ranch—rancho
canyon, wash—arroyo
bay—bahia
cape—cabo
canyon—cañon
hill—cerro
bay—ensenada
lake—laguna
beach—playa
port—puerto
island—isla

Shop Talk:

groceries—abarrotes
beer—cerveza
tires—llantas
market—mercado
cold—frio
hot—caliente
hot (spicy)—picante
clean—limpio
dirty—sucio
for sale—se vende
large—grande
small—pequeño
bad—malo
good—bueno
expensive—caro
more—más
less—menos
high—alto
low—bajo

red—rojo
blue—azul
green—verde
yellow—amarillo
brown—café or moreno
white—blanco
black—negro

In Hotels—Cafes:

bedroom—la recámara
bathroom—el cuarto de baño
single room—un cuarto sencillo
double room—un cuarto doble
dining room—el comedor
hot water—agua caliente
ice water—agua con hielo
key—la llave
towel—la toalla
soap—el jabón
Where is the ladies' room?—Dónde está el lavabo de damas?
men's room?—de señores?
breakfast—el desayuno
lunch—el almuerzo
dinner—la comida
the bill—la cuenta
daily specials—especiales del dia
waiter—el mesero
waitress—la mesera or señorita

"Muchas gracias" **works wonders in Mexico, just like "thank you" brings a smile in the U.S.** Use it often.

INDEX

MISSIONS (CONTINUED NEXT PAGE)

Adios Amigos!

Tom Miller   Elmar Baxter

Tom Miller, co-author of the best-selling book, THE BAJA BOOK II, whose popular "Baja File" column appears weekly in **Western Outdoor News,** packs his 30 years of Baja angling expertise, plus that of dozens of others, into this informative book.

Pages of maps, charts and tips have been painstakingly researched, drawn and checked to give the best view of the where's, when's and how's of Baja California fishing from the Coronado Islands to San Felipe.

ANGLER'S GUIDE TO BAJA CALIFORNIA contains maps of the ten **Fishing Zones** and each has its own fishing calendar for the Onshore, Inshore and Offshore species.

Pinpointed are beaches, rocks and reefs for surf, skiff and charter boat anglers. Nearly 100 fish drawings are complimented by physical descriptions, plus information on habitat, angling tips and cooking suggestions.

Pictures and stories, including a few adventures from the "good old days," combine to give a warmth typical of Miller's writings.

You'll find ANGLER'S GUIDE TO BAJA CALIFORNIA the most valuable book on Baja fishing yet written. This book is as important to an angler as is his tackle box.

ANGLER'S GUIDE TO BAJA CALIFORNIA is on sale at B. Dalton Bookstores, local So. California bookstores and numerous tackle shops or it may be ordered directly from the publisher, Baja Trail Publications, Inc., P.O. Box 6088, Huntington Beach, CA 92646 for $5.95 plus $1.00 shipping. (Californina residents add 6% Calif. tax).

BAJA ADVENTURES by Land • Air • Sea

BY MARVIN & ALETHA PATCHEN

Adventures come in many forms in Baja California. One's imagination is the only limitation.

Today more and more Americans are discovering that the word "Baja" is synonomous with adventure. And they are also learning that it need not cost an arm and a leg to be a participant.

Marvin and Aletha Patchen have looked for adventure in Baja in more ways than perhaps anyone else. Jeeps, dune buggies, motorcycles, campers, three-wheelers, go-carts, yachts, canoes, kayaks, skiffs, helicopters, airplanes of all sizes and a lot of hiking and skin diving have all been their modes of exploration.

BAJA ADVENTURES BY LAND, AIR AND SEA is not a guide book, nor is it a scientific journal, yet one may learn much from it. The information on trip planning, outfitting and selection of vehicles, boats and aircraft is solid and easy to assimilate for it is woven into a collection of adventures dating back over 20 years.

If you're a first-timer to Baja or a veteran traveler, you'll enjoy BAJA ADVENTURES. It's fun reading and you'll learn from it too. It's bound to be an inspiration whether you travel by land, air or sea.

BAJA ADVENTURES BY LAND, AIR AND SEA is available at selected bookstores in the southland, or may be ordered directly from the distributor, Baja Trail Publications, Inc., P.O. Box 6088, Huntington Beach, CA 92646 by sending $9.95 plus $1.50 tax and shipping.

MEXICO WEST
TRAVEL CLUB

Now that you are ready to travel and explore in Baja California you'll need one more thing--a membership in the Mexico West Travel Club.

Mexico West Travel Club is for all the adventurers who cross the border because it offers so many benefits.

1. As a member you can save 20% on your Mexican auto insurance.

2. We'll send you monthly newsletters, ¡MEXICO WEST! and UPDATE, where our staff and reader reports will keep you abreast of road conditions and fishing hotspots; current events and people; announcements of coming events and new places to visit; restaurants; beaches; camping and trailer areas--just about anything you need to know about Baja California.

3. You'll be able to phone for current road conditions, fishing, hunting reports, where to go, where to stay and what to see.

4. Members receive 10-20% discounts at numerous hotels, trailer parks and sportfishing landings in the peninsula, as well as some portions of mainland Mexico.

5. Through us you can obtain boat and car permits, fishing licenses and tourist permits.

6. You'll feel comfortable traveling in Mexico with your passport-size Mexico West Travel Pass, for it is readily recognized by many officials and merchants.

7. All books from Baja Trail Publications, Inc. are discounted to members.

8. You'll be invited to parties and planned outings along the peninsula where you'll have opportunities to meet other members as well as our fine staff of experts.

Each day our members praise the Mexico West Travel Club, the newsletters, our information service, the discounts, easy availability of permits, and trip planning. Why don't you find out for yourself?

The cost? Only $35 a year, and this includes all the benefits. We'll even throw in a hard cover copy of Ben Hunter's fine book, "The Baja Feeling," when you say "yes"! Send check, money order or Visa/MC number today to:

Mexico West Travel Club, Inc., 2424 Newport Blvd., Suite 91, Costa Mesa, CA 92627, along with your name, address, telephone and spouse's name.

Our member's testimonials speak for themselves:

"I used my Mexico West Travel Pass to purchase auto insurance at a big savings, spent a couple of days at the best hotel in Ensenada and had some great meals, all at a discount. Using only the money I saved, I took my first deep sea fishing and caught my first yellowtail."
— John Lyle

"We enjoy your newsletter. Reading them has helped us enjoy our Baja vacations. Happily we're enclosing our check for another year."
-- Jay Fangman

Word gets around, as you've heard us on TV and radio and read about us in OUTDOOR LIFE, SUNSET, CONSUMER'S DIGEST, SPORTS AFIELD, LOS ANGELES TIMES, CHICAGO TRIBUNE, SEATTLE POST-INTELLIGENCER, PORTLAND OREGONIAN, DENVER POST, and numerous other small publications.